'David and Maureen Craig are a re  ministry, they have remained faithful t have sought to follow the leading of the brought them through dark and uncert lives have been like beacons of light to own light. They have been illuminated ｊ ...ᵤ ᵤgᵢₗ of Christ. This book is moving, humbling, inspiring and challenging. I am privileged to have crossed their paths and been a small thread in the tapestry of their story. Their faithfulness has impacted thousands, and their story will inspire many more. May God take this book and use it as a flame of hope to all who read it.'

Rev Malcolm Duncan FRSA – *Senior Pastor Dundonald Elim Church, Author and Theologian-in-Residence for Spring Harvest*

'David Craig's autobiographical account is a treasure from beginning to end. The author's humility and honesty are what you see and what you get. David recounts how he and his wife Maureen unashamedly developed a ministry of the Word and the Spirit in team ministry both locally and on a worldwide scale. My only regret is that I did not find such a book at the beginning of my discipleship journey. This is a must read book that focuses on the grace of God working through human weakness.'

Dr Kenneth Scott – *Missiologist, Lecturer and Author of 'Life Stories of an Unworthy Servant' and others*

'Aberdonians are world renowned as "Cannie-folk". Christian, Spirit-filled, Aberdonians are a special blessing. David's account of their life and ministry is a must, for those who wish to "walk the Christian walk", rather than "talk the Christian talk".'

Dr G. Stewart McIntosh – *Missionary to Latin America and former Director of MAC research (Serving Church and Mission, Worldwide)*

'David is, by nature, a details person who remembers dates and figures like an encyclopaedia. I'm not! For me though, two things stand out in his leading with Maureen. One is large and one smaller but together they had a huge cumulative effect in his leadership. The first thing was that David consistently led a church (BCC) for over 30+ years while it continued to grow - very rare for any pastor! How did he do it? By, secondly, consistently doing small things well. Loving God and loving people, laying down truth and sometimes, just showing up! I guess it's a bit like long-term saving; the accumulative effect of the interest over many years has more sizeable implications the longer you invest in the kingdom of God (David started out as a banker – so he'll love that!). Their story is a life lesson on leadership, from which I have had the privilege of learning from them. I'm sure you will when you read it!'

Roger Constantine – *Senior Team Pastor,*
Bournemouth Community Church , UK

'David and Maureen have been faithful servants of Christ for many decades and this book explains their unique story of how God has used them. It is a story about the work of God in Bournemouth, about the global reach of the gospel, but also a story about how to pastor a Church through change. Written with such honesty and warmth, David has provided a rich resource to gain insight into how to lead a congregation through both times of blessing and times of challenge. Read this for a down to earth encouragement to seek more of God in your own life too!'

Dr Chris Sinkinson – *Lecturer at Moorlands College, UK*

'I found myself completely held by this book. David offers readers 'Seven Key Principles' as an outline of wisdom for the journey. The writing is illuminated by a clear devotion to Christ who called him and evidences how Jesus has sustained him over five decades of service to God.

David's honesty, vulnerability, humility, tenacity and pastoral heart, coupled with a passion for Jesus, His Gospel and other people, shine through. It is this humility and honesty about the joys, challenges and sorrows, of a life of service to God and His people, which speaks so powerfully to those who share that calling. But there is much to encourage all disciples here. Pastors, ministers and Christian leaders of all kinds will benefit hugely from reading this account. They too will be aided and encouraged in practical ways of keeping the lights on. Whether newly commissioned or a seasoned, experienced servant of God, there is a goldmine of sustaining and encouraging material here to reflect upon and challenge readers. Reading this book, I felt Jesus speaking to me personally and profoundly in many ways.'

Rev Dr Clive G Burnard – *Regional Minister,*
Yorkshire Baptist Association, UK

KEEPING
THE
Lights On

A JOURNEY IN
CHURCH LEADERSHIP

DAVID CRAIG

British Library Cataloging in Publication Data.
A record of this book is available from the British Library.

ISBN 978-1-80068-231-3

Printed and bound in Great Britain
Published by the Independent Publishing Network

All paper used is certified by PEFC
(Programme for the Endorsement of Forest Certification Schemes)
and FSC® (Forest Stewardship Council®).

Cover design by Simplicate
Branding, design, print and publishing support by Simplicate (www.simplicate.org)
The Simplicate logo is a trademark of Simplicate Ltd.

For enquiries or to contact the author regarding book-related events,
please email: craigshome.co.uk@gmail.com

DEDICATION

I thank God for His forgiving grace and steadfast love.
I thank Him for the gift of His Son to be my Redeemer
and all in all and for the gift of His Spirit,
wonderfully with me until the work on earth is done.

I thank Maureen for loving me and being my best friend.
I thank her for partnering me in these years of ministry
and for teaching the character of God
and sharing the love of Jesus with so many
through the gifts God has given her.

I thank Kevin, Fiona and Stuart
for their love, forgiveness and patience
with us both as we were learning to be parents
at the same time as we were seeking to learn
from the Lord Jesus how to lead His church.

CONTENTS

Val

With our love & prayers

David Ramen

PROLOGUE

On a visit to the USA many years ago, my wife Maureen and I were trawling around a fascinating store selling all kinds of creative and fun items and I picked up a fridge-magnet which was a must have. It has winked at us knowingly ever since, from its place above the oven ('if you can't stand the heat, stay out of the kitchen' comes to mind) and it carries this message:

'Leadership is the ability to hide your panic from others.'

I never had any thoughts of writing an autobiographical account of my experiences of local church leadership. I had thought there might come a time when I would put together a history of Bournemouth Community Church for its centenary in 2021. When I was asked to do that by Roger, my successor as senior leader of the church, I did that during the early months of the COVID-19 lockdown in 2020.

During that project I began to have a desire to sketch out the journey Maureen and I have made from our beginnings in Aberdeen and Edinburgh, followed by my years at London Bible College (now London School of Theology) and student pastorate in Buckinghamshire leading to fifty years of being involved in local church leadership in London and Bournemouth.

I have attempted to be very honest about our journey. There was a severe scarcity of fathers and mothers in God when we started out and little if any published material which spoke to the reality of what God was calling us to do. Even now, a lifetime later, many church leaders often feel as if they are furiously paddling under water while attempting to present a calm and unruffled exterior. My hope and prayer is that there will be those presently in church leadership – whether salaried elders and staff or non-salaried elders – and those who have heard the call of the Lord Jesus to prepare themselves for leadership roles, who will discover encouragement, warning, wisdom and vision as they read these pages.

The world has changed hugely over these years. Church life and witness is also very different in many ways from what it was. But I have attempted to underline various biblical principles which are unchanged and unchanging and which provide bread for the journey today and every day.

> ▶ **As a father has compassion on his children,**
>   **so the Lord has compassion on those who fear him;**
> **for he knows how we are formed,**
>   **he remembers that we are dust.**
>
>   ● **Psalm 103: 13-14 (NIV)**

'Since God has put His work into your weak hands, look not for long ease here: You must feel the full weight of your calling: a weak man with a strong God.'

– Lady Culross to John Livingstone of the Scottish Covenanters.

Aboyne Aberdeenshire August 2021

CHAPTER 1

The Silver City with the Golden Sands

1941 – 1967

During the 50s and 60s, if you took a train on the East Coast Main Line from King's Cross, London, you would have travelled in one of those 'corridor trains', off of which there were sliding doors leading into various seating compartments.

Had you opened one of those doors, entered the compartment and sat down, above the heads of the passengers opposite you would have been various posters in glass frames. Those posters were advertising the glories of resorts on the East Coast of England and Scotland. There was often a poster boasting Aberdeen's attractions. The posters were artistically excellent, so much so that they are highly sought after today. 'The Silver City with the Golden Sands' was the moniker given to the poster which was attempting to push you to book your next holiday in Aberdeen. 'Silver' referred to the granite stone, which had been used in the erection of a great many houses and most of the major buildings, such as the Town House and the University. Rubislaw Quarry, from which most of the stone had been extracted, was a frighteningly huge hole, 450 feet deep, which drew me like a magnet but terrified me in equal measure when I lived not far away as a small boy. 'Golden Sands' doesn't need any explanation. The beach at Aberdeen extends for miles. If it were situated in Spain, it would always be mobbed. But Aberdeen, on the edge of the North Sea, is a different matter.

Maureen and I were both born and brought up in this city in the northeast of Scotland. We are proud Aberdonians. 1941 saw the arrival of Maureen. She grew up with her grandparents, who treated her as their daughter, and she called them Dad and Mum. Dad was a blacksmith and Mum worked part-time as a cashier in a cinema. Her grandparents lived around the corner from the local Baptist Church. They did not go to church, but as parents quite often did in those days, sometimes to have a quiet hour or so to themselves, they would send their children to Sunday School. So, in the providence of God, Maureen would go down the stairs of the tenement (block of flats) in Rosemount where she lived, walk around the corner and into the Sunday School at Gilcomston Park Baptist Church. She was three years old. It did not involve crossing a road, but in those days, children had much more liberty to make their own way, and no one thought anything of it. Maureen went, Sunday by Sunday, and two of the women who helped with the children took her under their wing and prayed for her for many years.

When Maureen was eight years old, she was in hospital for six months. She loved dancing and, from an early age, did tap, ballet and Scottish country dancing. However, while dancing, she began to collapse. They discovered that she had been born with duplex kidneys and so, serious surgery was required. Maureen remembers being taken to hospital, with no information about why she was going there. Visiting was one hour twice a week and 30 minutes three times a week. In recent times, we have rightly been concerned about children missing out on their education due to COVID-19. For Maureen, in hospital for six months, there was a teacher who came in twice a week to give one hour of lessons each time to Maureen and another girl of her age. The girls knew when she was due to come and would do their best to hide from her. They were usually successful.

One day, when she was about 10 years old, Maureen was out shopping with her 'Mum' and overheard her say to someone in conversation, referring to Maureen, 'Oh, this is my granddaughter.' Having always assumed she was a daughter, she asked her 'Mum' about what she had overheard. All that her 'Mum' said to her in reply was, 'Mabel is your mother and I am your grandmother.' Maureen had always regarded Mabel, who was married, as an older sister and enjoyed visiting her. Nothing else was ever said about this to Maureen by her grandmother or by Mabel, or if it was Maureen has no recollection of it.

Maureen kept on going to Sunday School and these two women continued praying for her. After Sunday School it was Christian Endeavour. Christian Endeavour was common in many evangelical churches at that time. Its aim was to enable teenagers to get to grips with the Bible and prayer and to encourage them to take responsibility in leading, serving and caring. It was in fact at Christian Endeavour that I first set eyes on Maureen.

In 1955 the American evangelist, Billy Graham, was being greatly used of God in the USA and the UK. It was the 1954 Haringey Crusade in London which brought him to the attention of the British media. 'Souls in Conflict' was a film depicting that Crusade and the impact of the Gospel on people's lives. One of the women who had been praying for Maureen since she was three years old had a daughter with whom Maureen was great friends. So, the three of them went to the YMCA in Aberdeen to see the film and Maureen, at the age of 14, responded to the Gospel and came to faith in Christ. A year or so later she was baptised on confession of her faith in Christ at Gilcomston Park Baptist Church.

Maureen had wanted to be a nurse when she left school. but was unable to do so due to her renal history. She ended up in office work, which, as she says today, was the last thing she should have done. Administration is her bête noire. The two offices where she worked were both situated by Aberdeen's large, busy harbour and if ever there was a windy, chilly area to walk to work, that was it.

◢

I was born in 1944, a few months before the Normandy Landings of the Second World War. My parents had met at a Christian Endeavour Holiday in Wales. My mother was technically a Cockney because she was born within the sound of Bow Bells in East London and my father was an Aberdonian through and through. Due to the war, my mother had to move out of London and was living and working in Surrey, while my father was running the fish merchant's business in Aberdeen which he had inherited from his father, who had died in 1941.

It was a long-distance courtship, but in due time they married in Sutton, Surrey and then settled in Aberdeen. My parents were both Christians and so my younger brother and I were brought up in a home where we heard about Jesus from our earliest years. My father, reared with a Presbyterian background, had become convinced of the biblical basis for baptism of believers by immersion. So, he and my mother, who came from an independent evangelical background where believer's baptism was practised, decided to move to a Baptist Church in Aberdeen. They made that move while my brother, Philip, and I were still young as they wanted us to grow up with the understanding of baptism that was being taught and practised.

When I was about six years of age, there was a Children's Mission at our church, Union Grove Baptist Church. It was led by George I. Stewart, an itinerant children's evangelist in Scotland. While he was leading the week of mission, the evangelist stayed in our home. One morning, he explained faith to me, in a simple and memorable way that a child could grasp. He illustrated to me what it meant to put all my trust in Jesus. By the grace of God, that was the time when I did begin to trust in the Lord Jesus. Going to church with my parents, attending Sunday School, hearing the Bible read to me at home and engaging in family prayers, all provided a foundation, for which I was not always thankful.

My father had a big heart to see Christian leaders working together in Aberdeen. For many years he was one of the prime movers in what was called the Aberdeen Evangelistic Association (AEA). Although the word 'Evangelistic' is there in the title, in practice the AEA was more involved in arranging bible teaching meetings and conferences, bringing in well-known bible teachers and preachers from across the UK. When Billy Graham came to speak in Aberdeen in 1955 the AEA was heavily involved in helping set that up. Tent Missions were common in those days and AEA often helped in facilitating those, so there were certainly occasions when evangelism was very much their raison d'etre.

My parents were also committed to Christian missionary work overseas, my father being on the Scottish Council of the Regions Beyond Missionary Union (RBMU). When RBMU missionaries were home on leave and came to the northeast of Scotland to speak about their work overseas, they often stayed with us for a few days. So, I grew up hearing what God was doing in various nations, seeing the transparencies which would show where they were working and listening to everything. In those days, children were to be seen and not heard, but there was nothing to stop children from listening.

When I was about nine years old the family moved to Bournemouth. We had been on holiday to Bournemouth for four years in succession, driving the 600 miles from Aberdeen in our Austin 12. I loved those long journeys. The purpose of the move was the decision my parents had made to go into business with friends who owned a guest house and with whom we always stayed on our summer holiday in Bournemouth. For some reason, that business arrangement did not work out and within a year we were back in Aberdeen. During that year in Bournemouth, we worshipped at Lansdowne Baptist Church and I remember Rev Francis Dixon running up the steps into the pulpit. We also occasionally worshipped at Moordown Baptist Church and Winton Free Evangelical Church. Little did any of us realise that I would end up living the majority of my life in Bournemouth and leading Winton Free Evangelical Church.

Some years after the end of the war, quite a number of the smaller fish merchant's businesses were bought by national companies and Dad's was one of those that became absorbed. Subsequently, that was the year we moved to Bournemouth and then, on our return, he had a grocer's shop in Aberdeen for a year or two. It was a difficult time for him and there were one or two periods of unemployment.

Some years after we returned from Bournemouth to Aberdeen, my parents moved to Gilcomston Park Baptist Church. I was now in my teens and I began to attend Christian Endeavour at that church, which is where I first saw Maureen. I was baptised at the age of fifteen. I had also been attending Boys' Crusader Class every Sunday afternoon since moving to senior school. Crusaders was a national movement in which I continued to be involved when I later moved to Edinburgh and at Winchmore Hill in North London when I was at bible college. Christian Endeavor and Crusaders gave young people good bible foundations and the opportunity to learn to serve.

I left Aberdeen Grammar School and then completed a year at the newly opened Aberdeen Commercial College. I decided to sit the entrance examination for the Clydesdale and North of Scotland Bank (now Clydesdale Bank) and began my banking career at the Northern Branch in George Street, Aberdeen in 1960. If you wanted to progress in banking, it was necessary to sit the examination of the Institute of Bankers in Scotland and in 1965 I passed my finals and became an Associate of the Institute.

Aberdeen had an excellent Youth for Christ meeting on Saturday evenings at the YMCA in Union Street in the city centre. Many young people from different churches met up there. We enjoyed singing songs, many imported from the USA, which was just a touch different from the Baptist Hymnal. I had learned to play the piano in my last few years at junior school and enjoyed being one of those who would accompany the singing. There was good bible teaching, and many friendships were formed which have lasted through the years. Maureen and I were both involved in Youth for Christ and it was another commitment that helped us to learn to serve and lead.

When I was around the age of 15, two women visited Aberdeen and spoke at the Salvation Army Citadel. Their names were Marj Saint and Elizabeth Elliot. Their husbands, Nate and Jim, along with three other young American missionaries, had been killed two years previously as they attempted to reach the Auca Indians in Ecuador with the Gospel. The martyrdom of these five young men made an impact on many Christians in the UK.

The Citadel was packed out to hear the two widows speak.

God was powerfully present and when there was an appeal given to offer yourself to serve Christ, I stood to do just that.

This is perhaps the point at which to mention another significant occasion. When I was about eleven years old, I remember saying to God one Sunday morning as the church service was going on, 'God, if you want me to work for you, I am not just going to keep things ticking over.' I do not know where that thought of working for God came from, in the sense that I cannot remember God speaking to me about that previously. In the arrogance of youth, I felt that things at church just went on the same way, every week, month after month. Somehow, I didn't think that was how God wanted it. It certainly wasn't how I would want it if I was involved. It reminded me of some words of an old hymn we used to sing which has the line 'Nothing changes here.' Of course, I was taking the words of the hymn totally out of their context, but they just expressed how I felt about it all. However, looking back, God was evidently stirring something in me at an early age.

In the light of these two occasions, it is not surprising that in the years ahead I was unsure if God was going to call me to serve Him overseas as a missionary or ask me to lead a church in the UK. But by my middle teens, I was increasingly aware that God's call for some form of Christian ministry was on my life.

✎

Maureen and I saw a lot of each other at church, Christian Endeavour and Youth for Christ and we had many mutual friends. I fancied her from the start and was attracted to her feisty personality. However, my parents were on the move to Edinburgh, as my father had secured a post with the Scottish Special Housing Association, where he worked until retirement. I didn't want to move with them. I had many friends at Youth for Christ. And there was Maureen. But there seemed to be little alternative. If Maureen and I were to continue our friendship, the train journey between Aberdeen and Edinburgh was going to become familiar. The Bank transferred me to the Leith Walk Branch in Edinburgh. Maureen and I saw each other every second weekend. We both knew we were serious about our relationship and so, later in 1962, Maureen moved south to live and work in Edinburgh also.

My parents had begun to worship at Charlotte Baptist Chapel, a large well-known church in the West End of Edinburgh. It was a church with a revival history, where Dr Graham Scroggie and Rev Sidlow Baxter were previous ministers. Dr Alan Redpath, who had been minister of Moody Church, Chicago since 1953 and before that at Duke Street Baptist Church, Richmond, Surrey, came to Charlotte Chapel in 1962. His life and ministry were to have a considerable influence on both Maureen and me. There was a crowd of us in the Young People's Fellowship (YPF) and Alan Redpath made a big impact on us all. He was a breath of fresh air. At that time, he was in his mid-fifties but full of life and energy. His preaching was biblical with practical down-to-earth life application. He was a man's man, but deeply caring and pastoral. He had been an evangelist with the National Young Life Campaign in England before he became minister at Duke Street Baptist Church. His heart for young people and desire for them to know Christ and make Him known was transparent. YPF at Charlotte Chapel was a not-to-be-missed experience in those days. We grew in God through the preaching of the Word of God and by taking up the many opportunities to serve. Through YPF I had the opportunity to preach at various mission halls and smaller churches. It was at one of those mission halls, in Methil, Fife, just across the Firth of Forth from Edinburgh, when, after a service at which I had just preached, someone came to me and asked if I had thought of going to bible college.

After this kind of question had been asked on multiple occasions over a period of time, I spoke to the elder with oversight of the YPF and to other older Christians. I wanted to check out if they had any sense from God that this was a route I should be seriously considering in the future. I was planning to ask Maureen to marry me. We had talked about my sense that God was 'on my case' concerning training for Christian ministry of some kind. I explained to her that I was now growingly convinced that my career in banking was going to be cut short and that bible college training lay ahead. What did she think about that? How did she feel about that prospect? Would she be willing for that? To my joy, but not to my surprise, Maureen said she would be willing, although, like me of course, not really having a clue what that would involve.

Alan Redpath married us and his gift to us was his own book, 'The Making of a Man of God – Studies in the Life of David'. We still have the book of course in which he inserted, along with his greetings, Proverbs 3:5-6. He had a way of saying things that tended to stick in your mind: 'Better to burn out rather than rust out' and 'The conversion of a soul is the miracle of a moment, but the manufacture of a saint is the task of a lifetime'. Dear Alan suffered a serious stroke a year later and although he continued preaching afterwards, he concluded his ministry at the Chapel, as it is fondly known, in 1966. In the years following he authored many books and preached around the world at conferences under the banner of the Capernwray Missionary Fellowship and Bible School.

Maureen and I started married life in a flat over a branch of the bank in Leith Walk, which is the main artery joining Edinburgh to the Port of Leith on the Firth of Forth. By that time, I was working in the Chief Office in Edinburgh and enjoying the varied experience of the investment department, the foreign exchange department or working with the public as a cashier. I had almost completed my final banking examinations. The prospects were good. In those days, opportunities in banking at home and overseas for my age group were there for the taking. If I stayed with the bank, a big perk was an interest-free mortgage for the first five years and then 2% interest forever. In fact, I began to enquire about serving overseas with a large international bank and there was an open door for me to proceed with them.

As we contemplated our future direction, we remembered Alan Redpath's testimony. One day, he went into his work at Imperial Chemical Industries (ICI) in London and told his manager that he was leaving to become an evangelist with the National Young Life Campaign. His manager told him not to be foolish and immediately offered him a promotion, with a large raise in salary. Very tempting. The enemy is adept at offering what appears to be a juicy career and financial plum if he sees we are on track to obey God. At the same time, we are often aware that it is more than likely that our income will lessen, if not take a nose-dive, if we choose some form of Christian ministry. Alan Redpath rejected the poisoned plum and chose God's way for his life. Maureen and I, along with countless others, are so thankful that Alan Redpath continued to say 'yes' to God's direction for his life then and all his days.

We agreed together that I would apply to London Bible College (LBC), now London School of Theology, for three years of training. My professional qualifications, as an Associate of the Institute of Bankers in Scotland, was the basis for my acceptance for the London University Theological Courses that training at LBC involved. It was agreed that I would start at LBC in September 1967. During that application and acceptance period, the bank invited me to take up a position at the Head Office in Glasgow. It was an attractive proposition and bode well for my career and our financial future. We decided to reject the 'plum' and continue with what we believed to be God's direction for us.

We were able to find a first-floor flat in Crouch End, London N8 and prepared to move south with our son Kevin, born in 1964. We were sad to say goodbye to our many friends at Charlotte Chapel. Maureen's family in Aberdeen and mine in Edinburgh would miss so much of Kevin growing up. Life for Maureen and myself would be very different down south. Perhaps we would return to Scotland in three years to lead a Baptist Church?

Perhaps, instead, we would be going much farther away than London, as missionaries to a distant nation?

Jeremiah 29:11 rang in our ears: ' "For I know the plans I have for you," declares the Lord.'

And Proverbs 3:5-6: 'Trust in the Lord with all your heart... and he will make your paths straight.'

CHAPTER 2

Wisdom for the Journey

Generally, when you are younger and busy with life, as we were at that time, you do not think much about your husband or wife dying. It is said that young people think they are immortal. Actually, it is not so much they think about death at all, they just live and act as if life will always be as it is. When we are no longer young people, but family and work are keeping us more than occupied, that can quite often be true of us too. Since we retired, in 2009, we have become increasingly aware that we will not always be together. It is, as with the dawn, the light increases and you see things more and more clearly, even the detail that was missing in the early light. When close friends lose a husband or a wife, whom you too have loved and valued, your thoughts often turn to the surviving partner. You think about the pain of the loss of a friend and lover that they are experiencing and so you begin to face, with more reality, what awaits you when you have to endure such a goodbye.

There is huge comfort in the truth and hope of the Gospel of Christ. How we need Father, Son and Holy Spirit and how immeasurably blessed we are that the Triune God loves to journey with us, alongside us and in us at every stage and every season of our lives.

I've been writing in the midst of the COVID-19 pandemic. This is a time of confusion, difficulty and stress for many. Thousands have died, particularly, but not only those who are elderly and have underlying health conditions. Some husbands, wives, sons, daughters and grandchildren have not been able to visit family members shut away in care homes or even say their farewells to those who are dying. Thousands are losing their jobs and others are facing a serious reduction in income with the resulting anxiety of losing the roof over their heads, be it rented or mortgaged. Not surprisingly, there is a concerning increase in mental health issues across the population.

However, this is also a season of a multitude of new opportunities to reveal the love and compassion of Jesus in many different ways. Some churches are providing for their communities through Foodbanks and the provision of lunches for children of families in need. Across my own area of Bournemouth, Christchurch and Poole, Faithworks and local churches have commenced a Prayer Line, staffed by volunteers, providing anyone with the opportunity to call, talk to someone and receive prayer. Many church leaders are being confronted with some tough decisions about how the church can and should work in this new environment. Many non-believers, who never usually darken the door of a church building, are following streaming church services. Countless numbers are googling the subject of prayer online. This new experience called lockdown has caused so many to reconsider their lives and realise those things that are truly important. God is never taken by surprise and He is powerfully at work across the world to fulfil His purposes and to draw, by His Holy Spirit, a harvest to His Son.

One of the key issues which COVID-19 has brought to the fore for church leaders is the question of discipleship. Have we been making disciples? Or is the reality that we have developed a consumer/provider model which has not in the main grown Christ-centred disciples? Are our churches primarily designed to preach the Gospel and make disciples?

Looking ahead to whatever the new normal looks like poses other challenges for church leaders. There will inevitably be significant pastoral issues arising from those in the church family who have fallen into spiritual disrepair and those affected by loss through illness, death, mental health issues, unemployment and income reduction.

It is possible there will be a drop in giving due to a reduction in the number of people committed to the local church and the significant impact of the above issues. Added to that, the baby-boomer generation, which can often provide a large percentage of the income will need to be replaced in the next 10-15 years. There may well be pressure to return to the old 'normal' in a post-pandemic world by picking up with everything that was part of that pre-pandemic time, and many will speculate about what God is saying to the church about the days ahead.

This is a time to listen to what the Spirit is saying to the churches: it is an opportunity to rethink in the presence of the Head of the Church and to prepare to put in place what He is saying.

In every generation, Christ's church has been faced with new challenges. Some of the issues that the local church in the UK has had to wrestle with in the last fifty years will be laid bare in succeeding chapters. As we journey, I will be attempting to share something of the enduring wisdom of the Word of God which has been given to guide and teach us in every age, interpreted to us by the inspiration of the Holy Spirit. In this, I will include some lessons in leadership which Maureen and I have discovered to be foundational in our learning to follow the Lord Jesus in local church leadership.

Many years ago, I came across a book by Steve Farrar with the title, 'Finishing Strong'. At the time there were few books of value that were particularly orientated to men and addressed issues pertinent to them. But 'Finishing Strong' was certainly one of those. Here is a commendation that is found at the beginning of the book:

'My old track coach told all his sprinters and middle-distance men that the last third of the race was the most critical. Same with the 'race of life.' This is the time to lengthen your stride, focus on the fundamentals and above all else, don't trip up! No one ever got a gold medal for the 95-yard dash. Stay in the race. Finish strong.'

Farrar tells the story of three rookie evangelists, who suddenly appeared on the scene in 1945. Billy Graham was 27 years old, a full-time evangelist for Youth for Christ and began to fill auditoriums across the USA. But Billy Graham was not the only preacher packing them in at that time. So was Chuck Templeton. One seminary president called Templeton 'the most gifted and talented young man in America today for preaching'. Both of these men in their mid-twenties ministered for Youth for Christ.

At that time, The National Association of Evangelicals published an article on men 'best used of God' in that organisation's five-year existence. The article highlighted Templeton but made no mention of Graham. Farrar asks the question: 'How come you have never heard of Chuck Templeton?' Just five years later Templeton left the ministry to pursue a career as a radio and television and newspaper columnist. He had decided he was no longer a believer in Christ.

There was another young evangelist at the time, Bron Clifford. Have you ever heard of him? At the age of 25 it is said that he touched more lives, influenced more leaders, and set more attendance records than any other of his age in American history. Within 10 years, Clifford had lost his family, his ministry, his health and then his life. Alcohol and financial irresponsibility had resulted in him leaving his wife and their two Down's syndrome children. He died at age 35 from cirrhosis of the liver in a run-down motel on the edge of Amarillo. Some local pastors took up a collection among themselves in order that he could have a decent burial.

'In the Christian life,' says Farrar, 'it's not how you start that matters. It's how you finish.'

As I write these words it is 50 years since I was ordained to the Christian Ministry in Charlotte Chapel, Edinburgh. I do not know how many more years God will choose to give to me before, by His grace, I see Him face to face. But 'Finishing Strong' is as relevant for me now, at the age of 77, as it ever has been.

During the years of my journey in church leadership, I have sadly witnessed more than a few who were on the same journey but are no longer travelling. Billy Graham, Chuck Templeton and Bron Clifford were well-known names in 1945. But the names of the great majority of those of us who have been called of God into Christian ministry are unknown, except to those to whom God has called us 'to preach the Word' and 'shepherd the flock of God that is under your care'. We may be grateful for this, as with a name that is 'known' widely comes some unique challenges and temptations.

But why is it that some of those who were travelling on the road of church leadership are no longer on the journey?

Some have been tripped up by their own sin and some by the sins of others. There is no doubt that some have been brought down by the failure of churches to truly pray and care for their spiritual leader or pastor. In some cases, the failure has been culpable and brought pain and lasting injury to the person involved and their family. This is dishonouring to Christ and His Church and is often a stumbling block to faith in younger family members who have witnessed at first hand the impact upon their father and mother.

I have witnessed church leaders and pastors, whose church is in a denominational structure, being poorly served by those who are tasked with the pastoral care and support of the churches and the spiritual leaders. In my experience, in such cases, it tends to be the church that is prioritised, rather than the church leader or pastor. On the other hand, leaders of independent churches can be left high and dry when the tide goes out for them and their families. When you have sat with leaders and experienced their pain and confusion in such scenarios, you are sad and sometimes angry at the way in which some leaders and pastors are treated by their elders, deacons, church councils or whatever form of church governance is involved. In such cases, the grace of God, the shepherd heart of Christ, and the ministry of the Holy Spirit are all too often conspicuous by its absence.

Some are no longer on the journey of church leadership due to the sins and failures of others. But others are tripped up by their own sin. Sadly, the lives of Templeton and Clifford are examples of this. Money, sex and power are the old enemies of consistent faithful testimony to Christ. There are some who have been brought low by one or all of these. It is instructive to note that in 'Just as I am', Billy Graham's autobiography, he mentions how, in their early years, while on a mission in Modesto, California, his team came to agree together on the need for them to maintain the Bible's standard of 'absolute integrity and purity' in their ministry as evangelists.

The first point on their combined list was money. The second item was sexual immorality. 'From that day on,' says Billy, 'I did not travel, meet or eat alone with a woman other than my wife.' The third concern was not to carry on their work separate from the local church, but always to work with all church leaders who would cooperate with them in the public proclamation of the Gospel. The fourth point on their list was publicity: never to exaggerate attendances. They committed themselves to integrity in all their publicity and reporting. This agreement became known as the Modesto Manifesto and laid the foundations for a lifestyle that honoured Christ and the Word of God and brought godly protection to the team and their work of evangelism.

But for others, who are no longer on the journey of church leadership, it is not because of personal sin but due to their life and ministry being undermined by fault lines in their personal foundations. I refer to the evidence of this in the lives of some of the students we met during the years we were chaplains at Moorlands College. I have known church leaders who are no longer in ministry for similar reasons, including lack of awareness that earlier life experiences rendered them vulnerable and their lack of security in God. Church leaders need ongoing, consistent, committed relationships which will provide a place to share life and its struggles with their peers and others who have taken the journey before them and understand the stresses that can cause anyone to trip and fall. I and many other leaders have benefited from a model which provides just such a resource and is a proven help to those in church leadership.

Throughout our journey, Maureen and I have found **seven key principles** which proved to be enduring wisdom from God for the journey:

1. *Walk humbly with God*

Micah 6:8 sets this out in memorable fashion. Let the Word of God and the Spirit of God daily teach you what this means. This verse also directs us to act justly and love mercy in all our relationships with others.

> ▶ He has shown you, O mortal, what is good.
>   And what does the Lord require of you?
> To act justly and to love mercy
>   and to walk humbly with your God.
>
> ● Micah 6:8 (NIV)

> ▶ He guides the humble in what is right
>   and teaches them his way.
>
> ● Psalm 25:9 (NIV)

2. *Forgive and keep on forgiving*

In Matthew 18:21-35, Peter asks Jesus where the limits are when it comes to forgiving. The Master's reply rocked him back on his heels. Forgiveness must be without limit and from the heart.

> ▶ **Then Peter came to Jesus and asked,**
>   **"Lord, how many times shall I forgive my brother or sister**
>   **who sins against me? Up to seven times?"**
> **Jesus answered, "I tell you, not seven times,**
>   **but seventy-seven times."**
>
>   ● **Matthew 18:21-22 (NIV)**

3. *Keep your spirit clean*

'Let's keep our spirits clean' became the phrase Maureen and I would speak to each other when things became tough. We knew we were 'done for' in our walk with God and our ministry if we allowed our hearts, minds, and spirits to become sullied by ungodly responses to people or situations.

> ▶ **Create in me a pure heart, O God,**
>   **and renew a steadfast spirit within me.**
>
>   ● **Psalm 51:10 (NIV)**

4. *Trust God and His promises at all times*

> ▶ The one who calls you is faithful, and he will do it.
>
> ● 1 Thessalonians 5:24 (NIV)

> ▶ But the Lord is faithful, and he will strengthen you
>   and protect you from the evil one.
>
> ● 2 Thessalonians 3:3 (NIV)

> ▶ Trust in the Lord with all your heart
>   and lean not on your own understanding;
> in all your ways submit to him,
>   and he will make your paths straight.
>
> ● Proverbs 3:5-6 (NIV)

The verses from Proverbs were given to me by my parents when I began in ministry and they sure are wisdom literature.

5. *Pursue God and the course He has given you to walk*

Jeremiah 1:4-19 tells us not to be deflected from the way God has shown you how to live or from the way He has shown you to lead His people. But pursue Him and follow the course He has set out for you with grace and courage.

> ▶ "... You must go to everyone I send you to
>   and say whatever I command you."
>
>   ● Jeremiah 1:7 (NIV)

6. *Guard your time with God, your wife or husband, and your children*

Ephesians 5:15 - 6:4 teaches us to let love, compassion and care mark out our foundational relationships at all times. Your first calling is to love the Lord your God with all that you are and then to love your wife or husband, and children, in that order of priority with the self-same love.

> ▶ Be very careful, then, how you live –
>   not as unwise but as wise,
>   making the most of every opportunity...
>
>   ● Ephesians 5:15 (NIV)

7. *Keep on seeking after God*

Let it be the consistent choice of your will. There are always times, seasons when the last thing you want to do is seek God. At such times let your will be aligned with your Father's in heaven, who eternally loves you and whose Son, the Lord Jesus Christ, offered up Himself for you.

> ▶ ... When my heart whispered, "Seek God,"
> my whole being replied, "I'm seeking him!"...
>
> ● Psalm 27:8 (MSG)

The Master has taken Maureen and me by the hand, very often by a route and through circumstances we could never have imagined. It reminds me of God's call to Abram in Genesis 12:1, '... "Go from your country, your people and your father's household to the land I will show you." ' In the next two verses, God speaks out His unbreakable promises to Abram. As David Livingstone, the renowned missionary and explorer, once exclaimed: 'His is the word of a Gentleman and you can rely on it.'

CHAPTER 3

Training and Tupperware
1967 – 1970

We had left our country, our people and were now in the land God had shown us to move to – it was North London. Maureen and I and our three-year-old son Kevin settled into our new home and in the few weeks before I was due to commence the three years at London Bible College (LBC), we enjoyed exploring the area just south of Highgate Woods, Muswell Hill and 'Ally Pally' (Alexandra Palace). We found a church, Tollington Park Baptist Church, where we would worship for the years I was at LBC. TP, as the church was fondly known, lies just east of the Holloway Road, in Finsbury Park. The pastor had recently arrived at TP after graduating from London Bible College and in the years we were worshipping there he dedicated both our daughter Fiona and son Stuart.

Travel to College involved a bus journey from Crouch End to Finsbury Park, then the tube to Baker Street followed by a short walk to College nearby on the Marylebone Road. However, one of the students I met early on lived in Haringey and came to College on his motorcycle. So, from then on, for the years that followed, I waited for John under the railway arches at Finsbury Park and completed the journey on pillion. Never a dull moment on the back of John's bike.

My three years turned out to be the last years the College would remain in Marylebone Road. In the summer of 1970, when I graduated, the College moved to Northwood, Middlesex to take over the premises recently vacated by the London College of Divinity which had moved to Nottingham. So, in fact, I was in the last cohort of students to study in the Marylebone premises.

College life was somewhat of a culture shock on a number of levels. Having been in banking for eight years I found myself in an academic institution with an international student body. It was a very new and sometimes unsettling situation to be in an environment where my years and experience in the world of finance counted for little or nothing. Suddenly, I was in an unfamiliar place where, although some students came from the world of work, others came to LBC with university degrees. For the previous six years, I had been used to studying at home in the evenings for my Institute of Bankers examinations, but this new life was of a different order with lectures and study filling out almost all available time. It was my Institute of Bankers examinations success which provided me with the qualifications required for entry to the London University Diploma in Theology course. Studies at LBC included the Diploma in Theology lectures and also the subjects set by LBC to gain its own graduation qualification.

When I began my banking career, it was as the office junior and you were left in no doubt that was your position as you shopped for the cream buns and chocolate goodies for the staff coffee break. Commencing at LBC sometimes felt very much like starting again from scratch, except I was no longer 16-years-old and had the responsibilities of a wife and family.

In the years to come, I would find myself in similar situations where I felt like a 'fish out of water'. Early on in this journey, I needed to learn to live out what the prophet says about 'walking humbly with God'. One of the great benefits of heeding this biblical command is that it sends you to God for His grace and it instils in you a teachable spirit.

I had been privileged to be interviewed by Principal Dr Ernest Kevan, but in the intervening time he had died and now Rev Gilbert Kirby had been appointed. There were some excellent lecturers and one or two very entertaining ones too. Dr H. Dermot McDonald's (or 'Derry Mac' as he was known) lectures on Philosophy and Ethics were memorable, thought-provoking and entertaining. I rather thought I would struggle with philosophy, but his strong Irish accent and witty asides, combined with his teaching style, enabled me to enjoy and value the subject. I expected to enjoy Old Testament, having been brought up on many of the fascinating personalities and events recorded there. Rev. A.E. Cundall was the OT lecturer, or 'Thumbs Cundall' as some of us called him. Why? Simple really. As he stood giving his lecture, with each hand on either side of the lectern, his thumbs stood to attention. I did enjoy OT, but sadly, although not unexpectedly, the London University course examination questions on the subject, for which we were being prepared at College, were concerned with issues that were much less riveting than the biblical record. That I was successful in completing the London University's Diploma in Theology and the College's own raft of subjects was a cause for thanksgiving to God.

While at London Bible College there were reports from some students of people in a number of churches having encounters with the Holy Spirit. I almost felt, like the Ephesians, 'we have not even heard that there is a Holy Spirit' (Ephesians 19:1-2). I had been privileged to experience some excellent bible teaching ministry in Scotland, not least in my own home upbringing, but had no memory of ever hearing any teaching or preaching about the Person and Work of the Holy Spirit. God, yes, although little about His Fatherhood. The Lord Jesus, yes. But the Holy Spirit? Little or nothing at all. These reports of people experiencing the presence and power of the Holy Spirit were avidly discussed among some of the student body, but it was quickly evident that it was a point of considerable disagreement. I listened to these conversations and debates, often very aware of my biblical and historical ignorance and seldom participated. By and large, I remained unsure, if not often sceptical. Unbeknown to me at the time, God would be speaking to me much more about His Spirit in the days to come.

✎

There were important opportunities during those years to gain experience by preaching in various churches primarily in the London area, although sometimes as far afield as Norfolk and Bristol. In the summer of 1968, I was involved with a College mission team in Cork, southern Ireland organised by Irish Evangelistic Treks. It was an eye-opener in terms of the spiritual and economic needs of the people. But the primary opportunity for practical experience while at LBC came in the form of a year as Student Pastor at Hyde Heath Union Chapel in Buckinghamshire, a few miles from Amersham.

Hyde Heath Chapel originally served a farming and agricultural community, hence, in order to be culturally relevant, the first service was at 3pm rather than in the morning when so much had to be attended to on the farm. Although few, if any, who attended Hyde Heath in 1968 were still involved in farming, an afternoon rather than a morning service continued to be the arrangement, with an evening service following soon after at 6pm.

In my second year, every Friday after lunch at College from September 1968 to the summer of 1969, I would take the Metropolitan Line from Baker Street to Amersham, where I would be met by someone from the Chapel who would drive me the few miles to Hyde Heath. I would spend the afternoon visiting in this rural community from where many commuted into London. After a wonderful tea at Den and Joy Swains' home with their young family, I would walk up the road to the Chapel and lead the youth group.

Then home via the Tube to North London, which usually meant arrival home was about 11.30pm. On Sundays, we would travel out to Hyde Heath as a family and after lunch with Roderick and Jean Ling, I would lead and preach at the afternoon service. Following tea with the Swains family, I would lead and preach at the 6pm service and then home to London N8.

I discovered that visiting people in their own homes was valued and appreciated and it provided an opportunity for me to learn about people's lives and circumstances. By the same token, I became not simply 'that young man from the College' but a friend. These afternoon visits at Hyde Heath taught me much about the love of Father God for His children and laid an important foundation for me in the way I would set about future ministry. I learned that meeting and listening to people in their own homes provided insights that were invaluable for effective prayer and pastoring. They were also indicators as to areas the preaching of the Word of God could or needed to be directed. Very few, it appeared, had ever had the opportunity to build a relationship with someone they regarded as their church leader and I began to realise the immense privilege of being freely given entrance into the joys and sorrows of their lives.

My second year at College was very pressurised. I was not only attending the lectures at College and studying at home in the evenings but now, with the responsibilities at Hyde Heath, there were two Sunday services to prepare. In those days, most churches expected you to organise and lead every element of the Sunday services as well as preach. Up until this point in my life, I had only been preaching from time to time. It was a tough, but very necessary preparation for the years to follow in church leadership.

If you know Maureen, you will know she is no shrinking violet. So far, all our married life I had spent almost every evening after work studying for the Institute of Bankers qualification. Now I was at College, every evening was still taken up with study, plus now preparation for the weekend at Hyde Heath. As well as caring for the children, Maureen was working part-time as a Tupperware agent, very successfully too I might add. She had a large blue suitcase crammed with Tupperware of all shapes and colours and would go off on the bus and tube to sell at Tupperware parties held in various homes across North London. She did very well because she believed in the value of what she was selling. She would explain its value to friends who were going overseas as missionaries, 'It will keep your food completely free of creepy-crawlies.' She would then give them a gift of Tupperware and they sang its praises to her in the years that followed.

There was little money available. I had a mature student grant from the Scottish Education Department which paid my fees at College, but the living allowance was hardly sufficient to cover the basics. So, Maureen's Tupperware exploits were significant in our family budget. We would never have been able to make the move south for me to study and prepare for whatever the Lord had for us in Christian ministry unless Maureen had been wholeheartedly committed to what she also recognised as God's will and way for us. She would not hesitate to tell me if she thought I had things out of kilter between study, Hyde Heath and family life. I had better take note and I usually did. Her love and commitment to the Lord Jesus and to me have never failed and in the years that followed, she began to discover and grow into her own gifting in ministry.

In August 1969, at the conclusion of my time at Hyde Heath, I arranged for a College team to work with me in a week of mission to the children and youth of the community. The team included Geoff Gobbett, who followed me as Student Pastor at Hyde Heath, and John Houghton, he of the motorcycle from Finsbury Park to College. In the mornings we had a varied programme for the children based on the Chapel having been made out as a Space Centre and the children (Mininauts) arriving at 10am for 'space training'. In the afternoons there was football, scavenger hunts and the rest.

In the evenings, invitations were given to teenagers to come to the Gantry Club at the Space Centre. Here there was a coffee bar (very contemporary at the time), table tennis, darts and board games, followed by a relevant teaching session with questions and discussion. We ended the week with a barbecue on the ground next to the Chapel. It was fun for everyone, the team included, and we were understanding more and more how to lean on God and learn from Him and from one another.

I was privileged to have that year in Hyde Heath. There were very few similar opportunities available through the College. It was a year of learning on the job and having a growing sense of the privilege of beginning to explore the edges of what it means to 'shepherd the flock of God'.

In my final year at College, I was a member of the House Committee, representing the non-residents in the student body. The college had two hundred students and some organisation was required. I remember the House Committee Breakfasts, which, as a non-resident, meant I had to get up at the crack of dawn and get into Marylebone Road, whereas the others all fell out of their beds in the onsite student accommodation. However, it was worth it because there I met for the first time Joan's amazing pavlova. Joan was a New Zealander, and she produced these remarkable meringue desserts, with a crisp crust and soft light inside, topped with fruit and whipped cream, which for a Scotsman was a delight never previously encountered. It always made the early rise, bus and tube journey more than worthwhile. At Christmas, the tradition was that the House Committee put on a sketch poking fun at all and sundry, but especially the teaching staff. At the time, the Principal's daughter Ruth was going out with one of the students, by the name of Clive and it was suggested that as Clive had received the Church

History prize, it was a sure sign of favouritism at the very top. There was plenty more like that.

Life at London Bible College ended with Graduation Day in June 1970 which was held in the imposing St Mary's Marylebone Church situated next to the College. It was a time of joy but also tinged with sadness as we were saying our farewells to fellow students, who in the main we would never see again until we meet in heaven. However, there were some we would see again and often. During those three years, there were four of us who became particular friends, Geoff Gobbett, John Houghton, Keith Ives and me. We four, with our wives and families, began to meet up together. 2020 marks 50 years since we left London Bible College and our four families have been meeting about three times a year ever since. There were times in the early years when we were not sure our friendship would continue, as we represented differing expressions of church life and practice and we would discuss things with considerable fervour. However, our friendship has lasted long, and we have laughed and prayed and cried together as we have shared our lives and those of our children, grandchildren and now great-grandchildren.

Relationships built and formed at College and during the student-pastor year at Hyde Heath were instrumental in teaching and shaping me for the years ahead. Learning to appreciate listening and truly hearing what people were saying was invaluable. It provided a platform from which I could begin to learn to deal with people and situations in a Micah 6:8 manner. Our Triune God is relational at the heart of His being and has supremely and uniquely revealed Himself to us in the person of His Son Jesus Christ. Our Lord's desire is that those He calls to lead in His Church, love as He loves and forgive as He forgives. In other words, that we walk humbly before our God, acting justly and loving mercy.

The three years at LBC were a once-in-a-lifetime opportunity, over all too quickly in some respects. But by the end of that time,

I was more than ready to get out there and into 'the real world' as some of us described life outside of College.

In September we were back in Scotland visiting Maureen's family in Aberdeen and mine in Edinburgh. On Sunday 13th September I was ordained to the Christian Ministry at our home church of Charlotte Chapel by Rev Derek Prime. (Dr Alan Redpath, who had had such an influence on both of our lives and had been our Pastor until we went to London in 1967, had resigned due to ill-health while I was at College). Derek Prime, who had previously been Pastor at Lansdowne Evangelical Free Church, West Norwood, South London and President of the Fellowship of Independent Evangelical Churches (FIEC) in 1966, was now the Pastor at Charlotte Chapel (Derek led the church from 1969 to 1987, and died in 2020).

One morning the previous Christmas. when we were in Scotland visiting family, I was able to spend some time with Derek at the Chapel. I had no clue then as to where we would be serving God after graduating at LBC. Derek prayed for me, and for Maureen and the family, and gave me the verse:

> ▶ "For I know the plans I have for you," declares the Lord,
> "plans to prosper you and not to harm you,
> plans to give you hope and a future."
>
> ● Jeremiah 29:11 (NIV)

That verse has always been a source of assurance and a stimulus to vision and faith in the years that have followed.

CHAPTER 4

The Grove

1970 – 1978

When we moved south in 1967 Maureen and I had thought we would most likely return to Scotland long term, probably leading a Baptist church, as we both came from a Baptist background. While at College, the challenge and opportunities of overseas missions, for which we already had a large heart, had to be considered: was this His plan for our future life and ministry? In God's economy, overseas mission was always going to be integral to our lives in the years ahead, as it had been prior to coming to LBC, but God's calling on our lives was to find its primary focus in local church ministry in the UK. But not in the land of our birth! In August 1970 we moved from Crouch End N8 to Kensal Rise NW10. We had accepted an invitation for me to become Minister of Westbourne Grove Baptist Church in Notting Hill W11.

So, we were remaining in England and indeed London, which we had come to love. Edward Heath had just become British Prime Minister and would lead the country for four years. During that time, some significant decisions were made by his government, including the decimalisation of the currency and the accession of the UK to the European Economic Community. After the 'Winter of Discontent', James Callaghan would be elected and was Prime Minister from 1974 to 1979.

I visited Westbourne Grove for the first time in January 1970. It was a student preaching engagement arranged through the College. I preached again in June and in the August Maureen and I were settled before God that this was where he wanted us to serve Him. There had been another London church that had invited me, but by the early summer, we had peace that we should not accept that opportunity. Interestingly, the previous minister at Westbourne Grove was also from Aberdeen, where he had been my Sunday School teacher. At the same time, my father had been the Sunday School Superintendent (which was the terminology used in those days).

The eight years that we were to be at 'The Grove', as the church was fondly known, were to be significant in our lives. Kevin was six years old when we arrived in 1970 and fourteen when we left. Fiona and Stuart arrived during the years I was at London Bible College and were eleven and eight respectively when we moved to Bournemouth in 1978. These would prove to be important years for us in learning to parent and build family life. Father God taught us much about the biblical necessity of guarding and nourishing our marriage relationship and so ensuring our children were secure in our love for each other and for them.

Our Welcome Service (or Induction Service as it was called then) took place on Saturday 3rd October 1970. My parents and brother Philip were there as well as friends from Charlotte Chapel, our home church in Edinburgh. Other guests came from London Bible College, Tollington Park Baptist Church and Hyde Heath. By the next morning, our first official Sunday, almost everyone who had been present the previous evening had returned to their homes and there were only seventeen people in the congregation, including my parents and my brother. Seventeen in that massive Victorian building with a huge gallery on three sides. Commenting on the low numbers, my father said to me over lunch afterwards, 'Well, David, there is only one way and that is up.'

Westbourne Grove Baptist Church had a remarkable history. We celebrated its 150th Anniversary in 1973, three years after we arrived and writing its story involved pouring over old church records and visiting the Kensington Reference Library. These revealed some fascinating facts including the many visits of Charles Hadden Spurgeon, (known as the Prince of Preachers) when the building, with deep galleries, overflowed with 2500 in the congregation. Spurgeon and Garrett Lewis, the minister of Westbourne Grove Baptist Church from 1847 to 1881 were close friends and together formed the London Baptist Association. James Hudson Taylor, the founder of the China Inland Mission was a member of the church from 1861 until 1905. Garrett Lewis was instrumental in encouraging Hudson Taylor to publish his history-changing appeal in 1865 for '24 willing, skilful labourers for inland China'. Hudson Taylor encouraged Tom Barnardo, who he met in connection with Barnardo's interest in the possibility of serving in China, to continue and expand the work he had begun among the waifs and strays and orphans of London. Hudson Taylor also mentored the young evangelist Henry Grattan Guinness, who later founded Harley College, where 1500 people were trained for overseas missionary service. It was from Harley College that in due time the work of the Regions Beyond Missionary Union (RBMU) began – a Mission I had known from my youth. While at Westbourne Grove I was invited to become a member of the RBMU Board, and I would be privileged to be intimately involved with the mission for twenty-five years.

However, even with that rich history, when we arrived at 'The Grove' in 1970 the situation could not have been more different.

Victorian North Kensington with its wealth, palatial houses and thousands of people in service, had long since disappeared. The housing stock had sadly degenerated and the area was suffering from Rachmanism, which took its name from the worst of the unscrupulous landlords of the time. Immigration had brought many West Indians and Nigerians into Notting Hill and many were living in poor accommodation or in the recently built high-rise soulless tower blocks. There were also many hostels in the district providing accommodation for overseas students and young people from the Commonwealth and the USA who had come to London to study, work and 'see' the UK and Europe.

As I mentioned, there were very few people in the congregation on our first Sunday and the outside of the building gave reason to doubt that it was even in use. For this reason, the deacons asked if I would wear a clerical collar when I was out and about in the local area and although not at all enthusiastic about the suggestion, I could see that it had some merit. So, I did wear one for my first year. There was little money available, but at least we could paint the many massive doors of this cavernous Victorian building and erect a new noticeboard. Spending time every afternoon and evening visiting people in their own homes and building relationships with them and with the community was a no-brainer. It was rewarding, both personally and in laying foundations for the future.

In those days, doing what Christians used to call 'the work of God' was everything. The impression I received as a young man, growing up with parents who were very committed Christians, attending evangelical churches in Scotland and also while at College, was that you should give yourself firstly, secondly and thirdly to whatever work you believed God had called you to do for Him. There was no teaching or mentoring concerning where your wife and family came into all this. The result of such a background and the lack of biblical teaching on the subject of marriage and the family was that I threw myself into the 'work of God' at the Grove, studying in the mornings for two Sunday preaches and the mid-week prayer and bible study meeting. Afternoons and evenings I went out visiting, usually the older, retired people in the afternoon and in the evenings, young working people and students, who were beginning to come around the church. The only time I was at home, apart from meals, was a Saturday, which was my day off, on which Maureen insisted. Some years later, as I reflected on these early years in ministry, I was deeply saddened as I remembered that I had usually come home, at the end of afternoon visiting, about 5.30pm. We would have a meal together as a family and then I would be away by 7pm to spend the evenings spending time with people. I was sad that I had not been around to read, talk and pray with the children as they went to bed. I had been spending time with others but not with them those evenings. This reflection brought me to first ask God's forgiveness and then to speak to Kevin, Fiona and Stuart and tell them I was so sorry that I had not put them first in the way I ordered my days at that time.

Maureen, at the time, just accepted this lifestyle as part of 'the deal' in being married to a minister. At that time she learned to live with what appeared to be the commonly accepted status quo. However, she did point out to me, in no uncertain terms, that visiting young single women was not a good idea at all. This was absolutely true! But who would then follow them up on behalf of the church? There were no pastoral teams in those days, no expectation or indeed willingness that anyone else but the minister would engage in pastoral ministry. When we later arrived in Bournemouth, with the family having grown in years, Maureen became increasingly involved in pastoral care, discipling and counselling of women of all ages but at that time, it was not possible. What we did was run an open home, where many of these young working singles, men and women, came for meals, sometimes staying overnight, when the young women were able to talk and share and pray with Maureen. But Maureen's concern and warning to me was 'on the button'.

Sadly, bible colleges at that time were not at all geared up to teach the practical, down to earth stuff young men and women moving out into ministry needed to hear and take on board. Mentoring was a concept unknown at the time.

I am so grateful to God for Maureen for many reasons and this is certainly one of them: so often, especially in these early years in ministry, she pointed out to me areas where I myself should have known and lived better in the way I ordered my days and time. Living out that section of Ephesians 5:15-6:4 is foundational for a healthy, rich and God-honouring marital relationship and family life. Over the years we have been distressed by the knowledge that the marriages of some church leaders fall short of what could be termed 'rich'. Some of these marriages have failed altogether. We have discovered that unless you agree together to set in place time together and then steadfastly guard those times, you will both soon become like 'ships passing in the night'. This is not only about quality time e.g. a meal out together, it includes ensuring that you are engaging in real communication each and every day, truly listening to what that day has involved for your wife or husband. You may not always be enthralled by some of the stuff, but loving each other involves wanting to know and understand and care about what the other person has experienced.

It was in these years at Westbourne Grove that Maureen and I decided that we would also set apart a day a month for ourselves, without the children. After they had gone to school, we drove to Richmond Park and on the way bought yummy pastries. We would spend the day talking, walking and reading. Then we would get home in time for the end of the school day. Those days were a priority and we guarded them. I believe the best legacy you can give to your children is your love for each other and the security they receive from your loving commitment to and enjoyment of each other.

Back in the 1970s there were very few churches where a team ministry of salaried staff was in operation. It was not even in the thinking of most churches. These were the days of the so-called 'one-man ministry', except that many churches regarded the appointment of the minister, if married, as a 'bargain buy': in other words, they were getting two people for one salary and that salary or stipend as it was called, was very often insufficient to keep the wolf from the door without the addition of Government support through benefits. The church had a lovely house in Kensal Rise, just over two miles north of Notting Hill, along Ladbroke Grove and across the Harrow Road. Having lived in flats in Edinburgh and while at College, it was a luxury to have so much space and a garden as well. However, if you lived in the church house then the 'rent' was deducted from your stipend. In other words, your stipend was calculated on the basis you had free rent and utilities. At the Grove, money was certainly in short supply. Very few committed people and no bank reserves. The only way the church had survived financially and was able to pay some kind of stipend was through the renting out of the extensive basement halls as a storeroom for one of the many antique furniture businesses which plied their trade in our area of Notting Hill.

Following the Welcome Service, when greetings were brought from local churches and from people within the Grove itself, the leader of the Women's Meeting publicly announced how glad she was that Maureen would be taking up the leadership of the Women's Meeting immediately. There had been not a word about this previously and Maureen was flabbergasted and none too happy, to put it mildly. But she did it. This involved arranging and leading the weekly gathering and ensuring there was a Christmas Event for them including lots of food. It always amazed us how those ladies could pack the food away. Maureen decided to arrange an outing for them every summer to places like the Thames at Richmond and Kew Gardens. Again, food was rather important to the success of the venture. These women took us both to their hearts and their love and care and appreciation meant much to us as young things starting out.

We all enjoyed living in Kensal Rise. It was a fascinatingly mixed area. Our neighbours on one side were Londoners. The husband and sons revelled in large American cars and were forever working away on another wreck. His wife loved singing at the top of her voice one of the hit songs of the time, 'Stand by your man'. On the other side of our home, our neighbours were a family from our church. That was certainly not ideal, to say the least, and it could have made for difficulties. In fact, it worked well for all of us. The children of the two families were all good friends. There were increasing numbers of West Indians and other nationalities like a Greek family, whose daughter became a life-long friend of our daughter, Fiona. The children had many friends in the road and enjoyed their local schools. Kevin attended the school in Harvist Road, Kensal Rise and Fiona and Stuart went to a Junior school in Donnington, Willesden. One day Maureen had a call from the Headmistress, Miss Pardoe. Two young brothers had been bullying Stuart. Fiona saw it and being the big sister out to protect her younger brother, grabbed a book and hit one of the boys with it. Never a dull moment when you have a young family, but Fiona's care for her brother was rather endearing.

There was another family who lived a few doors away from us who also worshipped at The Grove. They were from mid-Wales originally and had a cottage there, which they generously offered to us as a family for a week around Easter every year. We had eight successive years of holidays there at Talley, between Llandeilo and Lampeter. The cottage was up a lane next to a sheep farm and as we used to go in springtime, the fields were full of new-born lambs and the cottage garden covered in daffodils. The farmers had two dogs and this was Fiona's introduction to her lifelong love of dogs. By the lane there was a stream. Kevin, Fiona and Stuart loved to kick a ball about in the lane and of course the ball often went into the water. 'Stuart, get the ball', the older two would cry and off Stuart toddled to retrieve it... he is not best blessed now by the memory. We would go for family walks in the many Forestry Commission forests in the area and the trip to Market Day in Carmarthen was always keenly anticipated. Fiona and Stuart would spend their pocket money very quickly on chocolate goodies. Kevin would spend just a small sum on a tube of Polos and eke them out for days, much to the chagrin of his brother and sister, who had long since consumed their chosen confectionery.

Our family holidays were very inexpensive affairs. Children were much more easily satisfied with simple things in those days, as you can tell from the above record. But their enjoyment of these weeks in Wales and other similar holidays in the summer was no less than had we been able to afford something much more expensive and elaborate. They still all recount these times with fun and laughter. Family holidays, away from work and school, are very important in building memories and in shaping family life.

Carving out time to be together as family must be a priority in the life of someone called to lead the local church. If we are called to lead others, then we are called to shape all of our life, family life included, in a way that honours Jesus, blesses our children and models love, care and protection.

Maureen's early insistence that I have a day off every week, Saturday as it was at that time, was to do with love, care and protection for myself, our marriage and especially our life together as a family. Failure to build these kinds of boundaries in some church leader's homes has led to children growing up with little love and respect for their parents and a similar attitude to their parents' God.

The congregation gradually grew in numbers. The intergenerational and cross-cultural dimensions added life and fun. The growing numbers of students brought about increasing opportunities to speak at Christian Unions, Nurses' Christian Fellowships and Scripture Union groups in schools. Before arriving at the Grove, I had no experience of uniformed organisations, but there were excellent Boys' Brigade and Girls' Brigade Companies in the church and so I soon learned. Fiona joined the Girls' Brigade and loved it, with particularly fond memories of camps on the Isle of Wight. Kevin was in the Boys Brigade and every summer we had a camp at Ringstead Bay, just west of Lulworth Cove, Dorset. Kevin remembers how one day we went over on the ferry from Studland to Sandbanks, Poole. It is the narrowest water crossing imaginable. I knew that when the ferry arrived in Sandbanks, we would be in a one-way system. The officers told these inner London lads that we were going to France and, of course, we would have to drive on the right. It was a while before they realised they were still in England. These Brigades were led by officers from the church who loved Jesus, loved the youngsters, and gave themselves to helping these girls and boys to understand and receive the love of God for themselves.

CHAPTER 5

The Fire of God
1970 – 1978

Commencing in your first church is a rather huge undertaking, but when you are young and fresh out of bible college, you go for it with alacrity. However, within a year or so, my early enthusiasm for serving God in Notting Hill began to disappear. The needs of the people in the community and the weight of the responsibility to lead the people in their relationship with God and their mission to make Christ known, pressed in upon me. I simply felt I did not have what it was going to take. You leave college ready to set the heather on fire and then you discover that, despite all the knowledge you have gained in three years of study, you are short of the essential ingredient, which no one appeared to have mentioned – that is, the fire of God.

This caused me to begin to seek more of God. I realised that in the goodness of God I had a large reservoir of biblical knowledge. Following the move to Edinburgh there had been the stimulating and challenging ministry of Dr Alan Redpath at Charlotte Chapel, Edinburgh, and more recently the years at London Bible College. However, my heart-knowledge and heart-experience of God – Father, Son, and Holy Spirit – was thin, weak, and lacked reality.

As I began to pray and tell God about my need, I decided to ask for counsel from some of the older church leaders in the district, men I respected in God. One was dear John Fidge, who was leading Kensal Gospel Mission near Ladbroke Grove, and the other Eldon Corsie, leader of Kensington Temple, a growing Elim church in Notting Hill Gate. Each of them encouraged me to continue to seek God while continuing with the ministry to which God had called me. I was rather disappointed. I felt like Naaman, the leprous commander of the Syrian armies, when he called on the prophet Elisha, expecting the prophet to heal him, only to hear him say, 'Go to the river and wash seven times and you will be clean'. (2 Kings 5) However, the counsel I received from these men was from God and I continued to pray for more of Him and to get on with the work of leading the church. Of course, God had his own agenda which I would soon discover.

Around this time Maureen and I had an evening with a couple we had known at College who were now ministering in Hammersmith, not far from us in west-central London. As the evening progressed, we remarked that there was something different about them. They had always been naturally quiet and reserved in their ways and when they explained to us that they had been filled with the Holy Spirit you could have knocked us sideways. In our last couple of years at College, there was a lot of talk about what was termed the neo-pentecostal movement and no end of non-complimentary stories about people who had had some kind of Holy Spirit experience. All this made us very wary of any talk of the Spirit. Reflecting on what God had evidently done in our friends' lives and on other ways in which God had been showing us that there was much more He wanted to teach and reveal to us about the Person and Work of His Spirit, I repented of my sinful thinking and heart attitude towards the Holy Spirit. I also asked God's forgiveness for things I had thought and sometimes expressed about some students at College who had shared their convictions and experiences in those days. I confessed my fears and ignorance. I asked God to forgive and cleanse me and teach and lead me into His truth and the freedom Jesus promised it always brings.

At the same time, an older woman began to worship at the church on Sunday mornings. One Sunday as she left at the end of the service, she said to me: 'David, thank you as always for preaching the Word of God. But you need the Spirit!' It was said with a smile and with gentleness. I knew the Lord was speaking to me through her. A little later I discovered who she was. Her husband was Rev Roy Jeremiah, an Anglican vicar who led the London Healing Mission just a few streets from the Grove. The London Healing Mission! The ministry of healing was something I knew nothing about. In all my considerable exposure to excellent bible teaching over the years, healing was a subject (one of many, it would turn out) that had not been remotely covered. Added to which, I had little, if any, experience of the Church of England and vicars, so all in all I decided to steer clear of this dear lady's husband.

A couple of weeks later the phone rang and it was Rev Roy Jeremiah. He mentioned his wife and her appreciation of my ministry and invited me to come and meet him so that we could get to know one another. This filled me with no joy at all. But how could I refuse? A few days later I arrived at the London Healing Mission, based in an attractive street in North Kensington, only a block or so away from the church. I was somewhat nervous to say the least. Over a drink of tea, Roy asked me about myself and, against my better judgment, I found myself sharing the same story I had previously chosen to share with John Fidge and Eldon Corsie. This time, however, I was doing so rather reluctantly: this had not been at my initiative. Perhaps God was taking the initiative? After all, I had asked Him. How quickly we can forget what we say to God.

Roy asked me if he could pray for me. Horror of horrors! An Anglican vicar, leader of the London Healing Mission, wanted to pray for me. I would have been delighted and thankful if one of those other leaders I had sought out had offered to pray for me – that had been my hope when I went to see them. They led conservative evangelical churches and were solid biblical guys (sure, Eldon was leading a large Pentecostal church, but I knew him), whereas Roy Jeremiah – I knew next to nothing about him and what I did know, Church of England and leader of a Healing Mission, did not make me feel at ease at all. Again, the story of Naaman and his reaction to Elisha's direction to him to bathe in that foreign little Jordan river came to mind. That was exactly what I was thinking and how I was feeling. However, thank you, Lord, I remembered the end of that Old Testament story too.

I indicated to Roy that he could pray for me. I didn't say I was happy for him to do so. That would have been going well beyond where I was at. I have no memory at all of what Roy prayed. He laid his hands gently on my head and prayed. Doubtless it was for more of God, as that was the journey I was on and which I had been describing to him.

I do remember very clearly what then took place. I began to feel as if all the energy and strength were being drained from me. I felt weak, very weak. I was a young man at the end of my twenties. I went out to my car and drove the two miles or so home along Ladbroke Grove and across the Harrow Road to Kensal Rise. To Maureen's considerable surprise and not a little concern I said I had to go and rest. I explained what had happened and how I felt so very weak. I reflected that this was the exact opposite to what I expected to happen when I wanted to have more of God and be filled with His Spirit. Later I was to realise that whatever else God was doing, emptying precedes filling.

In the weeks and months which followed Roy explained to me a little about the nature of the issues that would sometimes present when people came to see him for healing. There were times when deliverance was required for healing to be ministered. All of this was new to me and although I wanted to learn more about how to minister the grace of God to people in need, I was considerably nervous and cautious. On one occasion Roy telephoned to ask if I would be free one afternoon as he would appreciate prayer support.

I looked at my diary and realised that I could be available, although I wished I couldn't. I was still quite reluctant to move further into areas with which I was unfamiliar. I also felt very unprepared and lacking the spiritual tools I needed.

When I arrived at the Mission, Roy explained something of the issues that were presenting in the person he had arranged to see. He said that after he had spent an initial time with the individual, he would invite me to join them. I was left in a separate room where I began to seek God for His help: for insight, wisdom, and equipping. As I prayed, nervous and only too aware of my inadequacy, I found myself speaking out in a language I had never learned. I realised that this was the Holy Spirit gift of tongues described in the New Testament. I discovered that there was a new energy and passion in my praying; in fact, I realised and knew that in the unknown words I was speaking out there was a powerful declaration about God and the Kingdom of His Son, the Lord Jesus Christ.

I was very thankful indeed that God had answered my prayer for more of Him and His Holy Spirit. But the work that God was doing in me presented me with some additional difficulties. First and foremost, my wife Maureen. She understandably was somewhat unsure about what had happened when Roy Jeremiah prayed for me that day and I came home so physically weak that I had to rest. She was concerned that the work of the Spirit in my life would cause me to love the Lord Jesus Christ more and love her less and that she would 'lose' me. We talked much about these things, but despite my reassurance that although the work of the Holy Spirit is always to cause us to love Christ in increasing measure, the Spirit's work is also very much to cause husbands to love their wives as Christ loved His Church. In time, by the grace of God, Maureen became much less concerned and knew that my love for her was undiminished.

Then there was the church. What was I to do? God had met with me by His Spirit and had taught me – even with a physical demonstration in my own body – that His work was far too much for me. It would not be in my energy and strength but by His Spirit that His people would grow in their relationship with God and in their mission to make Jesus known. He was teaching me about the gifts and tools for ministry that the Spirit supplied and I was learning that the people of God needed the equipping of God in order to fulfill their calling to love God, love one another, and love the lost.

The congregation was still small numerically. Yes, we had grown but fragility in many areas was evident. I was conscious that the church had only just survived the collapse of the ministry that preceded our arrival. We were just beginning to build numbers and community again. If I were to start to teach and share my grace encounter with the Holy Spirit, revealing that I was speaking in tongues in my private devotions and was occasionally engaged in assisting in healing and deliverance at the London Healing Mission, surely the slow and steady build would swiftly collapse, and Westbourne Grove Baptist Church would perhaps cease to be.

In the 1970s, rumours and stories about the Holy Spirit were beginning to gain circulation among some Christians. There were exaggerated accounts of 'off the wall' neo-pentecostalists, or sometimes they would be called 'charismatics'. There was talk about the 'renewal movement'. Many were either fearful or antagonistic towards any mention of the Holy Spirit. As my experience had evidenced, there had been a serious lack of biblical teaching about the Person and Work of the Spirit, particularly in His equipping of the church for holiness, ministry, and spiritual warfare. That ignorance was fertile ground for fear, anxious talk, opposition, and indeed sometimes inappropriate expectation and practice.

So, what was I to do? In this rather febrile atmosphere, where some churches were experiencing painful disagreement, dishonouring talk, and indeed schism, I was extremely concerned about what I should do. If I were to nail my colours to the mast, as it were, this small company of God's people, who I loved, perhaps would be scattered to the winds and the cause of Christ in this corner of Notting Hill be forever lost beneath the waves.

I decided to keep silent. I would say nothing about what God was about in my life, nor would I teach what the Bible had to say about the ministry of the Spirit. From time to time, in pastoral conversation with people in the church who I believed would be helped, I would share some of my convictions about these things from the Word of God and would pray for them. But in the subsequent years at Westbourne Grove, I did not open up this subject from the Word of God in Sunday preaching or in mid-week bible studies. My use of the Holy Spirit's gift of tongues in my personal worship and prayer life became less and less until I almost ceased to use that gift at all. In the meantime, Maureen had begun to pray and seek God for more of Him in her life and was asking God about the ministry of the Spirit.

I thank God that, from the beginning of my years in church leadership, I had a longing to see church leaders and churches praying and working together in their localities. So it was that the North Kensington and District Evangelical Fellowship was commenced. In our area, there were several gospel churches which included Kensal Gospel Mission, Kensington Temple, and Peniel Chapel near the Portobello Road, with its renowned Market. It was a joy to have Lyndon Bowring, another graduate of London Bible College, arrive at Kensington Temple and we all began to develop supportive relationships and pray for one another and our churches. When the Grove initiated a summer outreach in the well-known local Portobello Road Market, we had the prayers and help of local leaders and churches.

As a young man just setting out on the journey of church leadership in a Baptist church, the Baptist Union expected me to become what they called an accredited minister. But the Baptist Union, at that time. was being led by men who were somewhat adrift from biblical moorings. Indeed, early in my time at Westbourne Grove, the Baptist Union appointed as President someone who had previously gone on record denying the deity of Christ. Ecumenism was the order of the day, but sadly, not the ecumenism of my brothers in the Gospel in the North Kensington and District Evangelical Fellowship. I resisted the pressure from the then London Baptist Superintendent, who suggested that there was no way I or this numerically weak church could survive without the aid of the Union. In the light of the biblical slide in the Baptist Union, Westbourne Grove Baptist Church seceded from the Baptist Union. Some Baptist churches, who also seceded at that time, lost the use of their buildings. Due to the nature of the Trust Deed of our buildings we thankfully retained ours.

In refusing to become an accredited minister of the Baptist Union, I could not therefore attend the area Baptist ministers fraternal. However, I had decided when I arrived at Westbourne Grove, that I would meet with the ministers of the local Fellowship of Independent Churches (FIEC). I had become a personal member of FIEC and that enabled me to do so. It was a joy and encouragement to meet with these brothers over my years at The Grove and their prayers, counsel, and support were invaluable.

Another strategic involvement in those London years was my attendance at the Westminster Fellowship, held monthly at Westminster Chapel and chaired by Dr Martyn Lloyd-Jones. Around 150 leaders from churches across England and Wales would gather to listen and discuss theological issues and practical matters relevant to church leaders. It was an immense privilege for a young man like me. I remember well a particular occasion when a young student studying music in London was attending our church. Maureen and I knew her well. Our home was always full of young single people studying or working in London. But there was something concerning about this young lady and we believed that it possibly had a demonic root. I decided to telephone 'the Doctor', as Dr Martyn Lloyd-Jones was fondly known, to ask his advice. He listened to me and then said, 'I will come and meet her with you at your church'. I was bowled over that he would want to meet us. He arrived at the arranged time and I sat and observed while praying quietly. He asked the young lady some questions and then stretched out his hand towards her. We met in the vestry which was a large room and the three of us were sat considerably apart. The Doctor prayed, commanded the demonic to leave her, and she quietly and undemonstratively slid off her chair to the floor. He wrote out a prescription for me to take to my GP and asked Maureen and me to take her home and let her sleep overnight. We did and she slept for 12 hours. The young lady was free, healed, and grew on in God.

Through this experience, God revealed to us that there were sometimes root reasons for a failure of growth in God in some Christians. This wasn't what I'd experienced before with common issues, such as lack of attention to the spiritual disciplines of biblical reflection, prayer, worship, and keeping short accounts with God over issues of sin and disobedience. In our next church situation, we would learn to recognise other barriers to spiritual growth and vitality, which although not requiring deliverance from demonic oppression, did require in the believers concerned, a recognition of an issue in their lives which, necessitated confession, repentance, receiving God's forgiveness and building new godly patterns into their lives to facilitate growth in God.

By the 70s, Notting Hill was becoming more widely known. The Notting Hill Carnival which had been going on since 1964, began as a street party to celebrate Caribbean culture. Notting Hill had a history of racial problems. In 1958 it was the scene of race riots instigated by the fascist British Union. However, the Carnival, which gathered increasing numbers of people each year, had been relatively free of serious public order problems. But in 1976 the

Carnival ended in a riot with more than 100 police officers being taken to hospital and about 60 carnival-goers also needing hospital treatment. The trouble appeared to start when the police attempted to arrest a pickpocket near the Portobello Road. The police were attacked with stones and missiles and they armed themselves with dustbin lids, milk crates, and wire fencing and charged the rioters. Gangs of youths took advantage of the situation and there was a lot of mindless violence. The 1976 riot did not negatively impact relationships among the local population, although relationships between the police and the black community, which had been problematic for some years, were, understandably, not helped.

The years at Westbourne Grove passed. The church continued to grow numerically, through some becoming followers of Jesus for the first time and others coming to us as they moved into the area and looked for a community of Christians in which to worship and serve. We were thankful to God for the growth of many in their relationship with Him and for all that we were learning and enjoying in those early days in Christian ministry. The church family at The Grove were a joy; so much fun and friendship together and a precious sense of being a community loved by God and loving each other.

Then around Easter 1978, on our annual week's family holiday in Tegfan, our friends' cottage in Wales, Maureen and I unaccountably began to feel that something was changing. We described it to one another through a gardening picture. When you prepare to move a shrub that is secure and growing well where it is, you begin to loosen the earth around the roots. We felt as if that was what God was doing with us – he appeared to be digging gently but firmly around us; in fact, He was preparing us to be transplanted. We could point to nothing at all which would have brought about this sense within us. We had no desire to move from 'The Grove'. We were all settled as a family and incredibly happy indeed in a loving and caring church community. But nonetheless, we both had this sense that in some way God was preparing to ease us out from where we were.

✎

A few weeks later, after our Easter break, I had an invitation to preach at a church in Bournemouth. Bournemouth, of all places. My parents had this connection to Bournemouth having honeymooned there and a fondness for the area after we had lived there as a family for a year when I was young.

One of the students who worshipped with us at The Grove had, without my knowledge, suggested to her father, who was a deacon in this Bournemouth church, that they should invite me to preach one Sunday. Winton Free Evangelical Church was in a situation where they were asking God to lead them to their next Pastor. I duly went to Winton and preached there and subsequently was invited back with Maureen to preach 'with a view'. This was the rather strange expression that many churches used when they thought they would like to hear someone preach a second time and quiz them and see if this could be a likely new Pastor.

In conversation with the Deacons, who in the absence of any Elders had the responsibility to explore the way forward to the appointment of a new Pastor, I asked many questions and so did they. In the course of this, I described my convictions concerning the ministry of the Holy Spirit, as I knew God was making clear to me that I must be upfront with them about these things. I also mentioned that I was involved on the Boards of two overseas missions and that I may well request time out, on occasions, to visit and minister to mission personnel overseas. The church community met and on the recommendation of the Deacons they invited Maureen and I and the family to move to Bournemouth and for me to prepare to become the pastor. We knew this was from God. We knew we had to be sure of that. But little did we realise then how important it would become that we had God's sure and certain call as an anchor when the storms came. Oh, and by the by, my parents were over the moon that we were moving to Bournemouth. They had already moved some years before from Edinburgh to Surrey and subsequently, in later years, they came to live in Bournemouth.

✎

One morning in August 1978, outside a row of terraced houses in Kensal Rise, northwest London, you would have seen a removal lorry crammed full, with some children's bikes last in, along with a few garden plants. The tailgate slammed shut and it drove off towards the North Circular Road, Richmond, and the southwest. Our white Morris Marina sat outside the house which had been our home for the past eight years. Precious personal possessions had been retained for the car and last in was Ben the rabbit and Mac the budgie, sitting on the children's laps in the back seat. Well, not exactly sitting – they were in a hutch and cage. Then we took a last nostalgic walk around the house. Checking that we had not left anything behind and that the house was secure, we said our goodbyes to neighbours and friends and drove slowly away. It was tough to say goodbye to a special church family at The Grove, but the journey towards a new season of life for us all had begun.

CHAPTER 6

Nailing My Colours to the Mast
1978 – 1979

Our first night in our new home in Winton, Bournemouth was vastly different. All the family was safely bedded down and Maureen and I were lying in bed chatting through the events of the day. We talked together about how strange it was, compared to living in northwest London, that cars were not parked nose-to-tail outside the houses on both sides of the road. And it was so quiet. Then, suddenly, at 11pm, the streetlights went out! We lay there, a bit shocked, and then chuckled. Anything less like Kensal Rise could not be imagined. There, the streetlights never went out at night, car doors banging, people shouting, the sounds of reggae music or country and western, especially loved by our neighbour, went on into the wee small hours. We felt as if we had come to a village in the depths of the countryside.

The church house (or manse as it is known in Scotland) was a lovely family home about a five-minute walk from the church. It had been bought as a new build by the first pastor and his wife. When he died, it was sold to the church and it had been the church's house in which all the pastors and their families had lived ever since. It would require quite a considerable amount of tender loving care to bring it up to speed as far as the interior was concerned and some persuasion to ensure that the church arranged for some essential kitchen work to be attended to. But it got there, eventually.

On Saturday 23rd September 1978, a coach load of the church community from The Grove, including many West Indians and Nigerians and their children in colourful national clothes, disembarked amid much shouting and exuberant greeting. Maureen and I thought, 'We are going to miss this so much!' There was almost no ethnic diversity in Bournemouth at that time and their arrival that day made us feel thankful and grateful for the love and friendships we had enjoyed over the eight years in west London. It also made us realise that whatever ministry God had for us in Bournemouth, it was likely to be quite different from what we'd enjoyed in London.

The Free Evangelical Church, in the Winton area of Bournemouth, began its life in 1921. Winton Baptist Church, a few blocks distant, had appointed someone to lead their church whose ministry, it discovered in due course, was not as biblically based as they had believed and expected. This resulted in some members leaving and beginning to 'meet together' in their own homes.

On 21st July 1921, thirteen people met and agreed to form a church. (Thus 2021 marks the church's centenary). One of those founder members was Dorothy Parr, who became the first person from the church to be sent overseas as a missionary when she sailed for Japan in 1927.

Walter Stalley and his wife Maud, who had met and married while missionaries in India had returned to the UK due to Maud's ill health. Walter was appointed as the first pastor of the newly-birthed church that summer. Not surprisingly, a significant aspect of the early foundations of the church was 'a keen missionary spirit' which evidenced itself in committed prayer and giving to overseas missions. In those early years, there was also considerable investment in open-air witness, door-to-door visitation, and children's ministry.

In 1928 a piece of land and a cottage were purchased in Calvin Road and the dedication service of the church's new premises took place on 6 March 1929 when E.J. Poole-Connor, the founder of the Fellowship of Independent Evangelical Churches (FIEC) was the preacher. It was of interest to me was that he had at one time been pastor of Talbot Tabernacle, a few minutes from 'The Grove' in Notting Hill.

In 1948, after 27 years, Walter Stalley retired and Harold Fife succeeded him as pastor. Harold Fife was a member of the council of the North Africa Mission and while leading the church he made many preaching and pastoral visits to the mission personnel in North Africa. In 1957 Harold Fife was succeeded by Arthur Rutt who had been President of FIEC in 1955. His ministry at Winton was very brief. He died suddenly in 1958, but it was not until 1963 that Peter Culver was appointed. Peter had been assistant to Francis Dixon at Lansdowne Baptist Church, Bournemouth, and led the church in Winton for thirteen years. During his time, in 1971, the church celebrated its Jubilee Year with many well-known preachers visiting including Dr Martyn Lloyd-Jones. Two years before I was invited to lead the church, in 1976, Peter Culver became pastor of Widcombe Baptist Church, in Bath.

When I commenced at The Free Evangelical Church, Winton in 1978, those people actively committed to the life of the church numbered around 65 adults. Winton was a typical independent evangelical church of its time. The previous ministry, which had ended just over two years before we arrived, was one where the Word of God was consistently preached week by week. There had been an excellent children's and youth ministry for some years, although the high-water mark had passed some time before we arrived. Three church members were working overseas as missionaries, one was a founder member of the church, so there was a strong commitment to overseas mission.

Beginning in ministry at Westbourne Grove Baptist Church in Notting Hill, I had given priority to visiting everyone in their own home, doing my best to get to know them as well as possible. That didn't take long at 'The Grove' as there were only about fourteen adults when I arrived. Here at Winton, 65 was hardly huge numbers, but it was going to take longer, and in my view, time well spent. So, I began to set aside afternoons and evenings (when there were no meetings) for visiting, listening and asking questions. I would then write up, on a card-index system, the information gained: family names and details, their employment, their salvation story and current discipleship situation, their church history at Winton and any previous church connection. It was important that these visits were a two-way street. In this way, it gave an opportunity for each of them to get to know me and learn about the journey Maureen and I had been on over the years.

I had discovered in London, where the congregation was much more 'on the move', that remembering people's names and other personal information they had shared with me was important for building relationships and helping people to feel 'at home' in the life of the church. Although people's lives here in Bournemouth were by and large very static and the average age was older, building relationship and friendship is strategic. Investing time and energy in people's lives was going to be just as vital here as in London; maybe a little more difficult and time consuming and stretching, but nonetheless essential.

As I visited, I discovered some large differences between Westbourne Grove Baptist Church and the church here in Winton. First of all, to my astonishment and concern, few people in the church knew each other to any depth. Many had been attending for years, yet too many lacked any real relationship with others. This was a complete contrast to London. It wasn't to do with numbers in the congregation, as by the time we left the church in Notting Hill, we had a similar number of people to Winton. Some people regarded others as in a different class. They felt they couldn't engage them in conversation and certainly would never dream of inviting them for a meal – not even a cup of tea! In the London church, people loved sharing food and fun together. Our home in Kensal Rise was a veritable thoroughfare of nationalities, ages and backgrounds, including those with addiction issues. At Winton it was as if people were billiard balls, bumping into one another and bouncing away again.

The second difference that very quickly hit us was the way in which we were regarded and referred to. In Winton, when I first arrived, I was referred to as 'The Pastor'. In London, I was 'David' and my wife was 'Maureen'. Maureen found it hard being introduced by one member to another in these terms: 'This is Mrs Craig, the Pastor's wife.' We laughed about it sometimes and would joke amongst ourselves about introducing one of the women to another woman as 'This is the solicitor's wife!' This contributed to the early months not being easy for Maureen. Whereas I was immediately visiting people in their homes, our children were still young and she did not have the opportunity and acceptance that comes with being 'The Pastor'. So, after being friends with everyone at Westbourne Grove, Maureen felt somewhat isolated in these early days at Winton.

Something that was exactly the same for Maureen, as in London, was that on the day of our Welcome Service at Winton the leader of the Women's Meeting said to her, 'Of course, you will be taking over the Women's Meeting.' And that was after I had particularly made a point of telling the Deacons about Maureen's experience when we first arrived at Westbourne Grove and requested that the same situation did not take place here. You can imagine that the moment we arrived home after the Welcome Service, Maureen immediately said to me, 'I thought you had told the Deacons that I would not be going straight into leading the Women's Meeting?!' Fortunately, I could insist that I had done as asked, so obviously, the Deacons had not passed the message down the line. A further difficult one for Maureen in those days, as she did in fact begin to get involved in the Women's work, was being told quite often: 'Mrs Culver didn't do it that way!' (Mrs Culver being the wife of the previous pastor).

On Sunday 24th September 1978, following the Welcome Service the previous day, we said farewell and prayed for Dorothy Parr, one of the founder members of the church. Dorothy was returning to Japan, where she had been a pioneer missionary since 1927, remaining in Japan through the Second World War, serving Christ and His church. Dorothy had some amazing accounts of God's provision through those years. As well as Dorothy, two other members of the church were serving overseas, Muriel in Algeria and Ann in her first term in Japan.

In those early days of visiting people in their homes, I began to recognise that some of the 'older saints' were 'prayer warriors'. In the main, they were single women who had been committed to the church since its earliest days. Two of those prayer warriors were Kitty and Ethel. Kitty had been a member of the church since its foundation and had prayed for the church and for her contemporary Dorothy Parr through all her years in Japan. Ethel became a member in 1950 and as well as interceding for the church, was leading the Missionary Committee when I arrived in 1978. Her love for Jesus was evidenced in her intercession for the church around the world. Discovering the church's prayer warriors heartened me no end. These were two of them – there were others. I thanked God so often for placing people in the church who knew God and gave themselves to prayer.

The church met twice on a Sunday, which was usual for almost all evangelical churches at the time. The pattern of service in the morning was four hymns, chosen from Hymns of Faith, prayer, bible reading, children's talk, and a preach. The evening followed a similar order.

On Sunday mornings I began by preaching through Colossians and in the evenings, I took the theme of Commitment to Christ. The work among children and young people continued week by week and there were a good number of home Bible Study Groups meeting regularly. The Church prayer meeting was on Monday evenings.

A special week of outreach and mission to adults had been arranged for March 1979 led by evangelists Derek Cleave and Peter Anderson. House meetings were one of the ways used to share the Gospel with friends and neighbours and a few people came to faith in Christ and were added to the church. Some of those were to become a great resource of prayer and spiritual wisdom in the years ahead. Subsequently, an Evangelistic Committee was formed to continue and move forward the evangelistic heart and activity which resulted from the mission week.

In the summer of 1979, when we went on holiday as a family, I was reviewing our first year at Winton. One of the issues that was in the forefront of my mind was my experience of preaching to the church week by week: the people, with a few exceptions, were expressionless and appeared unresponsive, almost dead, as it were. I was under no illusions about my preaching. I had never considered myself greatly gifted in that area and compared myself poorly to many of my contemporaries at College when we were in our first church in London. Indeed, during this first year at Winton God had clearly spoken to me from Jeremiah 1:17, 'Do not be terrified by them or I will terrify you before them.' There were men in the church who were gifted in the Word of God and in teaching and preaching and I considered their gifting in God to be way beyond mine. And in that judgement, I was correct! But God had been clearly speaking to me from the whole of Jeremiah 1, namely that He had called me to lead the church, not these men and I was not to make excuses about my youth and relative inexperience compared to them. Rather I was to 'Stand up and say... whatever I command you.'

As I continued to reflect on my experience of preaching Sunday by Sunday in that first year, I was asking God, 'What is it about this congregation? What is wrong? What is missing?' As God does sometimes, He didn't answer my question. Instead, He asked me a question, 'What about YOU?' The Lord Jesus took me back to my encounter with the Holy Spirit in London. He asked me if I was going to 'nail my colours to the mast', as it were, here in Bournemouth, in a way I had not done in the church in London. The Lord warned me, that if I obeyed Him, I would encounter difficulties and opposition and that I would be regarded by more than a few as having 'gone off the rails' biblically. By His grace, I was enabled to reply, 'Yes'.

This involved me in repenting of my London decision when I held back from sharing with the church there my experience and biblical convictions concerning the place of the Spirit in the life of the believer and in the life and worship of the church. I received God's forgiveness and opened up my life again to all that the Lord Jesus loves to pour out of His Spirit. Having allowed the gift of tongues to lie fallow in my devotional life for a few years, I began to pray in the Spirit again and seek more of Christ. It would not be the first time that God would speak powerfully to me through Jeremiah 1 – that Scripture was a constant source of encouragement, affirmation, strength (and heavenly warning) in the months and years ahead. Jeremiah 1:4-19 was one of the scriptures God used to encourage us to pursue the course He had given us to walk. Now that I had, after some years, 'agreed with God' it would soon be time to 'nail my colours to the mast' in my ministry and leadership at Winton. I would need to dig into God for all the courage and grace I would need in the days ahead.

CHAPTER 7

Learning, Forgiveness and Freedom
1979 – 1983

Before we go further in this journey, it helps to know some of what was taking place in the wider world. As Christ's followers, we need to be able to set personal and local events in the larger context of current world events. Praying for the church of Christ around the globe, whether personally or corporately, requires knowledge of contemporary situations as they affect the people of God, particularly as so many churches and church leaders are suffering severely in many nations. In 1979 Russia invaded Afghanistan and China instituted the one-child policy. Lord Mountbatten, while sailing with family members, was murdered by an IRA bomb placed in his boat and Margaret Thatcher became Prime Minister in May and was to lead the UK until 1990. All of these events were destined to be significant for countless numbers of people.

In our local context, the name of the church, The Free Evangelical Church, Winton, did not slide too easily off the tongue. Thinking about the man in the street, what on earth does the word 'free' mean or imply? 'Does it mean you don't take up offerings or have a collection in your church?!' We arrived at the point where we agreed to drop the word 'free' and simply called the church Winton Evangelical Church, even though many Christians in Bournemouth, when referring to the church, had called it 'Calvin Road' for years, as that was where the premises were located. But nonetheless, Winton Evangelical Church it was for now.

Up until now, the church had always been led by a pastor and deacons. From the time I arrived, I had been concerned to see us move towards appointing elders to be alongside the pastor in having spiritual oversight and responsibility. In the autumn of 1979, the church recognised the first elder who would serve with me.

The autumn of 1979 also saw the commencement of what would prove to be a long and profitable relationship, for the church and for me personally, with Moorlands Bible College (now Moorlands College). In September 1979 we welcomed a third-year student to be a student pastor with us during his final year. This arrangement with Moorlands continued over many years and the students were invariably a very real addition to the life of the church, helping and serving in a variety of ways according to their gifting. It fell to me to be their placement supervisor for the year, and this gave me many opportunities to get to know them well and discuss issues with them which were of a practical and down-to-earth nature. Remembering how my years at London Bible College had lacked that kind of input, I was glad of the opportunity to talk through with them the 'stuff of ministry', as it were.

Bournemouth had recently become a centre for the teaching of English as a foreign language. This was true all year round, but each summer saw an influx of younger students arriving for shorter courses during their summer vacation. A summer outreach to overseas students had been commenced ten years earlier, which involved Lansdowne Baptist Church, Moordown Baptist Church and Winton Evangelical Church. Team members were drawn from these local churches, along with university students from different parts of the UK who came to help after hearing about the opportunity through their Christian Unions. As a church we cherished being involved in this annual summer outreach, providing some of the morning bible teaching for the teams, who were often billeted at our Calvin Road premises.

The church also benefited from having an increasing number of longer-term overseas students worshipping with us and this was the case for many years. It was a joy to baptise some on confession of their faith in Christ and to witness others growing in their relationship with God while they were with us. The majority tended to be from Europe and quite a number of them were learning English prior to moving overseas as missionaries. Among this group, it was great to have a continuing number every year who were sent to Bournemouth for English language training by the Liebenzeller Mission. This church-planting mission emanated from Germany, but as well as Germans we had candidates from Austria and Switzerland. Maureen and I missed the international nature of leading a London congregation. Having these students year by year, helped us in that regard.

In 1980, the congregation was beginning to grow with additions through salvation and increasing numbers of young people and adults being baptised on confession of faith. In the two years to the end of 1980, we had had the joy of seeing 34 people baptised, including our son Kevin.

In London, when I had an encounter with the Holy Spirit, Maureen had uncertainty about what had happened to me, her main concern was that the work of the Spirit in my life would cause me to love the Lord Jesus more and love her less and that she would 'lose' me. In time, Maureen knew that her fears were totally unfounded, but she was still a little unsure about the work of the Spirit in terms of spiritual gifts and spiritual warfare. Maureen had continued to reflect on these things, study the Scriptures and talk to God about them. She was becoming increasingly hungry for more of God and His Spirit. One weekend in March 1980 I was away preaching in Liverpool. On Sunday, Maureen decided that she must go and ask a certain person in the church to pray for her to be filled with the Holy Spirit. When she went to look for him after the service, he was not to be seen. Later that day, at home, Maureen told the Lord Jesus about what had happened and asked Him to pour out His Spirit upon her. God met with her. A few weeks later she went to a couple in the church and asked them to pray for her to receive the gift of tongues. In His grace, the Lord Jesus answered her request.

By the summer of 1981, some expressions of disquiet had begun to be made by a few people in the church. The main areas of concern may seem shocking non-events now, but at the time, they were very real areas of challenge and breakthrough.

One issue that disturbed them was the fact that in 1980 we had produced a songbook for use in the Sunday services. The songbook did not replace the use of Hymns of Faith but enabled us to begin to use of some of the new songs that were being written and sung in some churches. But there were those who did not appreciate the use of these more recent expressions of praise and worship. There had also been some changes to the format of the evening service, with one Sunday evening a month being 'opened up' to give more time for worship and prayer.

It is perhaps worth explaining something of the background to what I have just described, as for many who are reading this, church as it was forty years ago is a foreign land. Churches had a hymnbook and that was it usually, as far as what was sung was concerned. Depending on the denomination you belonged to, it was their hymnbook you used. The same hymns had been used for generations. Fine if they were full of good theology, but like some of the songs we sing today, they were not all of that order. But even the excellent hymns were often sung too slowly and without enthusiasm so that they often felt somewhat like a dirge rather than joyful worship of the living God.

As God began to raise up new songwriters and musicians these new songs began to enter some of the churches. The words and music were rather different from the hymns people had been used to and if you combined that with introducing instruments other than the organ, you had a recipe for disturbance. We published a songbook with some of these new songs to go alongside the hymnbook we used, and gradually other instruments began to be utilised to aid our worship. Once a month on Sunday evenings more opportunity for an extended time of worship was given. For many these changes were welcome, but for some, changes of that order caused them to become uncomfortable and uneasy.

In the weeks before we arrived in 1978, two couples who had been influential in the life of the church for many years decided to move to another church when they knew I had been appointed. The issue in this scenario was due to my proposed use of the New International Version (NIV), which I had indicated was the version of the Bible that I would use for public worship. Their strong commitment was to the Authorised Version (AV). They had also heard that I was in favour of introducing some of the 'new songs' which were being increasingly used in some churches. These kinds of issues did not over concern most of the congregation, but the loss of such people from the church did raise questions about 'the direction of the church' in the minds of some (I was to come to know that phrase only too well in the coming months and years).

On Sunday mornings, having been preaching on the subject of 'The Church' for many months, I now began to tackle the theme of God's equipping for the church through the life and ministry of the Holy Spirit. I was preaching explicitly on the injunction to be filled with the Spirit and our need to be filled with all the fullness of God through the ministry of the Spirit. I also drew attention to the encouragement of the Word of God that we should earnestly desire spiritual gifts. To my surprise, the difficulties I had been expecting to arise from preaching these themes did not arise to any great extent. I had thought there were some who would 'haul me over the coals', as it were. Nonetheless, there were rumblings of concern and a couple of resignations which I thought were related, although other reasons were given at the time.

However, a severe disappointment and considerable source of surprise and concern to Maureen and myself was the resignation of two couples, as both the men were deacons. They thought that the pace of change I was setting in leading the church into the life of the Spirit was too slow. They may have been correct, but I believed otherwise and wanted to progress with respect for the other elder who was, to say the least, unsure. I longed for the whole church to experience more of their inheritance in Christ. Maureen and I were particularly close to one of the couples. They were our generation and had a young family like us and had helped us to feel at home in the church. They had also been a great blessing, especially among the young people over the years before we arrived. I had been expecting difficulties with some who I knew to have considerable reservations about the church 'going in that direction' (meaning issues to do with the work of the Spirit). But I was not expecting these brothers and their wives to leave, who were among the very few in the church who shared our convictions and experience. Maureen and I felt bereft at their going and it caused me to question, not for the first time and it would certainly not be the last if I was 'on track' in terms of the direction I was leading the church and now also the timing.

These situations are painful for everyone concerned. Some in the church ask why certain people have left and it is difficult, sometimes impossible, to tell the story when that story actually belongs to someone else. It is theirs to tell, not yours. As I have mentioned previously there was a great dearth of mentors and indeed, at that time, few who had any experience of leading a church through what became known as 'renewal'. It was in these and other situations that would follow, that Maureen and I began to hear God teach us the lessons of 'forgiving', 'keeping our spirits clean' and 'pursuing the course God had given us to walk'. Did we learn them easily and speedily? We wish! It required us to remind each other time and again and go back to God for forgiveness for ourselves and grace to build back better.

There is benefit in the passing of the years. Looking back now I am so thankful to God that He enabled me to stay 'on course' and that relationships with those who left us at that time have endured with mutual love and honour. Rather than the work of God being weakened, by the grace of God the cause of Christ's church in Bournemouth, Christchurch and Poole has been strengthened.

During 1981 and on into 1982 there were several people in the church who came to talk to Maureen and me about their desire for more of God. They also told us about areas in their lives which they believed to be a hindrance to their growth in God. Earlier in London, we had that learning experience with Dr Martyn Lloyd-Jones, when we witnessed God removing a demonic barrier in the life of someone in the church, which resulted in their peace, healing and new growth in God. Now the Holy Spirit was revealing to us other barriers to spiritual growth in the lives of some of His people, barriers, which in the main were not the result of demonic activity, but nonetheless required the taking of responsibility for sin, repentance before God and receiving His forgiveness and cleansing in order for them to be able to move forward again in God.

I remember one situation among many which illustrates ways in which God was teaching us and working to reveal matters which had been stifling growth in God. At the end of one baptism service, I spoke to the husband of a woman who had recently become a Christian and had just been baptised. It was his first time at church. I asked him if he believed in God and he said that he was not at all sure that there was a God. I suggested that if he was serious in wanting to know if there was a God he should say: 'God, if you are real, please show yourself to me.' A few days later, having asked God, he found himself in tears while having his lunch in his digger on the building site where he was working. This man became a follower of Jesus from that day and the change in him was immediate. He began to share his faith with the men on the site and led one of them to Christ. A month or two later he came to me with a problem. He was suddenly finding it hard to pray and felt his prayers were hitting a ceiling. His appetite for the Word of God had significantly reduced. I asked him some questions and soon discovered that he had been involved in freemasonry. As I explained the nature of freemasonry and the barrier this was in his relationship with God, he repented and received God's forgiveness. He destroyed everything relating to his involvement in that. Immediately he was free, and his joy and peace returned as did his free-flowing prayer life and desire for scripture.

Interestingly, I might not have thought of mentioning freemasonry, but for an experience Maureen had some years before. Her grandfather, who brought her up, was a freemason. He was not overly involved, but he was a freemason. Soon after he died, Maureen began to discover difficulty in her prayer life. As we talked together about it, we realised that this had begun around the time of his death. We remembered that he would have mentioned his family in 'prayers' in the ceremonies. Maureen told God about this connection through her grandfather, renounced any connection with freemasonry that this had brought about in her life and I then separated her from that in the name of Jesus Christ. She was immediately free from that restriction that had begun to affect her prayer life. The Lord was certainly revealing to us barriers to spiritual growth which we had never previously recognised or considered and this helped us to be able to help others.

As a consequence, some in the congregation were coming into a new freedom in their relationship with God, as He brought grace and healing to them. This revealed itself in a new desire to learn and receive from the Holy Spirit. This in turn brought newness and freshness of life in the Spirit, increasing love for Jesus and the desire to share Him with others.

It was as if, suddenly, there were people who were able to share their life experiences with us, things they had never told anyone previously. Often these recounted experiences had remained hidden and unspoken for decades. This was an immense privilege for us, but also rather scary. Maureen and I had received no training for this, and we were crying out to God to help us, to give us wisdom and direction. As far as we were aware, there was no one in the area at that time to whom we could go for advice and counsel. But in His mercy and love, the Lord Jesus held our hands and His Spirit began to teach us.

Maureen's desire to see people made whole and thereby able to grow on in God, led her to search for some teaching and training. Two significant opportunities were a conference at Swanwick, Derbyshire and a Crusade for World Revival (CWR) week in Surrey.

At CWR the Holy Spirit ministered to Maureen in a very personal and healing way through Psalm 139 and the truth it teaches concerning our identity, impacted her powerfully.

> ▶ **For you created my inmost being;**
>   **you knit me together in my mother's womb.**
> **I praise you because I am fearfully and wonderfully made;**
>   **your works are wonderful,**
>   **I know that full well.**
>
> ● **Psalm 139:13-14 (NIV)**

Indeed, the whole section from verses 13 to 18 was relevant, but these two verses, in particular, spoke to the truth that she was created and formed by God. She was no accident or mistake, but more mind-blowing was the truth and the realisation that she was one of God's wonderful works and she knew that full well. Maureen had discovered all those years earlier that the woman she thought was her older sister was in fact her birth mother and her parents were actually her grandparents. Psalm 139 being presented afresh brought her assurance of her identity before God. It became a lodestar section of Scripture for her in her person-to-person ministry to women over the succeeding years.

One day, Maureen was seeking to help a woman in her relationship with God. This person was seriously lacking assurance of the love of God for her personally and her place in his heart. She began to describe her insecurities and at one point mentioned that she knew she had never wanted to be born. As Psalm 139 was read to her and opened up to her by the Holy Spirit, she began to realise the truth and power of the Scriptures. She then told God that she was sorry that she had not wanted to be born and that she now knew that He had wanted her and loved her from before the foundation of the world. Now the woman was secure in her identity as a child of God and healing, joy and peace followed.

So it was, as the first few people in the church community began to be filled with the Spirit, that difficulties and opposition increased. Early in 1982, a further elder was appointed, which brought the number of elders to three including myself. There were discussions among us, as elders, in which the other two elders were representing a sense of discomfort which was being expressed to them by various people in the church. They also had their own concerns.

The value of taking time with people in their homes, in my first year, particularly, but also as an integral element in everyday ministry, was especially important. It always is! At this time and in the future, these times of two-way questions and sharing together enabled people to get to know me and my commitment to the Word of God and the mission of making Jesus known. It also gave them a chance to ask me questions they had and to discuss issues that they and others in the church were talking about.

✎

The life and witness of the church continued. The evangelism committee initiated the visitation of local homes every month on a Sunday morning. This was a time when most people in the area were at home and more willing to talk than in the evenings, especially in the dark evenings of the year. Worshipping together with the rest of the church family, being prayed for, and then moving out into the neighbourhood, was a real encouragement to the team who were visiting. While they were sharing Jesus door to door, another team was praying on the church premises. Over the next few years, we began to see quite a few local people come to Christ and be added to the church. In the summer months, occasional Sunday morning services were held in nearby recreation grounds and parks.

In 1981 it was decided to commence a weekly Mums and Toddlers Group at the church. Mums and Toddlers Groups were few and far between at that time and soon numbers of Mums and children from 0-4 years were packing the place out. Maureen still bumps into women, when out shopping in Winton, who used to come with their children years ago. Mums and Toddlers (now Parents and Toddlers) has been a staple ministry arm of the church down through the years and continues today to help build bridges with the local community.

Sunday School was integral to most churches in the 70s and 80s as it had been for generations and that was also the case at Winton. There was a Bible Class for teenagers on Sunday mornings and a good group of young people attending the youth work each week. A holiday Bible Club during the Easter school holidays began in 1983. It was a great success in terms of organisation, creativity and numbers of children attending and many made a commitment to Christ. Holiday Bible Clubs, either at Easter or Summer, have continued to be a special and fruitful aspect of the work among children over the years. God has given us highly creative, gifted and fun-loving people in the church over the years, who have given themselves to sharing God's love for boys and girls in this way.

From the early history of the church before we arrived you will have noticed that the pastors were people with a world vision and indeed two of them had lived and worked overseas. The commitment of the church to its missionaries and to those who were seeking God about the possibility of training and overseas ministry was of ongoing importance. The Missionary Committee arranged an annual Missionary Weekend for teaching, information, challenge and prayer.

This later became the Missions Group and was composed of people who had God's heart for overseas mission. Some of the members of the Group themselves were sent out by the church into long-term or short-term service or served on the Missions Group when they returned from overseas.

CHAPTER 8

Joys and Sorrows
1983 – 1986

By 1983 I had been leading the church for five years and there had been gradual changes taking place. On their own some of them may not appear to be significant: introduction of Home Groups (these replaced the former weekly prayer and bible study meeting which took place on the church premises, although we continued to meet all together once a month); use of a songbook alongside Hymns of Faith; introduction of an overhead projector; commencement of a worship band and less use of the organ. For some, these changes provided no issue at all, but for others, they were hard to accept. Some people discovered that their reaction to these changes indicated that their security was tied to the familiar and well-loved rather than to more significant biblical and spiritual issues. More importantly, as some of the congregation were entering into healing and freedom through encountering the ministry of the Holy Spirit, there were changes in the measure of open-heartedness, community and joy around the church. All of these things together contributed to causing some real difficulty and unease for a proportion of the church family. Perhaps the comment spoken to me by more than one long-standing member of the church at this time would illustrate: 'If I had wanted to go to a Pentecostal church I would have done so. Don't change my church.'

I was pretty disappointed by the comment, but sadly by this time, not overly surprised. The words highlighted a major blind spot for not a few Christians that, actually, it is neither your church nor mine, but Christ's who is its Head. The comment also indicated a working assumption about Pentecostal churches which was largely based on hearsay. For most Christians in those days, it tended to be, as the old children's hymn expressed it: 'You in your small corner and I in mine.' ('Jesus bids us shine': Susan Warner 1819-1885)

When we arrived in Bournemouth in 1978 it appeared that there were few evangelical churches across Bournemouth, Christchurch and Poole where there was an openness to learn about and a desire for the ministry of the Holy Spirit, particularly where that involved exploring the multi-faceted gifts of the Spirit. So, the relevance of the Lord's warning to me in 1979, that if I nailed my colours to the mast there would be many who would think I had gone off the rails or was no longer biblically orthodox, had context.

In the summer of 1983 one of the two other elders, the first to be appointed in 1979, resigned and he and his wife left the church. Losing him as an elder and losing them both from the church was very grievous for me personally. We could ill afford to lose people of their years and Christian life experience. This was especially so as the congregation was growing by the addition of those who had just come to faith, some of whose lives were quite broken and were in considerable need of love, healing and discipleship. Their decision to leave was unsettling, for me, but particularly so to those who had been in the church for many years. Over the succeeding three or four years, there was a steady drip, drip of one and another leaving at different points. I was so thankful to God that he kept us from a major division in the life of the church, but it was nonetheless very painful for those who decided to leave and for those of us who remained. There was no lack of respect and love between us, but, speaking personally, while that was a great reason for thanksgiving, it increased my sadness. These were brothers and sisters with whom I had worshipped, prayed and served for five years and I and the church had lost them from this community and all that they brought of the life of God. However, I was realising, sad though it undoubtedly was for all of us, that although you can fellowship with all who are in Christ, you can only build church with those who are in agreement about the nature of the vision. In the goodness of God, each one who moved away from the church in those years has gone on to worship and serve God in other local churches, strengthening the body of Christ elsewhere.

There were many times in the years from 1980-1986 when Maureen and I were wrestling with our thoughts and feelings about remaining at the church. I had questions about my ability to fulfil God's call to me to lead in the way He had asked. We both found it extremely hard to witness people we cared for very much being upset. Often Maureen would say she was leaving and at other times I was the one who was leaving. In our conversations on this subject, we used to refer to our desire to see a green for 'Go' light from God. But we never did see the green light, however much we wanted to – and we did want to! So many times, we felt that we just could not go on. But God! The promise in Hebrews 4:16 became very precious to us as 'our time of need' seemed to be coming around increasingly frequently...

▶ **Let us then approach God's throne of grace with confidence, so that we may receive mercy and find grace to help us in our time of need.**

● **Hebrews 4:16 (NIV)**

We often rehearsed to one another the certainty we had from God about coming to the church in the first place. We also remembered God's question to me in the summer of 1979 as to whether I was going to be obedient to Him in the matter of His Spirit, my 'yes' at that time and his warning that the way would not be easy. We anchored ourselves again and again into 1 Thessalonians 5:24:

> ▶ **The one who calls you is faithful, and he will do it.**
>
> ● **1 Thessalonians 5:24 (NIV)**

Now and for many years we have been so grateful to Him that He never did give us the green light to 'GO' that we had so often craved. For if He had, we would have missed all the joy and blessing that we have witnessed, as we have watched the work of His grace and His Spirit in the lives of so many. He is the GREAT I AM and our sufficiency, and yours, is in Him alone.

In January 1984 Maureen and I attended a conference for church leaders in Sussex arranged by Colin Urquhart and Bob Gordon and the team at Kingdom Faith Ministries. Colin formed Kingdom Faith Ministries when he left the Anglican ministry in Luton, to give himself more freely to speaking in the UK and overseas. He was a leader in charismatic renewal from the 60s to the 80s. Bob Gordon was a pastor and teacher with a passion for bringing together Word and Spirit.

At this time, an increasing number of church leaders in the UK were seeking more of God and longing to learn and experience more of the work of the Holy Spirit. This conference proved to be a significant time for us both. We can trace back to that week encounters with God and personal decisions about spiritual disciplines which have stood the test of time. We benefited much by receiving prayer and being able to talk through issues, particularly concerning the use of the gifts of the Spirit. As a result, we both experienced new liberty, especially in using the gift of tongues in our personal devotional life. Such opportunities were invaluable due to the lack of availability in our area of 'fathers and mothers in God'. The only downside and it was a downside, was that when we returned home, we wanted everyone in the church to run after God and receive all that He had to give them. But the whole church was not on the same page and so wisdom, discernment and patience were needed – along with courage.

A memorable and absolutely strategic moment for me took place during those days in Sussex. It concerned my prayer life. I had been in church leadership in London and Bournemouth for almost fourteen years. Until this time I had resisted what Alan Redpath had years ago whimsically described to us young people in Edinburgh as 'blanket victory'. In talking about our personal prayer lives Alan had talked about the importance, before the day gets going, of setting aside time to spend with God. (If he were alive today, he would probably use the term 'duvet victory').

Up until this time I had set aside space for personal devotions, as distinct from intercession for the church, when I started work in the morning. But as the years had passed and life became increasingly hectic with work and family responsibilities, my personal prayer life had suffered. I knew it and often felt guilty about it. This particular day, following a morning session, I went out into the grounds of the conference centre and was walking along a path that had a slight covering of sand. I was deeply troubled about the inconsistency and depth of my prayer life. I stopped where I was and told the Lord I was drawing a line in the sand and I literally did draw a line across the path with my foot. Then I stepped over the line and said to God that from now on, by His grace, I would set aside time to spend with Him before the rest of the family were up and about. And by His grace and building in the personal discipline that was my responsibility to do, that morning became a watershed for me in my personal devotional life.

Another spiritual discipline that I built into my life from that time forward was setting aside a day a month to spend with God. To ensure that actually happened, it was necessary to write that day in the diary for months ahead so that it took priority over anything else, except a family emergency. As I worked from home it was essential to spend that day at another location. If I had had an office on the church premises, it would similarly have been essential to spend the day elsewhere, away from those things that would cry out for attention and distract you from your stated purpose to be with the Lord. I often used the home of a friend, when he was out at his place of work. I would spend some time in the Word of God, reflection and personal prayer. Never in preparing a preach! I would usually have a walk somewhere where there would be as few people as possible. I would worship and talk to Father, Son and Holy Spirit. Such times need guarding for all you are worth. Once a year, after the first Sunday of the year had passed, I would go away for three days on my own. For some precious years, I used Ashburnham Place in East Sussex. They had a Prayer Centre, where you could book a prayer cell (a small room with just a table and chair) for the time you wanted. There was also overnight accommodation and wonderful grounds to walk in. When I first started to set aside those early January days, I confess I went with a list of church-related issues that I desperately needed God to speak into. Seldom did any of those issues receive an answer. I heard Father say to me, 'David, please may you and I have time together? Just you and Me?' I realised that God wanted me as a son and not as a servant. I needed to give attention to our relationship. I rarely went home after those days with any answers to my list of questions. But in the coming weeks and months, the answers were 'just there'. The lesson to 'keep seeking after God' was beginning to be learned.

> ▶ ... When my heart whispered, "Seek God,"
> my whole being replied, "I'm seeking him!"...
>
> ● Psalm 27:8 (MSG)

However, for that to be lifelong requires the consistent choice of the will, as there are always times and seasons when it is one of the last things you actually want to do.

The pattern of Sundays mornings and evenings continued to involve worship and consecutive expository bible teaching.

As well as preaching the Word of God, Sunday evenings provided an opportunity for extended periods of worship, where gifts of the Spirit could begin to be exercised. The church continued to grow as the Lord added in those who were being saved. There was also some transfer growth. We were around 100 in membership after those first five years, although the congregation was always larger than the membership.

The worship area could seat a maximum of 150. At the rear of the worship area, there was a hall seating 60, a kitchen and two other small rooms. In 1984 we began to investigate the possibility of erecting a first-floor extension at the front of the building in Calvin Road. Later that year planning permission was refused. We were situated in a narrow residential street and the neighbours were concerned that the number of cars would increase. This would be the first of many thoughts about how to create more space on the church premises.

In 1985 the church suffered a severe loss through the unexpected deaths of two young married people, one a father with two young sons. The other person who died was intricately connected to the church family. It was the first time we had faced two younger people being diagnosed with a life-threatening illness and the church set aside time to pray and seek God for healing. Any expectation that God heals today was lacking in most evangelical churches. It had been only in recent years that teaching and faith for healing had been experienced in some measure in a few church situations. As leaders and as a congregation we were very much 'wet behind the ears' when it came to physical healing, as in many other areas of life in the Spirit. Some were convinced that God was going to heal, and both would live. In fact, they both died and moved to heaven to be with Christ. It was a traumatic time for the families involved and indeed for the whole church. It was also a learning time. I had never been in this situation where I was seeking to lead a church with a strong desire, in some, to see God at work in physical healing and others very unsure that it was even appropriate to ask God for healing. And all the time there was my responsibility to pastorally prepare and care for the immediate families and the church family.

Around this time, it was good to be able to appoint another elder, which brought us back up to three including me. It would have been healthy to have had more elders over these early years when there were many strategic and difficult issues to discuss. However, the elders we had were men who loved God and loved His truth and always exhibited much grace. That is a reason for thanksgiving, especially in view of the fact that there were issues where we did not all agree.

I was at a point where I was questioning if my time of leading the church was at an end. My vision and understanding for the way forward for this community of God's people included:

- growth through people coming to faith, especially from the local community.
- the worship of God where gifts of the Spirit are used in a biblical and God-glorifying manner.
- freedom to explore the whole area of healing.
- prepare a team of people with appropriate gifting and training to be able to help broken people into wholeness.
- leadership training.
- development of a salaried staff team.
- growing numbers moving out into cross-cultural ministry.

All of this was on my heart.

However I knew that my vision was not shared by all the elders. I was questioning if I was the problem. Certainly there was a divergence of conviction among us as to how the church should develop. Reflecting on the pain of losing an elder a year or so before and losing others who had a leadership role while not being elders, I realised that we were perhaps at a crisis point, however painful to contemplate.

None of us wanted to precipitate a crisis that would hurt and damage the congregation, especially those who had come to Christ in recent months and years. One of the elders felt he should stand down, at least for a time, but we persuaded him to remain. I did not want to face the personal pain of losing him. I also shrank from the pain and unsettlement this would cause for many in the church. But I knew I was seeking to postpone something that had to be faced. We all knew that at some point these matters had to be resolved.

Sometime later I had an extended time with God. Two questions remained burning within me:

1. Am I on track in my vision and understanding of God's way forward for the church?

2. Am I the person to lead the church in this?

I heard God speak clearly to me in the affirmative on both questions. I was so thankful but recoiled from the implications. I did not want to lose another elder. He was a brother I respected and valued highly. But again, I had to face the truth that 'you can fellowship with all who love Jesus, but you can only build with those who are in agreement on the vision'.

On the one hand, I had a clear vision for the way in which I believed God wanted the church to develop, but on the other hand, almost at the same time, I would be full of uncertainty about my suitability and ability to fulfil the task. This conjunction of thinking and feeling was not something of a moment. This conflict within me continued on and off for a few years. I was never someone who was full of self-confidence. I would often compare myself unfavourably with colleagues in ministry and sometimes look out on the congregation and see someone I thought would be much more able than I to lead the church.

There are seeds in those thoughts which could easily have derailed me completely. But in the goodness of God, in the midst of it all, I knew that God had called me to the church, and I knew that it was He who had given me the direction in which to lead, however unwelcome that was to some, both in the leadership and in the congregation. I had been well-taught from my youth about the necessity of keeping heart and spirit clean. I knew that walking humbly before a holy God and loving my neighbour was foundational for inner peace and welfare. Because God had called me, I wanted to do my very best in leading His church His way. But if I failed in that, I wanted most of all to retain a heart and spirit that would not grieve the Holy Spirit and would not spoil me for anything else the Lord Jesus may call me to in the future.

✎

Spring Harvest had recently commenced at the initiative of the Evangelical Alliance. It took place around Easter each year, held at Butlins Holiday Camp sites and gathering Christians from all different church backgrounds for a week of preaching, seminars, worship and fellowship. This does not appear at all radical now but, take my word for it, it sure was radical then. It was still unusual for Christians to get together across denominational boundaries.

In 1985 we decided to lead a group from the church to Spring Harvest at Minehead. It involved people sharing accommodation, making meals together and generally 'mucking in'. All good for building relationships. There was excellent bible teaching in the mornings, seminars on a variety of subjects and evenings of worship and preaching. It was a time of challenge from the Word of God, learning new worship songs led by gifted musicians who were worshippers and being so blessed in the company of hundreds who loved Jesus and wanted to grow in God.

Spring Harvest was much used by God to bring new life and patterns of worship and ministry to many churches in the UK. Many Christians, who had felt discouraged and lacked vision, were renewed and went home to their local church with a new joy and expectation in God. Like many churches, Spring Harvest was a rich channel of blessing to our church and an increasing number of people from the church went with us to Spring Harvest in those years. There was a Spring Harvest counselling team at every location and Maureen was a member of that counselling team for many years. These annual weeks of working and fellowshipping with other counsellors, sharing and learning from one another, was a stimulating, growing and sharpening experience for Maureen in terms of using the gifts God had given her.

We had the joy of continuing to see many coming to faith. From our arrival in 1978 through to 1987, 128 people were baptised on confession of their faith in Christ. Included among them I had the special joy of baptising our daughter Fiona and our sons Kevin and Stuart. As I have looked at the records of these years, many of which were not the easiest, to be able to recount the blessing of God in the midst of it all is praise and glory to Him.

In these years God was bringing an increasing number of people to the church who were in considerable need. I often asked God, 'Could you please send us some mature Christians with a heart to bring help and healing to the broken?' In those years there was no shortage of those in need, but a distinct lack of those who would sit where they sat and weep with those who wept. One evening, I had a phone call from a young woman in the church, who was deeply concerned for a female work colleague who was staying with her temporarily. Maureen and I went together (how often have I thanked God for a wife who loves Him and loves His people and longs for Him to heal the broken). As we entered the house and walked into the kitchen, we were met by a young woman shouting at me while wildly brandishing a large kitchen knife. In the goodness of God, she did not cause me physical hurt and in due time she calmed down and the knife was set down out of harm's way. We were to have an interesting journey with her over the coming days. Her story included abuse as a young girl and living as a novitiate in a convent for some years where she was exposed to transcendental meditation and drugs. Not surprisingly, she was deeply insecure, confused and suffering from demonic influence. We discovered later that she had suffered abuse by a priest years previously. When, that evening, her friend told her she had called her pastor to come to help her, she reacted. By the grace of God, this young woman fell in love with Christ and experienced the Father's loving acceptance of her in the Lord Jesus.

Maureen and I have met more than a few people, many of whom have been Christians for years, who could not bring themselves to share their life journey with us for a considerable period of time. Afterwards, they explained it in this way: 'I thought you would hate me (alternatives were 'reject me', 'not want anything to do with me'). It often takes time and consistency of care and prayer before sufficient trust is established to enable truth to be told. The telling of that truth is usually very painful for them as they recount their own sin and failure and the harm they have experienced. It is so wonderful to be able to tell them of One who has loved them from before the foundation of the world and who knows everything about them yet loves them without limit. His Name is Jesus: Saviour, Redeemer, Healer, Lover of their souls.

There are many Christians who do not truly believe that God loves them.

> ▶ **For he knows how we are formed,**
>   **he remembers that we are dust.**
>
>   ● Psalm 103:14 (NIV)

Commenting on this verse Sam Storms says this: 'I think we run from God rather than to Him because we know our own hearts only too well and His barely at all. If you stop and think about it, you'll realise how this affects the way we relate to other people. Convinced that if they knew the truth about us, they would be repulsed, we work to hide our true selves from sight. So we keep a safe distance.'

Storms continues: 'If we react that way to people whose knowledge of us is limited, imagine how we react to God whose knowledge of us is infinite.'

Here we have a clear and obvious barrier to active and confident trust in God and intimacy with Christ. So many Christians of years standing do not truly believe in the God who is declared earlier on in verses 11-13 of that Psalm:

> ▶ **For as high as the heavens are above the earth,**
>   **so great is his love for those who fear him;**
> **as far as the east is from the west,**
>   **so far has he removed our transgressions from us.**
> **As a father has compassion on his children,**
>   **so the Lord has compassion on those who fear him.**
>
>   ● **Psalm 103:11-13 (NIV)**

Maureen and I have delighted in the privilege of sharing these truths about the character of God from Scripture with many believers whose relationship with God was distant and lacking the fullness promised in being His children. To see the Spirit of truth at work in them revealing the lies they have believed about God and themselves and then bringing them into forgiveness, assurance and joy in the love with which He loves them – that is the best!

In 1986 I raised with the other elders the need to consider the development of a salaried staff team. Team ministry, while very evident in the New Testament church, was almost unknown, especially in independent evangelical churches such as our own. I knew that if the church was to grow, and if that growth was going to be consolidated through discipling and building a children's and youth ministry, we had to plan ahead. I suggested that we aim for the first appointment later that year and although 1986 soon became 1987, one year late was not bad at all.

When I came to the church in 1978 the leadership was in the hands of the pastor and the deacons. When we began to appoint elders, the deacons continued to serve the Lord and the church in all the usual practical and essential ways. Although the elders had responsibility for the spiritual leadership and oversight of the church, the deacons were godly men who had their own individual thoughts about the changes that had been taking place in the life of the church. There were some people in the church who shared their concerns with the deacons and so it was not only among the elders that questions about the direction of the church were being discussed.

Therefore, in January 1986 it was arranged that the elders and deacons would have a weekend away to pray, discuss, discover, and agree together God's direction for the church. I am sure all those who were going to be involved were nervous. From my notes at the time, two days before the weekend, I recorded feeling low, discouraged and apprehensive. One of the men in the church, who was not involved in the leadership, phoned me and asked if he could come and pray with me and for me. What a blessing! That night as I slept the Lord spoke into my mind and heart the words 'Dove of Peace' and I saw 'the Dove'. As I awoke, I remembered what had happened in the night and from that moment I enjoyed His Peace in a remarkable way throughout the weekend.

It was nonetheless a tough few days for all of us. We discussed at length the meaning of the terms 'baptism in, or with, the Spirit' and 'filled with the Spirit', Ephesians 4 ministries and various gifts of the Spirit, including tongues, prophecy and healing. We also talked about Sunday preaching, Home Group teaching and public participation in worship. It became clear that there was a divergence of conviction on more than a few of these issues. One of the elders, who had been on the verge of standing down some months previously, decided that he should now resign. He was not in agreement with the other elder and me over some of these matters which as elders we had been discussing together for some time previously. We were all very grieved about the loss we and the church would sustain. Some of the deacons were also in a similar place concerning either the relevance or the exercise of the gifts of the Spirit. In the coming months, we were to lose some of those brothers. For all of us as a church family, it was a painful and unsettling time. The elder who resigned at this time and who, with his wife and family we subsequently lost to the church in Winton, was another huge loss to me personally. He, like the previous elder who resigned a few years before, was gifted in teaching and preaching the Word of God and much appreciated for his discipleship teaching. In the goodness of God, he and his wife have used their gifts and experience to strengthen and bless another church in the succeeding years.

That weekend was difficult and painful in so many ways. It was one of the worst times for me and I am sure for many if not all of those who were present. The period this chapter covers were certainly years of joy and sorrow. In fact, the seven years from 1980 to the end of 1986 were the most difficult years I experienced in the journey of church leadership. Maureen and I have often said that we would never want to go through such a time again. However, God was teaching us so much during those years which we needed to learn and to put into practice in the years ahead. In the process, God did a strengthening work within us which, as we look back now, was essential for the challenge of the growth that was to come in the following years. In it all, the words of Micah 6:8 were constantly with us:

▶ He has shown you, O mortal, what is good.
And what does the Lord require of you?
To act justly and to love mercy
and to walk humbly with your God.

● Micah 6:8 (NIV)

CHAPTER 9

Clearing the Ground
1986 – 1987

Returning from a holiday in France at the end of September 1986, there were three letters waiting for me in the mail.

One of them contained a resignation, which, like others over the preceding five years or so, gave us much sadness. However, this time there was something which was quite different. Both of us had a sense in our spirits that this was the end of the steady drip, drip of people leaving. And so it was.

The other two letters had been sent by two women in the church, quite independently of each other. Neither knew the other had written to me. Both referred to the same Old Testament prophecy and both were suggesting something they had heard from God. The essence of these letters was that God had drawn them to Joel 2:12-27 and they believed that God was calling the church to a time of prayer and fasting.

> ▶ "Even now," declares the Lord,
>   "return to me with all your heart,
>   with fasting and weeping and mourning."...
> ... Blow the trumpet in Zion,
>   declare a holy fast,
>   call a sacred assembly.
> Gather the people, ...
>
> ● Joel 2:12,15,16 (NIV)

As I read the letters, I knew immediately that this was from the Lord. Not for the first time, I was so thankful to God that there were people in the church who were listening to God and willing to share what they believed He was saying to them with me.

The fact is that in the mid-eighties there were still many areas of biblical teaching and practice which had seldom been taught or practised in church life in the UK. Fasting was one of those.

We set aside Monday to Friday 25-30 January 1987 as a week of Prayer and Fasting. But how do you plan and arrange for something the church, as far as we were aware, had never engaged in and which, individually, none of us had ever experienced? New ground surely sends you to God – and that is always a good thing!

I had a paper in my study with the title: 'Preparing for Personal and Corporate Revival'. I cannot remember how it had come into my possession, but it had been undoubtedly sent from the Lord to us for this time. We made it available to everyone in the church and we encouraged everyone to use it in their personal time with God during the week.

"Father, please search my heart by your Holy Spirit and reveal to me everything that hinders your purpose for me and among us as your people. In the name of Jesus and for His sake, Amen."

The week required considerable preparatory work. We provided teaching material with relevant Scriptures under such headings as: What does it mean to seek after God? Why should we do this and how do we do this? What does God promise if we do seek after Him?

We provided teaching on fasting and some practical suggestions as to how this could be approached. We encouraged everyone to individually set aside time each day to be with God. We came together each evening at our premises in Calvin Road for a brief time of worship and the reading of certain bible passages relevant to the theme of the evening. Then each of us found a quiet space in the building to spend time with God. Everyone was asked to share with the elders, in writing, anything God had said to them which they believed to be for the whole church. After the week concluded I collated the many responses and later published a record of the commands and promises we had heard from God, which was, has been and still remains significant for us as a church.

I learned to depend on God. Every day I was seeking God for direction. "Lord, how do we approach this evening?" The first evening we dedicated ourselves to seek God's face, to seek after Him with all our heart, individually and corporately. We prayed for protection from the evil one. We asked God to restore the honour of His Name.

Another evening we expressed our repentance to God, as His people, for anything in the history of the church which had grieved the Holy Spirit and had never been previously recognised and confessed. We told God that we did not want anything to remain which would hinder His blessing and purposes in us and through us. We wanted to 'clear the decks', as it were, and knew this was of vital importance. We then confessed those specific areas in our corporate life which we knew had grieved the Spirit of God in our time in the life of the church. We expressed our repentance and received, with thanksgiving, forgiveness through our Lord Jesus Christ. We particularly repented of the church's rejection of His desire to pour out His Spirit upon us all.

We then thanked God for the gift of His Spirit and welcomed the Holy Spirit and expressed our desire to learn and receive more of His life and truth and power.

One of the older women in the church (one of those prayer warriors) had received a vision, many years previously, of the Spirit as a Dove wanting to alight on the church. But in the picture, some were waving their hands above their heads, as if to prevent Him from settling upon us. She had held it, for 31 years, waiting for God to reveal to her when she should share it. This evening she did, believing this was the time. We recognised this as a powerful representation of what had been taking place in recent years and also earlier in the church's history. When I had arrived in 1978, I discovered in the desk in what had been the minister's vestry and subsequently became the church office, a leaflet containing strong teaching against the gifts of the Spirit.

On the final evening of the week, we shared communion together. Many described how God had spoken to them personally and gave testimony to the blessing of God. There was a wonderful sense of the presence of God and a beautiful oneness among us. Maureen and I went home and sat up in bed talking about the week. We knew, although we couldn't accurately express what we felt, that this had been a strategically significant week in the life of the church. Wanting to celebrate, we remembered that there was some Vienetta (a mint and chocolate-layered ice-cream block) in the freezer and proceeded to rescue it and scoff it with huge thanksgiving to God with great joy.

Over the years since God taught me personally and us as a church the strategic importance of setting aside time to seek God with prayer and fasting, including when there is a need to 'clear the decks' individually and/or corporately. I have become more sensitive to situations that call for such biblical action. I have been able to suggest this to individual believers and witness the godly change that has resulted where they have wholeheartedly taken these steps. But in some local churches, the lack of such action by the leaders and church community has meant that situations which grieved the Holy Spirit have not been resolved before God with a humble heart and so the churches, which were already suffering, cease to grow and continue to regress and lose life and light. If a church community grieves the Spirit and there is no recognition, confession and repentance of sin, in due time the evidence of this begins to be seen. There are many Scriptures that speak to this apart from Joel 2. Examples of the spirit with which God wants us to come to Him and His promise of restoration are numerous: here are a few:

> ▶ There, by the Ahava Canal, I proclaimed a fast, so that
> we might humble ourselves before our God and ask
> him for a safe journey for us and our children, with all our
> possessions. I was ashamed to ask the king for soldiers
> and horsemen to protect us from enemies on the road,
> because we had told the king, "The gracious hand of
> our God is on everyone who looks to him, but his great
> anger is against all who forsake him." So we fasted and
> petitioned our God about this, and he answered
> our prayer.
>
> ● Ezra 8:21-23 (NIV)

> ▶ ... if my people, who are called by my name, will humble
> themselves and pray and seek my face and turn
> from their wicked ways, then I will hear from heaven,
> and I will forgive their sin and will heal their land.
>
> ● 2 Chronicles 7:14 (NIV)

> ▶ Submit yourselves, then, to God. Resist the devil, and
> he will flee from you. Come near to God and he will
> come near to you... Humble yourselves before the Lord,
> and he will lift you up.
>
> ● James 4:7-8 (NIV)

> ▶ Be shepherds of God's flock that is under your care,
> watching over them—not because you must, but
> because you are willing, as God wants you to be... Humble
> yourselves, therefore, under God's mighty hand, that he
> may lift you up in due time.
>
> ● 1 Peter 5:2-6 (NIV)

> ▶ For I have not hesitated to proclaim to you the whole
> will of God. Keep watch over yourselves and all
> the flock of which the Holy Spirit has made you
> overseers. Be shepherds of the church of God, which he
> bought with his own blood.
>
> ● Acts 20:27-28 (NIV)

If you know God is speaking to you about taking such action, with all my heart I encourage you to do so. Perhaps, in the words of Mordecai to Esther, and recognising that you are a child of the King of Kings...

> ▶ ... who knows but that you have come to your royal
> position for such a time as this?
>
> ● Esther 4:14 (NIV)

Since 1985 increasing numbers of people from the church were attending Spring Harvest and this brought us great encouragement from God. When it came to arranging for a party to go to Spring Harvest in 1987 we discovered, to our initial huge disappointment, that something had gone awry in the booking process and there was no space for us. Instead, we booked a hotel in Exmouth and planned our own Spring Harvest there. We called it CRASH '87 (Calvin Road's Answer to Spring Harvest). Calvin Road was the road in which our church building was situated and locally many called the church Calvin Road rather than Winton Evangelical Church, its name at that time. There was considerable mileage to be gained in the name we chose for the week, as the people were going around asking each other, "Are you going to CRASH?"

"CRASH '87" provided many fun moments as we ate together, enjoyed the indoor pool plus outdoor games. Lots of time to chat over coffee and get to know one another in a different environment. Coming only three months after that significant January week we could all see the hand of God in the opportunity to have a week on our own as a church. We enjoyed excellent bible teaching, increasing freedom in worship and the use of the gifts of the Spirit. There were significant prophetic words given during the week (and again the following year at CRASH '88), which were added to all that we had recorded during the Week of Prayer and Fasting in January.

Towards the end of 1986, the elders asked for the prayers of the church concerning the possibility of the appointment of another salaried member of staff, who would also become an elder. In May 1987 the church agreed to appoint Tony Seymour as Associate Pastor and elder with responsibility for the oversight of evangelism and discipling. In August of that year, Tony was ordained at Winton Evangelical Church and began his ministry among us. Tony, who with his wife Sandie, had been worshipping with us while he was studying at Moorlands College, had been student assistant to me during this academic year and was due to conclude his studies that summer. So, Tony and Sandie were well known to the church family and his evangelist's heart and wider gifts were recognised by us all. His giftedness in the use of the sketch board in evangelism was often used to great effect. Tony, a great walker, was instrumental in arranging many men's outings, usually ending up at a country pub for refreshment of some kind.

Although Tony's appointment would be the first time the church had ever had two salaried pastors and his appointment would immediately increase the annual budget by 40%, there was unanimity and joy at his appointment. When you think about it, that was quite remarkable. Here was a church that had suffered the loss of a fair number of consistent financial givers in the previous few years and did not have a substantial bank balance to cover the 40% increase which would be needed over the next twelve months to cover Tony's salary. But the leaders and church family had faith that this step was from God and that He would provide through the giving of His people. And He did.

The decision to begin to build a staff team, for this indeed was the first step in that strategic process, was significant for me personally and for the church. I had been eight years in London and now nine years here at Winton without a full-time colleague by my side. As you read through the Gospels and the Acts of the Apostles, colleagues, partnership, and team are very evident in the ministry of the Lord Jesus and of the apostle Paul. So I was very thankful to God for God's gift to me of Tony and I began to quickly learn to value Tony as a brother in Christ, his love for Jesus and people, his faith in God and his wisdom. What a joy to have in harness alongside you someone who is bringing gifts you don't have. And what blessing Tony's appointment brought to the church family! It is always healthy for people to have options in terms of who they would find it easier to speak to on different issues and Tony's arrival offered not only another voice to listen to and receive from in the preaching of the Word of God, but someone else who was an excellent listener and wise counsellor.

Soon after Tony became an elder, Richard (the other elder), Tony and I began to meet monthly with our wives, Adrienne, Sandie and Maureen, for a meal in one of our homes. It was an opportunity to build relationship, share news and information and pray together for the church and ourselves. The elders met on their own each month, but this gave the three male elders the benefit of female input across a range of issues, which was of great benefit to us. Time given to relationships is absolutely vital and our relationships as elders and when we met with our wives, strengthened us and brought us all much joy.

✎

In 1987 we commenced a link with Ichthus Christian Fellowship, based in south London. In 1974 a small group of Christians began to evangelise in S.E.London under the leadership of Roger and Faith Forster. From that base, Ichthus began to plant new congregations and resurrect dying churches. There was a commonality between us on the work of the Spirit and they had considerable experience in training leaders, evangelism and beginning new gatherings of believers, with the aim of establishing a worshipping and witnessing community where none presently existed. Our link with Ichthus did not involve us coming under their leadership or submitting to their oversight, but they were open-handed in inviting us to attend their half-yearly leaders' conferences, where we gained from excellent and practical bible teaching. There were also many opportunities to receive from their wisdom and experience in the areas where we knew we required input, as we looked to fulfil what we believed to be God's way ahead for us as a church. We formed a close relationship with one of their leaders, who was our speaker at 'CRASH 88', and was always very willing to hear and answer our many questions. Some years later, we were to send a young couple from our church for a year of training with Ichthus, which would help them to prepare to lead one of the new congregations we were to plant.

✎

Meaningful and God-honouring relationships between church leaders in Bournemouth, Christchurch and Poole had been sadly lacking for as long as anyone could remember. When I arrived in

Bournemouth in 1978 Harry Kilbride, then Minister of Lansdowne Baptist Church, had been gathering some leaders on a monthly basis, but that ended when he left the area. There was no networking across denominational boundaries or church streams. A few local leaders, including myself, attempted to gather a wider group of church leaders across the town, but that came to nothing.

In early 1987 our church, Winton Evangelical Church, became a member of the Evangelical Alliance (EA). At that time, the EA was beginning to endeavour to build area networks of EA churches throughout the country. Those of us who had recently attempted to encourage church leaders to network together recognised that this move by the EA was a possible way forward locally. The Alliance was beginning to exercise a more influential ministry in the nation than had been the case for many years. The EA banner did prove to be the way forward and in 1988 South Wessex Evangelical Alliance (SWEA) was formed and I was privileged to be the first Chair.

Fifty local churches were registered at the outset, representing the greatest coming together of evangelical churches of all different denominations and none, in this area, in living memory. In 1991 one of the leaders of Cranleigh Community Church took over from me as Chair. He was released by Cranleigh to give a day a week to this and SWEA prospered so that by 1994, there were about 70 churches and organisations in membership. A significant appointment made by SWEA at that time was to employ someone to lead the local ministry to overseas students. As our church had been a significant participant in commencing ministry to overseas students in the town many years previously, we were delighted with the appointment and funded our contribution to her financial support from our Missions Budget. That budget has been strategic for sustained financial giving to the local international student ministry and to many other local outreach projects. Of course, it has also been the vehicle for funding our overseas workers, whose numbers were to grow considerably in the next decade.

The church's financial report for the year ended 31st December 1987 recorded that, despite the 47% increase in expenditure, the year had ended with a surplus. The blessing of God, which was so evident following the January Week of Prayer and Fasting and Seeking God, was also, not surprisingly, seen in the church's finances. During the years 1982 – 86, when there was a slow but steady loss of people from church commitment, we sometimes wondered if we would survive financially. Often those who left the church were people who had given generously, whereas those who were coming into the life of the church were usually people with little or no church background and quite often moderate to low incomes. But throughout the years, God was indeed Jehovah Jireh, the Lord Who Provides. Pursuing the course that God has directed and learning to trust Him and His promises, even through days that are dark and when God seems to be hiding, is the way that leads to deeper roots in Him and grows greater confidence to move forward on larger challenges to faith in the future.

CHAPTER 10

Restructuring for Growth

1988 – 1990

I had been involved on the Board of Regions Beyond Missionary Union (RBMU), particularly, since 1978, as Chair of the Personnel and Candidates Committee. The mission worked in five different areas of the world and I had a special responsibility for members of the mission serving in Peru. The church had always encouraged me in this and released me to make many visits to Peru between 1980 and 1996 for which I was extremely grateful. My involvement and experience in interviewing candidates and their subsequent pastoral care in RBMU benefited the church too as it was to become a sending agency in its own right in the coming years when we commissioned and sent many of our church family overseas. Reflecting more broadly, most of the pastors at church had either spent time overseas as missionaries themselves or, in the same way as God had led me, were intimately involved in the governance of overseas missions and in visiting mission personnel overseas. To have leaders with a world view of the Church's mission and to have people from the church community serving overseas provides a New Testament marker which is sadly lacking in more than a few churches in the UK today.

In February 1988 Maureen and I spent three weeks with the Peru personnel, visiting them in situ from the capital city of Lima and the Pacific coastal area to the high Andes, from Lake Titicaca in the south travelling north through the Cusco and Apurimac Departments. Having space with each one where they lived and worked was a privilege. There was time to listen and pray with them over a variety of issues, both personal and ministry-related. The final week all the mission personnel gathered from across Peru for the annual conference, which was held just outside Lima in the foothills of the mountains. These were special times for everyone, catching up with each other, relaxing in a variety of ways including fun evenings (they were hilarious and reminded me of similar times at bible college) and enjoying the swimming pool. We worshipped together and prayed for each other and the various areas of our work in Peru and I was privileged to bring teaching from the Word of God. We both look back upon these visits to Peru with huge thanksgiving to God. It didn't take us long to discover that these missionaries were just ordinary people like us, with similar personal and ministry challenges, although facing issues of climate, culture, economics and separation from home and family which were very different. So many Christians imagine that missionaries and pastors are a breed apart – untouched by the usual waves and troughs of life. We wish! It was such a joy to build precious relationships with the Peru personnel over our many visits and to count them as dear friends. We have been hugely blessed and enriched in our walk with God and in our ministry.

Maureen and I were due to fly out the day after the conference ended, so we returned to the mission flat in the Miraflores district of Lima. A Swiss couple came back with us to chat through one or two matters before we headed home to the UK. I had first met them some years before when they came to the Personnel Committee in London. At that point, they had been waiting for a few years to be granted visas to move to Irian Jaya, Indonesia with RBMU, but few visas were being issued to Christian missionaries there at that time. They came to meet with the Personnel Committee concerning the way ahead for them. I will never forget what they said to us that day: "We will eat whatever you set before us." In other words, they were saying to us, "We believe that whatever decision you make and wherever you direct us will be God's direction for us and we will respond accordingly." What a responsibility that was for us on the Personnel Committee. We asked them to go to Peru instead of Indonesia and they had now served in Peru for some years and would, in time, become leaders of the Peru work.

When we had finished talking together, I asked if Maureen and I could pray for them before they left us. They asked if they could pray for us first of all. We gladly agreed. As they prayed for me, I began to weep. And weep. And weep. I cannot remember any of the words they used as they began to pray, it was as if a pent-up flood of tears was suddenly released within me and I wept for what seemed a long time but was probably a few minutes. When I ceased from my tears I remember saying, somewhat embarrassed, "Well, I don't know what that was all about." Maureen looked at me, as wives do sometimes as if to say, "How do you not know? Of course, you know!" Then light dawned. We had been through joys and sorrows in the almost ten years since coming to the church in Bournemouth. But the sorrows of losing dear people from the church family, plus words spoken to me and about me and the times of personal heart-searching I had been through had taken an emotional toll. It was all there locked up within me and Father God had chosen this safe place to bring release that I had not even recognised I needed. Grace upon grace upon grace.

Only God knows what my future in local church ministry would have been if He had not created that safe space in which to bring me release and healing. I was pressing on in the ministry God had given me as if nothing were out of order within me, completely unaware of my silently ticking emotional clock. And I was unaware, as evidenced by my exclamation, "Well, I don't know what that was all about". There is only so long that you can live and work like that before the dam bursts or before you wake up one morning, not knowing what is going on, but realising that you cannot go on.

Burnout, breakdown, call it what you will, it happens. All too often it removes men and women from the ministry to which God called them and for which God gifted them.

So many suffer. The individual concerned, if married their spouse and family, the local church where they have been serving or whatever ministry they are pursuing.

I have friends and colleagues in ministry who have walked this very painful path. I have witnessed the spiritual, emotional, relational and physical toll it has taken on them and their loved ones.

Church leaders need a safe space. They need a place where they can, in confidence and safety, be unburdened and freed from whatever is weighing on them and where the Holy Spirit can heal them from the wounds of battle. I will describe later how in the years ahead God in His grace opened up for me just such a place that provided ongoing relationships with others in local church leadership. Since retirement, I have been privileged to facilitate such a network of trust and prayer among church leaders.

Elijah was a servant of God who very much needed a safe space. The account of his sudden collapse, burnout, breakdown is laid bare in 1 Kings 19. His beginnings in ministry were marked by remarkable miracles, a great victory over the ruling Baal worship and unusual evidence of the anointing of the Spirit. Here surely is a man who will not be troubled by the kind of vulnerabilities that mark lesser men. Not so. A threat on his life by Jezebel, a leader in the demonic worship ravaging Israel under King Ahab, sends Elijah, this mighty man of God, into a panic and he runs for his life.

God knew Elijah needed a safe space. The account of how God provided all that Elijah needed is described in compassionate detail. Elijah just wanted to die. "I have had enough, Lord". Have you been there? Have you said that to God? I certainly have. Elijah needed rest and sleep. He needed food and drink (what better than newly baked bread?). Elijah slept some more. Only after about six weeks was he at a point where God knew Elijah was ready for the gentle whisper of heaven into his soul.

Our Father in heaven cares for us as whole people. He created us, breathed the breath of life into us and knows that we are dust. Sadly, we are often unaware of ourselves and our needs and we heap pressure on ourselves rather than getting aside with God and asking our Father to speak to us. We so often need what an old friend once described as 'a skin face'. In other words, someone to sit alongside us, walk with us, listen and pray. Ecclesiastes 4:9-12 says it this way:

> ▶ Two are better than one,
>   because they have a good return for their labor:
> If either of them falls down,
>   one can help the other up.
> But pity anyone who falls
>   and has no one to help them up.
> Also, if two lie down together, they will keep warm.
>   But how can one keep warm alone?
> Though one may be overpowered,
>   two can defend themselves.
> A cord of three strands is not quickly broken.
>
> ● Ecclesiastes 4:9-12 (NIV)

These words of Scripture remind us that close, trusting relationships are critical to healthy living. Church leaders need to be able to forge and invest in such relationships year on year. Such friends can ask you the questions about yourself which need asking, but you are either unaware of what they are, or you are only too well aware and do not want to go there. They can give you the wise, straightforward advice you may need about the basics of caring for yourself when you are in danger of being blind to the essentials for health and wholeness. Just as God in His love and care for Elijah provided him with bread for the journey, so He wants you to have 'friends for your journey'. Do you have such friends? If not, ask your Father in heaven to bring them to you. They may in fact be already at hand and He is asking you to recognise His provision and reach out to them.

Do read on in the story of God's dealings with Elijah. God recommissions him, and Elijah has the joy of anointing his successor in Elisha. God continues to use Elijah for His purposes in the nation of Israel. His sinking down under the broom bush was not the end. It was the beginning of his restoration and fresh anointing for the next season of his ministry. Whatever your 'broom bush' experience, God loves to lift up the fallen and restore the downtrodden. If that is you at this time then perhaps God's word to Elijah is His word to you today: "Go back the way you came… " (v15) Standing before God and encountering His gentle whisper is the way forward. And inviting a 'friend for the journey' to sit where you sit and pray for you can prove to be bread for your journey.

The issue of what to do about our premises, in order to provide more facilities for the growing congregation and the work in the community, continued to be a matter for discussion and prayer. In 1988 we made an approach to the owner of the house and land on the western boundary of the church premises in Calvin Road to ascertain if he would be willing to sell. The plan was to extend the worship area through to the rear hall and to use the house for small room accommodation and increased parking space. The expected costs of acquisition and conversion were reckoned to be in the order of £250,000. However, the offer to purchase was refused.

In the light of our difficulties in attempting to expand on our present site, we were growingly of the conviction that God was speaking to us by means of these closed doors. We believed that, at this time in the life of the church, He was directing us to invest finance in personnel rather than in buildings. This was a significant conviction and guided us in our decision-making on many occasions over the next few years. In particular, we did not consider again the possibility of expanding our own premises in Calvin Road or look for new premises to purchase. Rather, we gradually built a staff team, adding in those who had the mix of gifts we believed we needed to grow the church in its life and witness.

Growing churches have a number of solutions they can follow to resolve the issue of more people, including children and youth, but restricted premises. Having considered a number of options, the elders recommended to the church that we consider developing a 'Three C's Model': Celebration, Congregation and Cell (meeting in homes in small groups). This model of church growth would be supported by a diverse and growing staff team. The local Congregation would comprise of a number of Cells. Everyone would meet together in regular combined Celebrations, where the whole church would receive input. This would maintain a sense of belonging and corporate identity in the midst of growth. We envisaged these proposals coming into being sometime in 1989.

The finance report for the year ended 31st December 1988 continued to give great cause for praise to God. Giving to our Missions Budget (through which we funded local and overseas mission) was also up. A further cause for thanksgiving was that in 1988 an extension to the manse (the church house in which Maureen and I lived) was built, which provided a study, enlarged dining area, replacement garage and other benefits. This was completed by men from the church at a cost of £10,000, a huge saving on estimates from external builders. The treasurer underlined for thanksgiving that this had been funded from revenue and not capital, as had been anticipated when the project was given the go-ahead.

✎

1988 also saw two significant events take place for Maureen and me in that both our son Kevin and daughter Fiona were married. These were special days of thanksgiving and joy for us all as a family. With our youngest, Stuart, no longer desperate to come with us on holiday, we began to roam further afield for our three-week summer break. Having a three-week break in the summer each year was ideal for us. We found two weeks was too short a time to leave responsibilities truly behind. With two weeks, no sooner were you away than you were thinking of going home. We both loved having that time away, just the two of us. The pressures on you in church leadership are immense which is why, as I have said previously, it is so important to set aside uninterrupted time off each week. Your responsibility to Jesus for your marriage relationship and your responsibility to your spouse demands stretches of time together such as these holidays far away from people. We both love people, but we love each other first after Jesus! And that is the way God wants it to stay forever.

For some years, about five times between 1987 and 1995, we drove to the south of France, to the area of the Camargue, which lies to the east of Montpellier. We had found a campsite we loved and rented a large static caravan. There were many fascinating historical sites to visit, glorious beaches and plenty of beautiful walks to enjoy together. One of the church's missionaries, Muriel, who had served with the North Africa Mission since 1957, was then living and working among North Africans in Montpellier, having spent many years in Algeria. We so much enjoyed meeting up with her and being introduced to some of the beautiful mountain villages of the Cevennes.

There were quite a few years when, at the beginning of the third week of our holiday, my thoughts would turn to returning home. The prospect of leading the church for another year and the weight of responsibility involved would often cause me to say to the Lord, "I cannot do this anymore". I felt weak and lacking in all that was needed to take up the reins again. After struggling with this for a day or so, I found the answer. I knelt down before the Lord and recognised afresh His call upon my life and His call to lead this church in Bournemouth. I surrendered anew to Him and told Him that I would follow Him in this. I asked for the aid of His Spirit again for the task, which otherwise was totally beyond me. From that act of surrender and obedience there always came the peace of God, and His resources were there when I returned home.

In 1989 the continuing growth of the church required the setting up of a church office and the appointment of some help. Up until this point, I was banging away on a typewriter and the accounts and membership details were on the treasurer's computer. So, a computer was purchased, the existing vestry converted into an office and our first part-time office secretary, one of the church family with the appropriate gifts, was appointed. This was a major and essential change.

Little wonder that the gift of administration is included in the New Testament's gifts of Christ to His Church. I am so thankful to God for those in the church who served in this role over the years from when it was only a day a week, through to when it became a full-time role. The fact is that if you intend to grow a staff team then you need to give priority to the appointment of a competent, patient and 'full of grace' secretary/administrator. They are key to the success of the whole enterprise.

The appointment of a Youth Pastor had been proposed by the elders and in 1989 it was agreed to proceed, and we appointed Stewart, a young Scotsman, to the post (his nationality was 'not' a factor in him securing the job!). At this point, there were 120 children and youth connected to the church. The person appointed would have oversight of all the children's and youth work and take up growing opportunities to access local schools. The work among the children and youth included Mums and Toddlers, Creche, and Sunday School. There were also various age-related clubs and bible classes, which provided for all those of senior school age. This further addition to the growing staff team was again a large step of faith financially. The year had already seen commitments to begin to pay a part-time administrator, to fully fund the training of one of our young couples at Ichthus Christian Fellowship in South London and now the church was committing itself to the salary for a Youth Pastor.

It had become clear, as the church grew and faced the financial costs of building a staff team, that there was a need to teach a biblical approach to discussing and agreeing these appointments. The usual question from a church when a funding question arises was and probably still is in some cases, 'Can we afford it?' or someone would say, 'We haven't the money'. I realised that it was necessary to teach the church that the primary issue that needed to be in focus was not money. Rather, the issue to be considered and the question to be asked was this: 'What is God saying to us about this proposal? Is this God's direction for us or is this an appointment that God is leading us to make?' Prioritising this question enabled the church to operate from first principles. In other words, always seek God first for a revelation of His will. Yes, of course, it is necessary to then consider the issue of finance. But only once you have together ascertained the direction of the Holy Spirit in the matter. This approach to issues of funding stood us in particularly good stead in the much larger financial projects that would follow in the years ahead.

N

The elders had been progressing the preparations for the introduction of the Cell, Congregation, Celebration model. It required prayer and consideration. A decision was taken to establish a new Congregation in September 1989 in Charminster, which is a district just about two miles from the church centre in Winton. The new Congregation met for a while in an upstairs room at the Five Ways Hotel, which is a local pub. Later, we were able to rent a large hall on the main road from the local Catholic Church, which provided ease of access and much better facilities all around. The church family had been given the opportunity to join either Winton Congregation or Charminster Congregation, depending on where they lived. Their Cell (formerly house group) involvement would also be guided by where they lived and to which Congregation they chose to belong.

From this time, Winton Evangelical Church met in two Congregations, Winton and Charminster. On Sunday mornings, Winton Congregation met at our premises in Calvin Road, Winton and Charminster Congregation at the Catholic Church Hall, Charminster. On Sunday evenings we joined together for Celebration at our church centre in Winton.

Maureen and I led Winton Congregation and Tony and Sandie were the leaders of Charminster Congregation and so on Sunday mornings the four of us were at our own congregation. In the light of our experience in the early months of these arrangements, it was decided that it would be helpful to both congregations and to us as pastor and associate pastor of the church, to have one Sunday morning each month when the leadership couples changed congregations. This enabled leaders and people to feel more in touch with each other, especially as we were feeling our way into something which was new to us all. Tony and Sandie continued to be the congregational leaders at Charminster until 1993, when Lloyd and Rosemary, who had been involved with Tony and Sandie in leading the work at Charminster since 1989, took over as leaders of that congregation.

These were obviously major changes for the whole church including the leaders and had many implications for everyone. But the driving force behind the changes was the growth the church was experiencing, for which we thanked God. Problems stemming from growth are much to be preferred to the problems that arise from a work that is weak and lacks vision. But if growth is to be facilitated and if it is to increase year on year, the vision has to be wedded to practical thinking and effective future planning. And all of that has to be the subject of honest, thoughtful discussion that is soaked in prayer all the way.

At the same time as we began to meet in two congregations, September 1989, the church sent a young couple, Peter and Linda, to Ichthus Christian Fellowship in London for a year of training. We had in mind to plant another Congregation in a couple of years and the elders and church community believed that Peter and Linda were being called by God to prepare themselves to lead that new plant. It had been arranged that when they had completed their year at Ichthus in the summer of 1990, they would enter the next phase of their training by becoming assistant congregational leaders to Maureen and myself at the Winton Congregation. It had already been agreed that I would have a sabbatical in 1991, so we would need leadership cover at Winton Congregation during our absence. Therefore, by coming to work alongside us for seven months before the sabbatical commenced, they would be ready to lead Winton in our absence. All in all, good preparation to lead the new congregation for which they had been tasked to do further research and planning. The church had supported Peter and Linda financially through their training in London and from September 1991 they would become salaried staff. This was another large step of faith financially for the church, but we believed this was God's direction for us.

The church had been served by deacons throughout its history. The word 'deacon' had become rather institutionalised as an elected office, as opposed to the function of a servant as it appears in the New Testament. Many independent evangelical churches and evangelical Baptist churches, to name just two branches of the UK church, were still led by deacons rather than elders. Although we had appointed elders soon after I arrived at Winton, we continued to have deacons overseeing practical and financial matters. Only men had ever served in this capacity in the church over the years. Although women had been invited to serve as deacons in recent years, so far none had been willing, due to the history of men only. We needed to create a more flexible structure. Structures must always serve, not hinder, growth and development. Sadly, in many churches, sometimes due to a lack of openness to the ministry of the Holy Spirit, tradition and legalism can rule. In such situations, the existing structures can become sacrosanct, even if they are impeding the Gospel and the growth of the church.

As the elders and deacons examined the relevant New Testament teaching, we realised that while the church always needed people who were able and willing to 'serve', the word 'deacon' and the tradition attached to it in our situation was a hindrance rather than a help. We therefore agreed to bring the office and election of deacons to an end. This led to the formation of a Church Executive (CE), comprising Elders, Congregational Representatives, Administrator, Finance Officer and Buildings Officer. The CE would be accountable to the Annual Church Meeting, which would include people from both congregations, as we were still one church. The name of the church would continue to be Winton Evangelical Church, meeting in two congregations, Winton

Congregation and Charminster Congregation, both Congregations having a cluster of Cells. This new organisational structure came into being in January 1990. Deacons, as an elected office, ceased to exist. But the serving responsibility for finance and premises and any other necessary practical aspect of the life of the church was taken up by people with those gifts, men and women, as invited by the Church Executive and confirmed by the wider church family.

The church, and especially those who had been serving as deacons, accepted these new arrangements with much grace. Besides other benefits, it served to unlock the logjam where the election of deacons had prevented women from serving effectively. Some of the deacons had served for many years and no church can function effectively without people who are willing to use their gifts and time for the Lord Jesus and His people. It was a joy to see men who had served as deacons now beginning to use their gifts in other areas of the church's life. Often their gifts now more closely matched new opportunities, of which there were many.

The church holiday weeks in previous years (CRASH '87 and CRASH '88) had been a time of building relationships with God and one another. In 1989 we moved our church holiday time from Easter to the late summer and also had a new venue, in Cheshire. The theme for the week was 'Time to Advance' and again it was a significant event for many people and for the life of the church. It proved to be the last of these holiday weeks together. Although we explored arranging a similar week in 1990, with rising prices it proved to be too expensive and we did not proceed. However, these weeks had all been part of the purpose of God for us as a church. They brought us closer together, developed our heart for God, enabled us to develop in the use of the gifts of the Spirit and sharpened our understanding of His vision for us as a church community.

✒

March for Jesus was a recent national initiative organised by Ichthus, Youth with a Mission and Pioneer, working in concert with Graham Kendrick, an anointed worship leader. Saturday 16th September 1989 had been chosen as a day when local church leaders across the nation would organise a March for Jesus in their area. The timing of the founding of South West Evangelical Alliance two years earlier was superb, as for the first time there was a structure through which the churches across the area could organise effectively and participate in nationwide initiatives. On that day 5000 Christians from Dorchester in the west to the New Forest in the east gathered together at Kings Park, Bournemouth. There was an amazing sense of excitement as we all met together at Kings Park. There had never been such a gathering of the church in this area, preparing to go out on the streets to "bring the message that the church is here to bless, to love, to unite, to serve and to bring change". The day began around 11am with worship and prayer and then the march of witness moved westwards, through the shopping area of Boscombe and along the clifftop to the Lower Gardens in central Bournemouth. As we walked along the streets, we were singing many recent songs which proclaimed the name of Jesus and were praying for our communities. Forty other towns and cities throughout the nation from Shetland to the Channel Islands had similar Marches for Jesus on that day.

This was a memorable occasion! The church in the UK was out on the streets! There was singing, joy, worship bands, banners (many churches had created attractive banners with their church name) and people leaving their church groups to speak to the crowds of onlookers. I particularly remember that day, as I had lost my voice and was very frustrated at not being able to sing. At one point I went ahead and was waiting on the cliff top for our church contingent to arrive. As they came into view one of our older women was marching energetically along with the rest of the church, swinging her arms and singing, with balloons tied to her handbag. I found myself in danger of having to hurriedly wipe away tears. I was remembering her hesitations at the changes which had come about in the church in the last decade and her struggles with some of that. Yet she had stayed, when some of her friends had left (not at all easy for her), saying that she knew God had told her to 'stay' and she had been afraid she would miss what God was doing if she did otherwise. She was overjoyed at being a part of such a witness to Jesus in her own town and said to me later that day, "If I had left the church I would have missed today and so much else that God is doing among us".

With the growth of the church, the restructuring on a Cell, Congregation and Celebration model, and a growing staff team, the elders had been giving continuous thought and prayer to the church's leadership structures. The elders proposed to the church that they should continue to be the overall covering, under God, for the life and ministry of the church. They then recommended that a Leadership Team (LT) be appointed, consisting of the elders and other men and women who were both called and gifted by God and recognised by the elders and the church. The LT would then be responsible, under God and the oversight of the elders, for the ongoing life and ministry of the church and for its vision and direction. It was also proposed that each congregation should have a leadership team. These Congregational Leadership Teams would be responsible, under God, for the life and ministry of their own Congregation and would come under the overall covering of the LT.

The church community wholeheartedly agreed with this new leadership structure, which came into being in early 1991. The church was going through considerable growth and change. Bringing into senior leadership those who had been called to lead key areas of the church's life and witness, including those who were bearing weight in the leadership of their Congregations, was a no-brainer. It gave the elders ongoing access to the knowledge and insight of others they respected in God and it enabled others to grow further in their gifting and begin to recognise the potential that God had placed within them.

CHAPTER 11

Sabbaticals, Setbacks and Celebrations

1991 – 1992

aster 1991 saw Maureen and I commence a six-month sabbatical. It is more common now for churches to have a sabbatical policy for their staff, which is wise provided careful thought and planning is involved by all concerned. In 1991 there was no such policy in place in most churches. In fact, during the seventies and well into the eighties I cannot remember hearing of any church leader having a sabbatical. Such an arrangement was simply not even considered or discussed as a possibility by elders, deacons, church councils or whatever form of church government was in place.

It was now twenty-one years since I had left London Bible College and for a few years, I had thought that it would be good to reflect and learn away from our usual situation. But then, I had to consider whether there would be adequate cover for the church and its ministry if I were to be away for a period of three or four months. By early 1990 I thought some time in 1991 would be suitable as Tony and Sandie and Peter and Linda would be in place to lead the two Congregations, and the eldership and church were in a strong and healthy place. Therefore, I broached the matter with the elders and suggested that I take a four-month sabbatical from easter 1991. When they agreed and then suggested I take six months I wondered if they had an ulterior motive. But I was so grateful to them and to the church family. As Maureen and I had thought and prayed about the sabbatical, one of our desires was to visit two of our church's overseas workers in Hong Kong. We also particularly wanted to be involved in a large charismatic church situation in another culture, but it would need to be English-speaking. Believing that God had promised considerable further growth in our own church situation in the years ahead, we wanted to learn more about the ways in which a larger church operated.

We had a month here in the UK first of all, enjoying a rest and some time at Spring Harvest, where Maureen was involved, as for many previous years, on the counselling team. Then we set out for Hong Kong. The approach to Kai Tak Airport in Hong Kong was an experience to remember, flying in low over Kowloon. It was as if you could reach out and pick up the washing on the rooftops below, not far below at all! (The new airport, opened some twenty years later on reclaimed land, is amazing in its design, space and rapid transport links with the city, but the landing approach is ordinary by comparison).

We had come to Hong Kong to spend time with Rob and Elaine and their family. Rob had trained at Moorlands College and the family worshipped with us during those years. Rob and Elaine had a clear sense of God's call on their lives for overseas service and on completion of his course at the College, they and the family moved out to Hong Kong. The church had sent them and supported them since that time. They had a heart to provide member care for missionaries in that region of SE Asia and for Hong Kong nationals, who were serving the church in the Territory. They had settled on Cheung Chau Island, one of Hong Kong's outlying islands, which was easily accessible by ferry from Central District. There was a property on the island, which needed a lot of attention, love and care. Rob and Elaine moved in, lived there and did a wonderful job of licking it into shape as a home for themselves and a base for ministry. So began Bethany Ministries, which has provided a place of rest, recuperation and spiritual refreshment for many years and continues to do so today.

During our time with Rob and Elaine, we discussed and prayed together about the possibility of our church in Bournemouth planting an English-speaking church, where they lived, on Cheung Chau Island. God was at work and even while we were speaking about this possibility, unknown to the four of us at the time, the Holy Spirit was preparing someone in our church in Bournemouth. Within six months, they were on the Island, exploring if this was the call of God to them.

While in Hong Kong we were able to visit some key Kingdom ministries, including Jackie Pullinger's remarkable work. At the age of 22 Jackie, believing God was calling her to be a missionary and unable to find any missionary organisation willing to support her, arrived in Hong Kong. (If you have never read her story of faith and venturing on God, find the account in her book 'Chasing the Dragon'). Jackie lived and worked in Kowloon's Walled City, which was notorious for being run by Chinese Triad gangs. She helped some of the gang leaders to find Jesus and be set free from opium addiction. We were able to visit one of the rehabilitation homes, provided by the St Stephen's Society, which she founded in 1981. There we saw something of the continuing work of providing a place of safety for those suffering from life-threatening addiction and met the Spirit-filled staff who were praying and caring for them. The power and effectiveness of praying in tongues, for providing release and bringing the presence of Jesus to those ensnared, was powerful and a cause for praise to God.

There were many opportunities to share Christ and preach at a number of churches over our weeks in Hong Kong. We had the joy of meeting and coming to know and highly value the ministry of a New Zealander, Lesley Leighton and spent time with her as she shared the good news of the love, compassion and power of Jesus with her team on the streets in Kowloon. Since that time Lesley has planted churches in places as far apart as Mozambique and Russia. Some five years later it was a special joy to welcome Lesley and five Russian church leaders to the Waves of the Spirit Conference at the Bournemouth International Centre. After the Conference, Lesley and her colleagues led a remarkable Sunday evening at our church, when the presence and power of God changed lives.

Our visit to Hong Kong led to the privilege of entering The People's Republic of China. Little did we realise that this would not be the first and only time that we would be visiting Hong Kong and China. The fascinating journey, in which we travelled with Rob and Elaine, began with the one-hour ferry from Cheung Chau Island to Central District in Hong Kong. Crossing the narrow strip of water that divides Central from Kowloon by the renowned Star Ferry, we took the train from Kowloon in Hong Kong to Guangzhou, just over the border into China. It was only one hour to the Chinese border and then suddenly it was like going back in history... to our old school geography books... so many people working the land... in the rice fields ... riding bicycles, slowly, sedately... unloading a lighter at the riverbank, 12 men walking up and down the plank between boat and bank, each with a bamboo pole across their shoulders with suspended baskets, carrying coal, sand, cement. After the state-of-the-art technology all around us in Hong Kong, the contrast was stark in the extreme.

The next day we boarded an internal flight from Guangzhou to Nanning, which is in the southeast of China towards the border with Vietnam. We were to be in Nanning for a few days visiting Karen, a Moorlands College graduate teaching English and living for Jesus in the city.

Karen was in the process of adopting a little girl from a government-run home for disabled children and she took us to visit. The condition of the home and the children caused anger to rise up within us. We found it almost impossible not to express our feelings to those responsible but had to restrain ourselves, as it would have resulted in Karen being unable to continue her ongoing compassionate ministry in that institution. We held one of the tiny infants in our arms. She was not from the majority and ruling Han-Chinese, but from one of the despised tribal groups. We longed to take her out of there and home with us. While in Nanning, Karen took us for an afternoon walk around the villages outside the city, when we were able to experience something of the reality of life for the vast majority of the population. We also had the opportunity of speaking at one of her evening classes. It was composed of 40 students, mostly graduates in their 20s. Another day we enjoyed spending time with students from the Agricultural Research Academy, everyone eager to learn and ask questions and many opportunities to share faith one-to-one or in small groups. The thirst for knowledge on a wide range of subjects, political, economic and religious among all the students we met was in marked contrast to what was common in the UK.

The journey back to Hong Kong included a 24-hour train journey to Guangzhou. People labouring in the open fields for mile after mile brought back a memory from youth. My parents read many missionary magazines, which included the one published by the China Inland Mission, later the Overseas Missionary Fellowship. The magazine was called 'China's Millions'. The scenes from the train reminded me of the cover of some of those magazines., All the time I was in China, I found it hard to believe that God had given us the privilege of visiting this nation, which God loves so much. Little did we know then that God was going to cause China to be a major focus for our little church in Bournemouth, in sending personnel and in prayer and financial support in the years ahead. But we certainly knew that God was 'up to something' – there was that inner 'knowing' that Hong Kong, certainly, was on heaven's agenda for us as a church in the days ahead.

It is just worth saying that when we both thought we should visit our two overseas workers in Hong Kong as a part of our sabbatical, we had no clue at all that visit would open the door on all that God had in mind to do in the years ahead. We had simply always believed that the local church should do everything it can to love and support those it sends out into mission, whether 'here, there or over there'. Our thought of visiting Rob and Elaine was therefore a natural consequence of that conviction, in the same way as visiting Muriel in Montpellier, when we were on holiday in the south of France.

We discovered, when visiting RBMU personnel in Peru, that our visits to them were highly valued in a way that we could never have imagined before we went. Why so highly valued? Because just our going to them told them that the Mission cared enough about them to send two people just like themselves to sit and listen to them and care and pray for them. (Often the Peru Personnel wrote to the church to thank them for releasing us to visit them. That is what it meant to them). It is extremely easy to think you are forgotten when you are on the other side of the world, away from your nuclear and church families and usual support base and in an unfamiliar culture and language. We all need skin faces to show to us in down to earth ways that 'You matter! You are loved, valued, appreciated and not forgotten.' In Isaiah 49:14 we hear this cry:

> ▶ **But Zion said, "The Lord has forsaken me,**
> **the Lord has forgotten me.**
>
> • **Isaiah 49:14 (NIV)**

And then in verses 15 and 16 comes heaven's reply:

> ▶ "Can a mother forget the baby at her breast
>   and have no compassion on the child she has borne?
> Though she may forget,
>   I will not forget you!
> See, I have engraved you on the palms of my hands;
>   your walls are ever before me."
>
> ● **Isaiah 49:15-16 (NIV)**

And in order to underline this wonderful strengthening truth, God often sends some of His children, like you and me – 'skin faces' – to reinforce His message: 'I will never forget you!'

Following our month in Hong Kong and China, we were now headed to Singapore where, in a remarkable way, God had arranged for us to be visiting staff members for two months at Church of Our Saviour. With the other aspect of our sabbatical desiring to spend some time in a large charismatic church in another culture, we could prepare ourselves for the further growth we believed God was going to give us in the church in Bournemouth.

Months earlier, when we had been thinking and praying about the sabbatical, we asked the help of Bishop Ban It Chiu, a former Bishop of Singapore, who was retired and living in the Bournemouth area. He was a godly man, with a powerful healing ministry. It was through his kindness that we were invited to be involved in Church of Our Saviour. How good is God our Father! But that wasn't all. While in Singapore, the Lord provided two amazing homes for us to stay in, rent-free, both with swimming pools on the grounds. Maureen learned to swim in our first month! We were also gifted the use of a BMW car! We were overwhelmed by the generosity of our Father in heaven through His children. The story of God's provision involves friends in a church in Singapore, who made it known in their church community that a UK couple were to be in Singapore for two months and asked if anyone knew of any accommodation to rent? A British couple and an American couple living and working in Singapore were to be back home for a month each and gave us their homes for our stay. As that old friend of my father's said to me when I was a teenager: "You will never be able to say to God, 'You owe me'. If you honour Him, he will honour you". There were many days in Singapore when we were looking back to the sadness and pain of some of the years in the 80s and so appreciating God's loving kindness, expressed in these facilities which were way above anything we needed.

Church of Our Saviour (COOS) is a large charismatic Anglican church with a multi-national congregation, reflecting the international nature of Singapore. The staff team was numerous and varied in ethnic background and age. They were so welcoming, and we went back subsequently on brief visits in the years that followed on our way to or from Hong Kong and China. The staff meetings were memorable for a number of reasons, but particularly because the tables around which we gathered were strewn with all kinds of nuts, dried fruit and other not so wholesome goodies. At lunchtime we would all meet up at a nearby eating house and did they enjoy their food? We could not believe what they could put away and remain so slim.

There were many aspects of church life that were understandably quite different from the UK, which is one of the reasons we were there. Their preparation of people for believers' baptism, even as an Anglican Church, was particularly instructive. New Christians were coming from a variety of cultural and religious backgrounds... Buddhism, Hinduism, ancestor worship to name just a few. Their preparation for baptism included detailed doctrinal teaching and discipleship, as you would expect. But there was also a deliverance evening when the whole group together would be taught about the need to be set free from the demonic influences involved in their former background. This teaching was then followed by prayer for deliverance, healing and the ministry of the Holy Spirit.

In Asia, you are very soon aware that people believe in the reality of the spiritual world. The church is therefore speaking into a different milieu in Asia than we do in the West and they do speak into it. In the UK we appear to have little awareness that Satan is just as active but wearing a different garb. People who are being born again by the Spirit in the UK require just as careful teaching and discipleship as in Singapore. But they also need to be made aware of areas of their lives where the enemy of their souls has been wielding a strong influence or indeed exercising baleful control. As they recognise and confess the truth of their condition and follow this with godly repentance, freedom and healing follow. This early clearing of the ground enables their growth in God to move forward unhindered. For lack of such teaching and ministry to new believers in the UK, more than a few are held back from experiencing the fullness that is theirs in Christ.

Our two months as visiting members of the staff team of Church of Our Saviour was a gift from God and we learned so much... it was excellent preparation for the years that were to come in Bournemouth when we would often refer back to those days with thanksgiving. But our involvement there was not yet finished: we were about to move from Singapore to the Philippines. COOS was a missionary church. Geographically Singapore is a jumping-off point for so many nations. Every Sunday we were praying for teams preparing to go to Malaysia and Indonesia and some further afield to Russia, Europe and the Middle East. COOS had a church-planting couple in the north of the Philippines and it had been arranged that we would spend a month with them. Just as we were due to fly from Singapore, Mt Pinatubo, a volcano to the north of Manila, the capital of the Philippines, erupted. Flights were delayed for a couple of days. When we eventually arrived in Manila, we travelled by coach to Laoag, in the far northwest of Luzon Province. On the way, we saw the devastation wreaked by the eruption a few days previously. It was as if a billion fireplaces had been emptied and the ash had been spread as far as the eye could see. A spire, isolated in a sea of ash, was the only visible sign that a church building existed below.

There had been many ministry opportunities in Hong Kong and Singapore, and many more here in this relatively recently-planted church. We led early morning bible studies and prayers for the Filipino team and travelled out into the area preaching and teaching. The response to the preaching of the Gospel was like nothing we had witnessed previously. There was a sense of open heaven in Asia.

We had been due to be there for four weeks, but after two weeks or so Maureen became quite unwell. There was no access to reliable medical care where we were in Laoag, which was a relatively remote area and the team of Filipinos did not seem to grasp that Maureen was becoming much worse. We felt increasingly isolated. My major concern was that Maureen had a lifelong renal condition and I was afraid that her kidneys were being endangered. By now she was quite unable to stand or walk. I could not get her to drink any liquid. In the mercy of God, we had a missionary friend in Manila and eventually, after many attempts, I was able to get through to him on the telephone. To hear Nigel's voice was a huge comfort. I told the team that we had to get Maureen to Manila. With considerable difficulty, we managed to get her on a small aircraft for a very unpleasant flight from Laoag to Manila, where Nigel met us at the airport and took us straight to the main hospital in Quezon City.

The consultant, who had trained in Europe, explained that Maureen had contracted typhoid. I couldn't believe it as we had both had our typhoid inoculations before we left the UK. He explained that the strain of typhoid in the area where we had been would not have been covered. Maureen was in hospital for a week and I lay on a mattress on the floor of her room, becoming very quickly adept at flattening cockroaches, which were everywhere at night.

Nigel found a wonderful Christian guest house in Manila where we could both stay when Maureen was discharged. While she began to recuperate, I had the opportunity of visiting one of the very large churches in Manila, which met in a cinema with six services every Sunday. (Little did I think then that our own church in Bournemouth would meet in an ex-cinema, ex-bingo hall building years later). I built a close relationship with the pastor and a few years later he preached for me in Bournemouth. I was also able to spend a couple of days visiting a remarkable ministry to the poor in the shantytown area of Manila. Although I had often been in all kinds of shanty town situations in Peru, these situations in Manila were of a different order of desperation.

We were due to fly home on British Airways. Maureen's continuing weakness meant she needed a wheelchair and I will always remember her joy and relief on boarding the plane and hearing the British voices of the cabin crew. However, as the flight progressed, the aircrew was concerned that Maureen was becoming too dehydrated and in Delhi British Airways arranged for us to stay over the weekend in a five-star hotel, while a doctor checked her condition. A couple of days later, with the doctor happy that Maureen could now resume our journey, we continued the flight to Gatwick, arriving home at the end of August after four months in Asia. We then had a clear month before I began to pick up the reins at church, which gave me an opportunity to reflect and prepare for the next season. Maureen was not back to her usual strength and energy levels until the end of the year. Despite the not-to-be-repeated experience of Maureen's serious ill health, these months were a special, indeed quite unique time in our lives for which we have always been very thankful to God.

While we had been away Tony Seymour had been heading up the elders and staff team in my absence. I was so grateful to him for taking on that responsibility, as it enabled us to have the sabbatical. However, it took its toll on him. Tony had always said that he was not a No1 (that is, a 'first among equals' leader) and therefore he was certainly out of his comfort zone during those six months. Tony was such a gift from God to me. He knew he was a No 2 and excelled in that role and it was such a joy to work together. He is a very gifted man and was greatly loved by the church family. Having Tony alongside me for those years since 1987 taught me so much. Among other things I learned that when a colleague knows what their gifting is and what it is not, it enables effective functioning both for the person themselves and for those in team with them.

If you are setting out to build a team ministry, or if you are already in such a situation and did not start from first principles, the first essential is for you to be clear about yourself: the gifts you have and equally the gifts you do not have. In that process, you also need to be able to recognise your primary gifts. It is not sufficient for you to engage in this important exercise yourself: you need one or two people who know you very well indeed and will not hesitate to disabuse you of your illusions about yourself. If you fail to give this process due weight you may well (will) lay elephant- traps for yourself and others in the days ahead. As you build a team, it is essential to be able to recognise what you do not bring to the table in order that you may understand the strategic gifts needed alongside your own.

Fundamental to building an effective and harmonious team is that you are secure in your value and worth to God. Strip away any achievements you may think you have and any gifts you believe you have been given. These are not safe foundations for personal security because they are not biblical foundations. They are sand, not rock. Your security and worth must be wholly in the truth, ministered to you by the Spirit of truth, that you are accepted, loved and made righteous in the sight of God through the Lord Jesus Christ and there is absolutely nothing you can add, nor dare you, to His sufficiency for you. It is never about your gifts or your achievements: it is always about Jesus your Rock. To change the analogy, roots in Him bring fruit for His glory. Jesus said...

> ▶ **"I am the vine; you are the branches. If you remain in me and I in you, you will bear much fruit; apart from me you can do nothing."**
>
> ● **John 15:5 (NIV)**

Towards the end of 1991, 'It's Time', an evangelistic outreach, took place in Bournemouth and our involvement as a church was led by Tony. It happened in this way. When Tony was appointed in 1987, he and I began to meet monthly with five other church leaders. Our desire was to see God bringing together many of the church leaders in the area, but this did not take shape until 1994. These years when we all met together regularly, were seminal for building our relationships and God was going to use this as a foundation for what was to come in the years ahead among church leaders and churches across the Bournemouth, Christchurch, Poole conurbation. So there was a lesson there: do not give up on something God has birthed in your heart. It is what God said to the prophet Habakkuk, who when he did exactly the right thing and went to God with his complaint, heard this:

> ▶ ... Though it linger, wait for it;
> it will certainly come
> and will not delay.
>
> ● Habakkuk 2:3 (NIV)

'It's Time' was birthed out of the prayer and conversations taking place at the monthly gatherings of these five church leaders. On one occasion, when Tony was on one of his walks, looking across Bournemouth Bay to the three towns spread before him, he heard the Lord say to him, 'It's Time': time to bring the churches together in evangelism across these three boroughs.

When Tony shared this with the other leaders, it was agreed that we would work together to bring evangelism front and centre in our churches. The vision was to encourage each of these local churches to evangelise in their community. Tony, with his gift for using the sketch board in evangelism, teamed up with Open Air Campaigners and provided training and led open-air evangelism in Christchurch, Boscombe and Bournemouth town centres. The churches worked together on some projects, but in the main churches arranged and carried through their own outreach in their own communities, while supporting one another in prayer. This was the early beginnings of the work God was about in drawing leaders and churches into fellowship and mission.

One of the changes I initiated after we returned from our sabbatical was to set aside Tuesday mornings for the staff team to meet for prayer and worship, to share personal news and information and then have coffee together. Attending to a rolling agenda followed, when we would all have an opportunity to hear and contribute to matters concerning church life. Maureen and I had recognised, through our attendance at staff meetings at Church of our Saviour, the strategic importance of gathering all the staff on a weekly basis. It was key to building relationships and to ensuring that everyone had an opportunity to speak into issues and no one felt side-lined in any way. The team at this time included our office administrator Doreen; Maureen and me, congregational leaders at Winton; Tony and Sandie, congregational leaders at Charminster; Peter and Linda, preparing to lead the new Hill View congregation to be planted in 1992; and Richard and Adrienne. Richard, one of the elders, had now retired from a career in banking and gave much time to pastoral visitation. His wife, Adrienne, had been a GP and was gifted in discipling and counselling. In November 1991 Peter joined Tony, Richard and me as an elder.

In 1992 I arranged for the staff team to spend a day together at Waverley Abbey in Surrey, the headquarters of Crusade for World Revival (CWR). I was keen for us all to go through the Myers-Briggs Temperament Analysis Course, to help us in our understanding and appreciation of each other. In the weeks before our day at CWR, we each had to complete a questionnaire and return it so that the CWR staff could prepare for our day with them. It was a valuable exercise. It enabled us all to understand the differences in the way each of us operated and helped me to know the most helpful way to utilise each member of the team and draw out of them gifts and abilities I might otherwise have missed. We also had lots of fun together, as we began to realise how differently we approached situations. Subsequently, we often looked back to that day and were able to see how valuable the exercise had been for us all, aiding us in our relationships and helping us to work together more effectively.

◢

In 1988, we had agreed that we would not invest major finance into extensive development of our premises as a way of accommodating increased numbers, but rather we would invest in staff and plant out new congregations. We had no doubt that was a decision from the Lord, but it was now definitely time to upgrade our church centre premises at Calvin Road.

A three-phase plan was proposed and, through the generosity of church members and a grant from the local Talbot Trust, we completed the work debt-free by the end of 1992.

God had given us a skilled team from the church who had costed, planned and project-managed these works. We were so thankful to God that we were able to complete something which honoured him and would commend His name in the community. On Saturday 23rd January 1993 we invited our neighbours and the local community to an Open Day. The leaflet which advertised the day read: "Join us as we celebrate the completion of refurbishments to our premises in Calvin Road. Come and find out more of what goes on in your local church and how it touches lives, both in the community and overseas". On Sunday we had special Thanksgiving Services.

CHAPTER 12

Extending the Church Walls
1992 – 1993

Soon after planting our Charminster Congregation in 1989, the elders had a growing sense that this would be followed by a further congregation in due course. Initially, we were discussing and praying about the planting of what would be the third congregation (after Winton and Charminster) in the Parkstone area of Poole. The raison d'etre for Parkstone, which was about five miles from Winton, was that quite a number of people who had become part of the church lived there and had expressed a desire to see the church plant a new congregation in their area.

However, after much prayer and discussion, the elders and congregational leaders believed the next congregation should be located nearer to Winton. Hill View was in the opposite direction from Winton to Charminster and there were enough people in the church who lived in that area to enable the formation of a viable congregation.

Easter Sunday 1992 saw the commencement of the Hill View Congregation, meeting in Hill View School. There was a core of 27 adults and 11 children. Peter and Linda were appointed congregational leaders. They had been involved in considerable research during the previous six months and had also spent time with the local Church of England vicar to explain who they were and the development of Winton Evangelical Church into district congregations. The area was visited for a month beforehand and there was a 'March for Jesus' around the district on Easter Saturday, in which the whole church, comprising all three congregations, was involved.

Peter was an excellent teacher and as well as leading Hill View Congregation with Linda, he developed a discipleship course for the church under the title 'Lamplight' and trained a gifted team to run the course with him. There were three modules: From Darkness to Light; Following the Light and Living in the Light. Lamplight was a superb course and over the next few years, more than two hundred people completed it. Lamplight was a foundational course for so many who were coming to Christ in those years. Others, having moved to the church from other church situations, recognised their need for teaching, healing and fullness in Christ and this course met them at the point of their need.

It was around this time that it was agreed that each congregation would use the name 'Community Church'. This was a much more appropriate name for use in local outreach. So each congregation became in its signage and publicity Winton Community Church, Charminster Community Church and Hill View Community Church. These three congregations were all part of Winton Evangelical Church, which continued to be the overall name of the work. The introduction of the word 'Community' was going to be significant in the future.

On returning from a sabbatical in 1991, Maureen and I shared the discussions we had with Rob and Elaine in Hong Kong, concerning the possibility of the church planting an English-speaking congregation on Cheung Chau Island. The elders, leadership team and church family agreed that the church should prepare to move ahead with this. In the same way that we had seen God going before us in calling and preparing Peter and Linda to be ready to lead Hill View Congregation, He had been preparing someone else in the church for congregation planting in Hong Kong. Heather had sensed for some time that God was asking her to visit Rob and Elaine and their ministry on Cheung Chau Island and when she shared this on our return from sabbatical, we believed this was evidence from God that we were on track with His plans.

Heather spent nine months with Rob and Elaine in 1992 and it became evident to the church and to Heather that God was calling her to be a member of that future church-planting team in Hong Kong. In order to help her prepare, Heather became a member of the staff team in 1993. She had also become a member of the new Hill View Congregation and now began to assist Peter and Linda in their leadership. During that year Heather fulfilled another aspect of her preparation, which was to complete a nine-month Teaching English as a Foreign Language (TEFL) Course here in Bournemouth. Heather had a grown-up family and had been serving in the life of the church for some years. I mention this as she was the first in what would become quite a number of people in the church in the coming years who were older and who were to hear God call them to serve in world mission.

In May 1993 Maureen and I were back in Hong Kong visiting Rob and Elaine. It was exactly two years since we had first visited on our sabbatical and there had been considerable developments in their ministry and of course plans were afoot for a team from the church to come and plant an English-speaking congregation on the Island. The Bethany Ministries team was growing and at that time included four ex-patriate couples, including two couples from the Philippines. The purpose of the visit had a number of elements: Rob and Elaine had asked us to come and minister to their team in teaching, training and pastoral care. Then they wanted to talk through with us the possible expansion of their work into Macau and perhaps the Philippines. Finally, there was the need for Maureen and me to review with Rob and Elaine, tapping into all their local knowledge, the progress being made so far and the journey still to be taken to see the new church plant on Cheung Chau brought into being. At that time, Heather was preparing to arrive the following year.

It is one thing to plant congregations in neighbouring areas of your own town or city, but quite another to pray and plan to commence another congregation on the other side of the world. But when you are walking God's way, He is always ahead of you. We discovered that the Lord had not only been preparing Heather. In September 1991 Rob, one of the young men in the church, had commenced a three-year course at Moorlands College. Rob had been leading our Evangelism Committee for some years, having come to Christ at the church through the witness of school friends, who had invited him to come along with them. Rob married Alison, another student from Moorlands in 1993 and in their final year at Moorlands they spent their College placement with Rob and Elaine at Bethany. They returned to the UK with the conviction that God wanted them to join Heather in planting an English-speaking congregation on Cheung Chau. The church affirmed Rob and Alison's calling to be members of the church planting team there. Heather was sent out by the church in August 1994 and Rob and Alison, with their first child Jotham, joined her in May 1995.

Historically, most missionaries from UK churches had served overseas with a mission agency taking the primary responsibility for arranging their job description, finance, health and pastoral care. But at this time, some UK churches were beginning to engage in world mission directly, without the aid of mission agencies. The number of churches that would forge this new path was going to increase considerably in the succeeding years. This was evidence of a fresh New Testament commitment by churches to obey the Great

Commission directly, rather than always looking to agencies to take the strain and bear the responsibility. All this was a joy and evidence of new spiritual life and health in church life. But it did involve, for churches like ours, the need to 'up our game' in areas usually the responsibility of the sending mission agency.

Personally, I was very thankful to God for my involvement, at the coal face as it were, with mission agencies, especially Regions Beyond Missionary Union and then post-1991, Latin Link where I had and continued to have experience in candidate selection, pastoral care and all the elements involved in sending and supporting overseas workers. I hasten to add that mission agencies had not suddenly become obsolete. Far from it! The Lord of the harvest would continue to use these agencies as experienced aids to the churches to help them fulfil their world mission mandate. But the command of the Lord Jesus, Head of the Church, was always directed to the gathered church and now, for some churches, they heard the voice of the Lord of the Harvest that it was time to get on and do the stuff directly.

There was a substantial financial cost involved in funding our growing overseas ministry. Our team in Hong Kong were going to be wholly funded by the church, which obviously included accommodation, health insurance and airfares. We were continuing to support Muriel, Rob and Elaine. In 1994 we also had three people in their twenties who were preparing for overseas ministry with mission agencies. One had been accepted to serve with Wycliffe Bible Translators and would, after training with Wycliffe in the UK and USA, serve in Ghana for three years. Another, after concluding her training at All Nations Christian College, was due to serve with Medair in Sudan, but health issues eventually prevented this. Then another, who had graduated from Moorlands College in 1992, completed an English for Speakers of Other Languages (ESOL) Course and began to fulfil her calling to work among Muslim refugees, asylum seekers and immigrants.

The Missions Group was increasingly involved in praying and working with those who were seeking to discern God's call on their lives. That summer, another five people from the church were in Poland to assist in an evangelistic English language camp organised by a church in Warsaw, with whom we had developed links. The 1994 church accounts reveal that the budget for the church that year was £100K and the mission's budget was an additional £20K. God wonderfully provided all we needed through the dedicated giving of His people, year on year. An important factor in the very generous giving to the church's commitment to world mission, which increased much more in the years ahead, was that the church community was intimately involved in recognising God's call on the lives of those who were sent overseas. The church family was kept fully informed in the process of testing the call of God and when the church confirmed their call everyone was 'on board'. The people being sent out by the church were known, loved and valued and would be greatly missed. If the people you send into Christ's mission in the wider world will not be missed from their local church community, there is strong reason to question whether they should be going at all.

CHAPTER 13

Refreshing and Renewal
1994

In January 1994, while the leadership team were attending a conference at Ichthus Christian Fellowship in London, Richard, one of our elders died suddenly here in Bournemouth. This was a great shock for the whole church community. His wife Adrienne was herself a member of the leadership team. Since their arrival in the church in 1980, Richard and Adrienne had given themselves wholeheartedly to us all. Richard had been an elder since 1984 and his ministry of care and encouragement had enriched and strengthened the church through these years of considerable change and growth. He was a great loss to me personally, as he had encouraged me and stood with me through some difficult situations when he first became an elder.

By 1994, I was at a mid-way point from commencing ministry at Winton Evangelical Church in 1978 and concluding with retirement in 2009. In February, I had somehow arrived at the age of 50; Maureen was a few years older, As regards our family, Kevin and Fiona were married and Stuart was in his early twenties. Life was busy for us both, the church was enjoying stability and there was healthy growth across almost all areas of its life and witness.

However, we were both aware of a dryness in our spiritual lives. It was not a sudden realisation, more a slow dawning that gradually awakened us to the fact that we had lost the sense of the blessing of God as a heavy life-giving dew upon our lives. I particularly remember one Sunday evening in the early summer of that year when, after preaching, I knew I should invite a response to God's Word in the form of inviting people to come forward and receive prayer. But I could not bring myself to do so. I felt unsure, nervous, and frankly, I was aware that I had no anointing from God to proceed in that way. Inviting people to physically respond was not the way I usually concluded after preaching, but that evening I knew that the Holy Spirit was speaking to me on the subject and in the process revealing to me my need in a way I could not deny.

I should pause at this point and explain. It is now, and has been for many years, a common element in many church services such as our own, for there to be an opportunity for people to respond to the preaching of the Word of God. Now there is always a prayer team available to pray and offer help to anyone to whom God has been speaking through the service. But an opportunity to respond to God in church in this way is relatively recent. We were used to seeing people respond to the preaching of the Gospel in Billy Graham evangelistic gatherings in the 50s and 60s, but a physical "getting up out of your seats and going to the front" was never a usual element in local church Sunday services.

So that Sunday evening in 1994, when I knew that God had been speaking by His Spirit through His Word and that the Spirit of God was nudging me to provide an opportunity for response brought home to me my need for God to do a new thing in me. I returned home, concerned, and asking God to meet with me. This was the moment when I began to cry out to God for more of Him and for fresh manna from heaven.

About a month later, I heard about a gathering in Birmingham, where there had been an unusual sense of the presence of God.

Subsequently, there were further reports of meetings where the presence of God was being manifested in unusual ways: unusual for those days, but certainly not unheard of, providing there was a knowledge of church history. Holy Trinity, Brompton in West London was mentioned, but in those days, it was a church that was hardly known outside of London, unless you moved in evangelical Anglican circles. I wanted to know more, but I was also cautious. I had a responsibility to God for the team I was leading and to our church community.

Then I heard from friends in London that weekly meetings, specifically for church leadership teams, were being held at Queens Road Baptist Church, Wimbledon. From my years in ministry in London, I knew the minister of that church by reputation and through friends. He was known for his commitment to Scripture and his longing and prayers for revival. There was nothing 'wacky' about him at all. At the time there was a variety of reports in the Christian media and by word of mouth about whatever it was that was happening in some churches and meetings in different parts of the UK. Some reports were decidedly against it. A fair amount of heat was being generated, but not very much light. I decided that the elders and leadership team should visit the church in Wimbledon for a day in late June.

Before we went to Queens Road, I made it clear that we were not going there to spectate or speculate. Due to the knowledge I had of the leader of that church, his biblical and evangelical position and the integrity of his lengthy ministry, we were going there believing that God was at work and desiring to receive from Him. I underlined that we can and must trust the Spirit of truth, that if there is anything which is not of God, or out of biblical order, He will reveal it to us.

The presence of God was very real. There was teaching from the Word of God and explanation and then the opportunity to receive prayer. Quite often that day, but not always, when people received prayer from members of the Queens Road prayer team, they would fall to the floor under the weight of the presence of God upon them. There were expressions of joy, some release in laughter, while others stood quietly or lay silently on the floor, receiving from God as the Spirit ministered to them and to specific areas of their lives. We also received prayer.

In the days that followed, there was much for us to talk through as elders and a leadership team. Although there were areas where we did not understand all that God was doing, we knew that God was about a work of grace and love and healing and there was a desire among us for more of Him. I shared with the church the background to our visit to Wimbledon and what we had heard and experienced and that we believed this to be a work of God's Spirit. In the summer months that followed there was a fresh anointing on our Sunday services and increased hunger after God. In September, the elders and leadership team visited Queens Road again for another leaders' day.

We knew that this fresh outpouring of the Spirit of God had first been experienced at the Airport Vineyard church in Toronto, Canada in January some months earlier. The leaders of that church had arranged a conference and invited a colleague in ministry to come and be the speaker. During those days, the presence of God had begun to be experienced in an unusual manner. In September Maureen and I heard that there was to be a 'Catch the Fire' conference arranged by that Vineyard Church in Toronto from 11-15 October. We very much wanted to attend, but certainly could not fund it ourselves and were reluctant to ask the church. As we prayed and asked the Lord about it, an envelope was put through our front door and inside was a cheque for £1000. We were very thankful to God and made the arrangements to fly out to Canada.

The meetings were held in a huge convention centre, which the Airport Vineyard Church had rented for the conference. It was packed with people not only from North America but from all over the world. To our surprise and joy, there were two or three other church leaders from Bournemouth and that was to be significant subsequently for our local situation. The worship was often led by David Ruis, a Vineyard worship leader, who was unknown to us at the time. In the mornings there were teaching sessions and seminars on a variety of aspects of life in the Spirit. In the evenings, the focus was on worship and preaching with prayer ministry following. John Arnott, leader of the Airport Vineyard Church led the evening meetings and sometimes preached, as did Mike Bickle, whose preach from Song of Songs remains powerfully with us. Mike Bickle was a Vineyard pastor at the time and went on to establish, in 1999, the International House of Prayer in Kansas City, USA. which we were to visit in 2001.

Although Maureen and I had continued to seek God for more of Him and His anointing for some months now, we were still very aware of our need. Initially, although we valued the worship, teaching and opportunity to receive prayer, we continued to feel very dry. It was, I thought, as if I am a plant in a pot and the soil around me is very, very dry and even though someone pours water on the soil, the water just runs off the top.

However, the Lord was continuing to pour the water of His Spirit upon us day by day and the soil of our lives was becoming, at first, damp and in due time saturated. One morning, as we were singing Reginald Heber's wonderful hymn 'Holy, Holy, Holy, Lord God Almighty', the presence of God became so weighty upon everyone in a manner I had never experienced before nor since. Some people were lost in wonder, love and praise. Others fell to the ground where they had been standing singing, some slowly sinking to the floor, some crashing down, yet sustaining no harm. I remained standing. The awesomeness of Almighty God was borne in upon me, so much so that I was in awe. I felt that I dare not breathe.

One evening, towards the end of the conference, I was sitting, quietly worshipping and reflecting, having received prayer a little earlier. A woman, not far from me, was lying flat on her back. She too had received prayer and was quiet and still. Then, with her eyes closed and making no sound at all, one arm began to move in a semi-circular motion and her hand touched the wrist of her other hand, on which was her watch. This action was repeated, slowly again and again and without any other movement or sound. I asked the Holy Spirit what the action meant. Then she began to speak, her eyes still closed. As she repeated the action and as her hand came down and touched the watch on the wrist of her other arm, she spoke the words, "It is time to seek the Lord". Every time the action was repeated, she said, quietly but firmly, "It is time to seek the Lord".

We were able to visit Niagara Falls one afternoon before returning home to the UK. It was a glorious October day, with a cloudless deep blue sky and the leaves of the trees stunning in their early autumn colours. As we watched the thundering of the waters of the river careering over the Falls and witnessed the clouds of spray rising from the depths, we were reminded of the words of Psalm 93:4:

> ▶ **Mightier than the thunder of the great waters,**
>   **mightier than the breakers of the sea—**
>   **the Lord on high is mighty.**
>
> ● **Psalm 93:4 (NIV)**

When we returned to Bournemouth, Maureen and I brought the elders and leadership team up to speed with all that we had heard, witnessed and experienced of God's grace to us in Toronto and then we prayed for each of them. We then discussed and agreed together the way in which Maureen and I would report back to the church. On the first Sunday evening after our return, we both spoke, sharing our own individual experience and then offered to pray for those who wanted to receive from God. Having never done this before, we were more than a little nervous and yet we knew that God had met with us and it was time to share what we had received from His hand. I remembered the Sunday evening earlier that summer when I had not been able to invite the response that the Spirit was prompting me to give to the people and our prayer journey since then. It seemed that everyone in the congregation remained. God met with one after another after another. We didn't leave the building until almost midnight. There was great joy and thanksgiving among us all that evening. God had met with His people in a new outpouring of His love and power and healing.

Since that Sunday evening, so many had contacted us to express the blessing they had received, as God met with them. At the Tuesday staff meeting, we all knew that we needed to cancel our usual Thursday evening programme and in its place, we arranged that we would have a Renewal Service at the church centre. On that first Thursday evening, I invited three people to share testimony and then I preached and shared. Since the Sunday evening, there had been further opportunities to pray for the staff and leadership team and some of them now joined Maureen and me in praying for people during the ministry time. It was late again before we were able to leave for home. These midweek Renewal Services continued for many months, with God in His grace continuing to pour out His love and healing, not only among us at Winton, but upon many who were coming from other church situations, where there was not a similar opportunity.

It was clearly important to pastor this move of God with wisdom and integrity. There is always a danger of the flesh intruding, spoiling and hindering the work of God. Reading the history of times when God has come unusually near, leaves you in no doubt of that. The first Sunday evening after I returned from Toronto I spoke plainly to the church about this and gave straightforward direction about the way in which I believed we should conduct these times of renewal. I was thankful to God that it was seldom necessary to redirect people or caution them. But when it was required, one of the elders did so.

This season impacted many. The common themes were new love for Christ, a breakthrough in an area of life where God had previously been speaking but there had not been obedience; forgiveness long needed and now received and believed; the Word of God, coming with conviction, leading to true heart repentance; a new heart and passion for prayer; longing for holiness and revelation concerning hindrances.

If individuals are encountering God, as they were, then the whole church is impacted. There was a new awareness of God in all His glory, grace and power; a fresh desire to press in for more of Him and the evidence of that was seen in passion for Jesus, love for one another and a new quality of unity in the church; heart for the lost and boldness to speak about Jesus and witness to Him; a longing for the churches across the area to come together and make Jesus known. Believe it or not, but generally speaking, up until this time, most churches regarded evangelism and reaching out to non-Christians as something which required a well-known evangelist and a city-wide mission, something after the order of Billy Graham and Louis Palau. But this began to change exponentially, almost immediately with us and across the nation. Holy Trinity, Brompton in West London had been impacted in the early summer of 1994 and from there the Alpha Course was birthed, which has been used as an evangelistic tool by churches worldwide. Like many churches, we have used and continue to use the Alpha Course since the mid-nineties. The 'success' of the Course has been down to the change in churches: since the fresh touch of God upon His church. Christians no longer have a mindset which expects a renowned evangelist to come to lead a Mission. They themselves are sharing their faith one-to-one with family, neighbours and work colleagues and inviting them to attend an Alpha Course with them.

That was such a strategic turnaround. There were other changes in the life of the church at Winton. The church had a clearer vision of who God truly is, informed by the Word and the Spirit of truth and as a result, the worship was more heartfelt and powerful. The increased desire to pray resulted in weekly prayer meetings before work and the continuation of days and seasons of prayer and fasting. With a new desire to receive from God, our three congregations appointed prayer teams that required care and prayer in the selection and training of the relevant people.

There were invitations to Maureen and myself to share what God was doing in our lives and in the life of the church with other church leaders in the region and further afield. Some of these opportunities brought us into touch with people who would be significant in the future story of the church. At the end of November, I attended the 'Cities for God' Conference at Ashburnham Place in East Sussex, which came at a significant time in view of what God was about to do among us as local church leaders across the area.

In the days following our return from Canada, there were many telephone calls between local church leaders. The few of us who had been to the Catch the Fire Conference in Toronto discovered that many other leaders were eager to hear from us, ask questions and receive prayer themselves. There was a strong desire expressed that local church leaders should meet together so that we could share what we had experienced of God, pray for each other and encourage each other to move ahead with God in our personal lives and in our churches. We therefore arranged to meet one Thursday lunchtime in November at a local Anglican church. Eighteen leaders came together from many different church backgrounds. What a turnaround God had brought about among us. For seven years, five of us had met monthly, always longing and praying for God to bring us together for His sake, for the sake of His church in the area and for the Gospel's sake. Now, God had done it, overnight as it were. It reminded us of those many times in Scripture when it says,

"When the time had fully come, God... " This was God's time, and it was God's chosen way. It would never have been in our thinking or our expectation, but isn't that just so often, if not always, the way in which God works?

That Thursday lunchtime gathering of leaders was the beginning of ten years when church leaders in Bournemouth, Christchurch and Poole met together monthly. We would bring our own lunch and enjoyed networking with one another and in many cases getting to know leaders, who although in the same town, did not know one another. Then, we shared news and matters for prayer which were relevant to us all. We worshipped, prayed for one another, and interceded for our churches and the three boroughs of Bournemouth, Christchurch and Poole. During those ten years, about forty church leaders would gather monthly. There was an honesty about us and our church situations. Everyone was open to being vulnerable and receiving counsel, prayer and ministry from one another. Many of the leaders had never had encounters with the Holy Spirit in ways which may be expressed by such terms as 'baptism in the Spirit' or 'filled with the Spirit', but by the grace of God, this was His timing for quite a number of our colleagues. This level of intimacy, encouragement and support among local church leaders was something few, if any of us, had previously experienced, anywhere. The words of exclamation in Psalm 118:23 expressed our worship and thanksgiving:

> ▶ **The Lord has done this,**
> **and it is marvelous in our eyes.**
>
> ● **Psalm 118:23 (NIV)**

A direct result of these gatherings was that Send Your Fire (SYF) came into being. But before I continue, I should say that both locally and nationally, there were many church leaders who were very doubtful that what was being dubbed, 'The Toronto Blessing', was a genuine work of God. (Personally, I very much disliked the term, 'Toronto Blessing'. The fact that Toronto was the place God chose to act initially was immaterial). Most distressing was when some of these church leaders spoke against this work of God by fiercely attacking it and making scurrilous accusations against the integrity of church leaders who were involved.

Send Your Fire was birthed by the church leaders who began to meet in November 1994. A steering group of five were invited to lead and I was privileged to be the first among equals in that group of leaders. A number of meetings, primarily for church leaders, were arranged in February and March 1995 at the Pavilion and Winter Gardens in Bournemouth and also elsewhere in the area. A Leaders' Prayer Retreat was held in May 1995 at Ashburnham Place, E Sussex, 'to seek God together for His sake, for development of unity and relationship among us and for direction regarding His way to reach Bournemouth, Christchurch and Poole and the surrounding area'.

On Sunday 18th June 1995, a Combined Worship Service was held in the Purbeck Hall of the Bournemouth International Centre (BIC). Church leaders were invited to close their evening services (which most churches held regularly at that time) and come together to worship the Lord Jesus Christ and hear from the Word of God. The evening was arranged by and led by SYF church leaders. Local churches provided the music, I clearly remember the sense of awe and thanksgiving as I watched crowds of Christians, (1200), from an amazing variety of local churches, filling up the Hall. There was a pervading sense of joy among the people. I remember so many expressing their joy and thanksgiving that church leaders were meeting together and their recognition that this evening was one of the consequences. So often God's people are waiting for His leaders to lead. Combined Sunday Evenings to 'Hear from the Word of God and Receive from the Spirit of God' took place three times a year for many years at the BIC or the Pavilion and monthly early Saturday morning prayer gatherings for our churches and communities.

Send Your Fire continued its ministry to church leaders and the churches for the rest of the decade. One outcome of our relationships together as local church leaders was an evangelistic mission one summer based at the Bournemouth Football Ground in Kings Park. The week included teams engaged in street witness, providing practical help to people in our local communities and children and youth outreach. In the evenings in the stadium, we worshipped God and the gospel was preached. Many came to faith and others renewed their trust in the Lord Jesus Christ.

As Bournemouth prepared to celebrate the millennium in the year 2000, a few of the SYF Bournemouth church leaders, working with other church leaders in the town, approached the local Council with the request that local Christians be given permission to install a witness to Christ in the centre of our town. The result was that Bournemouth Council gave permission to erect 'The Flame' in Bournemouth Square. 'The Flame' is an attractively designed structure atop of which burned a flame for the whole of 2000. Around the base are the words, engraved in the surrounding stonework: 'Jesus the Light of the World'.

Prior to the dedication of 'The Flame', on Sunday 2nd January, there was a Millennium Service in the Windsor Hall of the Bournemouth International Centre, where 5000 Christians gathered to worship Jesus. The crowds then walked to the Square and 'The Flame' was dedicated. ('The Flame' still stands in Bournemouth Square with the words 'Jesus Light of the World' for all to see). These events illustrate some of the benefits that can take place when church leaders are in relationship and in Gospel agreement from which to venture on God in witness and outreach to our cities, towns and communities.

After ten years of Send Your Fire, new leadership forums in the individual boroughs sprang out of the SYF relationships. Church leaders in Christchurch, Poole and Bournemouth decided to meet separately, in their own Boroughs, to pray, network and plan how best to share the love and compassion of Christ in their communities. Believing that there was still great value in charismatic leaders getting together, the Charismatic Leaders Network (CLN) was formed in 2004 and once a term a leaders' day was held, comprising worship and teaching on a subject relevant to current church life. CLN also provided a channel for news and prayer for one another and continued to serve as a support network for charismatic leaders across all three boroughs.

Many other illustrations could be given of the grace, courage and vision that has come to church leaders, churches and Gospel outreach in this area of South Wessex as a result of leaders and churches coming together to honour the Lord Jesus, the Head of the Church and live out their mutual life in Him.

CHAPTER 14

Strategic Decision

1994 – 1996

S eptember 1995 found Maureen and me visiting our five overseas workers in Hong Kong. It was becoming a regular part of our lives having first visited Hong Kong during our sabbatical in 1991 spending time with Rob and Elaine and their family and returning in 1993 to see first-hand the development of their work at Bethany, to meet and minister to their growing team, and talk and pray further about the preparations our church back home was making to plant an English-speaking congregation on the island.

Now, two years later, the church planting team from Winton Evangelical Church was in place on Cheung Chau. Heather had been on the Island for a year and had set up a thriving kindergarten and mother and baby club. Through these means and the teaching of English, Heather had been building good relationships in the community. Rob and Ali and their young son Jotham were just settling in as they had only been on Cheung Chau since May. Alison was expecting their second child in five months and we were all aware that the conditions surrounding the birth would be vastly different from those in the UK. There was much to discuss and decide about the church which was in process of being formed as Cheung Chau Christian Fellowship. It had to be registered with the Hong Kong Government and there was a lot of paperwork to be completed. We were also looking ahead to the coming handover of Hong Kong to China in 1997. For all these reasons it was important to have quality time with the church-planting team at this early, but strategic stage in the life and work of the team.

Some significant changes in the leadership of the church back home and its three congregations began to take place in 1994/95. In the light of the continuing growth of the church and the pastoral responsibilities I had for the increasing numbers of staff, both in the church and overseas, it was believed that it would be wise for me to be released from some aspects of the leadership of Winton Community Church, the new name for the Winton Congregation. Another factor in this proposed change was that I was about to commence a three-year term, which unexpectedly turned out to be four years, as Chair of the Board of Moorlands College.

Therefore, in May 1995, Adrian was appointed as Assistant Congregational Leader at Winton Community Church, working with Maureen and myself and relieving me of much of my responsibility. Adrian and Sue had been part of Winton Community Church for two years, Adrian teaching at the Christian English Language Centre (whose directors were members of the church) and Sue working part-time in the Eye Department of the local hospital. Adrian had trained at Moorlands Bible College some ten years previously and while at College had served with us on placement in the church.

A further significant change in the leadership of the church concerned Tony, who had joined me as Associate Pastor in 1987, at the point where we began to build a staff team. In 1989, Tony, with his wife Sandie, led the formation of our Charminster congregation, now called Charminster Community Church and continued to lead that congregation until 1993, when Lloyd and Rosemary became congregational leaders. In January 1995 Tony and Sandie concluded their ministry among us and moved to Cornwall. Some years later, after they had both renewed and restored the life of what had been a rather faded Christian guest house, Tony was ordained into the Anglican ministry. Following his retirement from full-time ministry, Tony continues to serve in the Cornwall diocese, taking services as needed. I remember personally the emotional difficulty of losing Tony: he was such a gift from God to me as the first full-time salaried staff member. Tony was greatly loved and valued by the whole church and to say our farewells to them both was anything but easy. He had been intimately involved in the prayer, planning and execution of the planting out of two congregations and all the structural changes that we had to make to facilitate the growth of the church in the years from 1987 to 1995.

During the academic year 1993/94, Andy and Carolyn, third-year students at Moorlands College, came to us on placement. During that year they were based at Winton Community Church, working with Maureen and me. At the end of that year, which also marked the end of their studies at the College, Andy and Carolyn shared with us that they believed God wanted them to remain in Bournemouth and be committed to the Hill View congregation, now called Hill View Community Church. They therefore found part-time work and gave themselves to the life and witness of that congregation and later became members of the congregational team led by Peter and Linda. In 1995, while still supporting themselves financially, they were appointed to the staff team. As well as being members of the congregational team at Hill View Community Church, they both had responsibilities across all three congregations in pastoral ministry, schools work and oversight of children's ministries.

Many of our staff appointments over the years were people who were already in the life of the church or we had known them as

Moorlands students or through other relationship networks. With the best will and taking great care over the preparation of person specifications and job descriptions, references and well-prepared interviews, there will still be many important, perhaps strategic issues, you will not discover until you are working together. Whereeas if God places people in your church community or if He gives you relationships with people through other means and you realise that they have the godly character, gifts and experience you think are required, then thank Him and share it with your fellow-elders and senior staff. If you are on the wrong track, they will be able to disabuse you. In my experience over the three decades of building team I and the elders have had many occasions to thank God for placing the people we need either right here among us or through relationships and networking.

From 1992, following our sabbatical the previous year, we began to set aside a few days, every spring and autumn, so that the leadership and staff teams could enjoy and benefit from a period of retreat and conference. This provided space to spend more time together with God and one another. Our relationship with God and our relationships together are crucial if the church is going to enjoy continuing growth and heaven's blessing. These times also opened up unhurried opportunities to discuss together major issues which needed more attention than we could give at our weekly Tuesday morning meetings.

In early 1995 we were having one of these few days away together when the Lord spoke to us very clearly about the need to re-order our priorities. It had been our practice for three years now, every Tuesday morning, to meet for Worship, Word and Prayer. Then after coffee, we would attend to a rolling agenda. However, during this time away we heard from God and agreed that in future we would not meet together on the first Tuesday of the month, but rather, individually, we would devote that day to personal prayer and seeking God.

During our autumn days of retreat and conference that same year, we recognised that there were three areas where the church was being less than effective. These were:

- reaching the lost
- discipleship
- equipping every member for ministry.

This was to lead to a strategic change in the direction of the church.

In the light of those conclusions, the leadership team decided to carry out an in-depth church audit in the first six months of 1996. It was over six years since Charminster Community Church had been planted and almost four years since Hill View Community Church was birthed. Added to this, there was again an expectation that the church may consider planting out a further congregation, probably in Parkstone, Poole. Quite a number of people who lived in the Parkstone area were worshipping at Winton Community Church and were interested in such a venture. It was clearly unwise to plant out another congregation unless we were sure that God was in it. We needed to carefully and prayerfully assess the effectiveness of the three C's model (Celebration, Congregation, Cell) we had been pursuing since 1989.

The congregational leadership teams of Winton Community Church, Charminster Community Church and Hill View Community Church reported on their assessment of the health of their congregation. There was common agreement that we were not 'cutting the mustard' in terms of numbers of people coming to faith, in every member becoming a disciple and discipling others and in equipping everyone for ministry. Other issues were also recognised: staffing congregations required a certain mix of gifts. But as a church, we also required staff with a specialised gift-mix to effectively develop and mobilise the whole of Winton Evangelical Church in areas such as children and youth ministry. Indeed, this was an area of the life of the church which was far from easy to develop in the congregational model. There was also clearly a limit on how many staff could or should be employed.

A further issue was that people who had come into the individual congregations since we commenced planting out Charminster in 1989 and Hill View in 1992, did not always think of themselves as belonging to Winton Evangelical Church, but rather and sometimes solely, to their own local congregation.

Had the three C's model been a mistake? Thinking back to 1989, with the doors closed on extending our church centre premises, we believed that planting congregations was God's way for us at the time and there had been many benefits. Those who had been leading the congregations and those who had been engaged in serving in those congregations in a variety of ways would not have had that opportunity otherwise. This included many people who had discovered their gifting and had grown in using those gifts for the glory of God and the good of the worshipping community. In each congregation, people had come to faith from those localities and had grown in God.

Our conclusion, after much prayer and discussing all the issues involved – and there were many strategic matters to be weighed, not least the impact of any decision we were to take upon the staff and church community – was that we should recommend to the church that we discontinue meeting in three congregations and commence meeting together as one church from 1st January 1997.

We recognised the transition involved would not be easy for any of us. We were embarking on a huge change and change always presents many varied difficulties. I confess I always shrink from bringing in major change because you know it will bring with it considerable extra pressure. But once you know that God has shown you this is His way forward, then you also know it is going to be more than worth it. By now He had proved that again and again. However, the people who belonged to the numerically smaller congregations at Charminster and Hill View would possibly find it especially hard to make the adjustment to meeting in a much larger space with many people, a fair number of whom they may not know. Where that larger space would be we did not know at this stage: it was one of the many issues where God was calling us to trust Him... after all, God had said to Abram:

> ▶ "Go... to the land I will show you.
>
> ● **Genesis 12:1 (NIV)**

> ▶ So Abram went, as the Lord had told him...
>
> ● **Genesis 12:4 (NIV)**

And God, as He always does, kept all His promises.

The decision to discontinue congregations underlined the need to provide an appropriate pastoral 'net' for the church in this transition and that was one issue that was uppermost in our minds.

Maureen and I had learned, from our 1991 sabbatical visit to Church of our Saviour in Singapore, that if you did not have effective structures in place, you may have many new people coming in through the front door, but others may be leaving by the back door. We had read and attended conferences about the cell church movement when in Singapore and since then here in the UK, but had never believed, up until now, that the time was right to initiate this in the church here.

When we made the decision to develop a three C's model for the church, Celebration, Congregation and Cell, we had implemented the Celebration and Congregational C's but had not truly followed through on the third C, Cell. We believed it was a step too far for the church at that time and so our existing house groups were used to cover the Cell aspect of the model, as that would be easier for everyone.

But now the time had come to explain to the church our desire to see everyone as a member of one of the cells. This would enable pastoral care, by providing a pastoral 'net' through the cell structure. It would also facilitate discipleship, every member ministry and would provoke a heart for mission to the lost across the whole church family. Previously, house groups had been regarded by some as an option that was not central to their involvement in the life of the church, a 'bolt on' if you like, to be involved if you preferred, but unimportant if you did not. We now underlined that gathering in 'cells' was just as much 'church' as being together in 'celebration' on Sundays. The main elements in the cell gatherings would be Welcome, Worship, Word and Witness. Two Area Pastors would give oversight and input to the cell leaders. We decided to call our cells, Life Groups.

Those of us who were elders, and members of the leadership and staff teams had needed time and space to think and pray all this through. There had been much to assimilate and consider. There would be many questions. The church family would also need time and space to take all this on board. We therefore arranged an Envisioning Week in early July (1996) and then two Open Forum evenings in mid-July. The purpose was to present the vision on three separate evenings of the Envisioning Week, so that, hopefully, everyone would be able to get to one of them. Then, having had up to two weeks to think and pray about what they had heard, we had the two Open Forum evenings, when clarification could be made, where necessary and questions asked. This was followed, a month later, towards the end of August, by the church family setting aside three days for prayer, fasting and listening to God. In the evenings of those days in August, we met together at the church centre 'to focus entirely on Him... to seek His Face and give Him space to speak to us whatever was on His heart'. Then in September, with this preparation of heart, mind and spirit, we met together to make a decision on the future direction of the church.

The church believed the vision presented was indeed God's way forward for us as His people and we agreed to become one congregation again from January and to pursue the cell model.

We now needed to consider, sensitively and prayerfully, our future staffing needs in the light of these changes, which were barely four months distant. As all the staff had been intimately involved in the praying and planning over the previous twelve months, we were blessed that everyone was aware of the implications of our recommendations to the church and the church's decision. Nonetheless, it was tough to face up to the changes this would bring about for us all as a team. As the senior pastor, and with oversight of these discussions and changes, I was very thankful to God and to all the staff for the way in which everyone approached the issues. There was a spirit of openness to God for His will to be understood and carried through, even though this involved large personal changes for some of the staff team in particular. From 1st January 1997, the staff team would consist of:

- Senior Pastor and two Area Pastors
- Five further staff were responsible for heading up
- Worship and Music, Children and Youth,
- Women's ministry, Discipleship and Counselling
- Church Office

In total there were eight staff, a mix of full-time, part-time, salaried and unsalaried.

As you can well understand, we were all going through a season of massive change and having to make many adjustments. One of the changes we made in preparation for the introduction of becoming a cell church, was to close down the house groups for a period of nine months. There were not many groups, and a relatively small proportion of the church was committed to them. In light of that fact, we thought that it would help everyone to have some clear water between the ending of the old house groups and the commencement of the new life groups. However, with the congregations being discontinued from January 1997 and the house groups ending at that time until life groups were due to commence later in the autumn of 1997, there were people who felt somewhat 'lost' in terms of valued relationships.

We began to realise that we had made a number of mistakes in our recent leadership decisions. There had been too many major changes taking place, with other changes in course of preparation in the same period of time. This had led to some confusion. The leadership team realised this and together we had asked God's forgiveness. In March 1997, at a gathering of the church family, I led us as a team of elders and leaders in apologising to God's people and asking their forgiveness.

One of the clear lessons along the way of learning to follow the Lord Jesus in leading His church is always to be ready to humbly confess where and when you get it wrong. Asking for forgiveness, whether in a one-to-one situation or as in this case, before the whole church community, is the way our Lord has taught us and shown us to live. Giving away forgiveness is similarly the Jesus way, again whether one-to-one or in a corporate setting. Acting in the manner of Christ never reduces true spiritual authority. Failure to so act undermines the work of God in individual lives and in His church. There are many Christians today who are not involved in the local church because, at some point along the way, they observed or experienced the failure of a church leader or leaders to 'fess up' and shoulder responsibility for sin or wrong judgements. Those Christians have their own responsibility of course for their response to such a scenario. But that does not obviate the responsibility of church leaders in the first place.

CHAPTER 15

Changes and Challenges
1997 – 1999

The year 1997 was to be significant in the life of the church as we all began to meet together rather than in three congregations. It would be a memorable year for the UK in ways that would impact the wider world. In the British General Election, Labour won a landslide, placing them in power for the next thirteen years. J.K.Rowling, an unknown author, had her first book published. Harry Potter and the Philosopher's Stone was the title and by 2001, 5 million hardback and 6.6 million paperback copies had been sold. That same year, the world was shocked by the death of Diana, Princess of Wales, killed in a high-speed crash in Paris. Floral tributes quickly appeared in key locations and Kensington Gardens were to see mourning crowds and carpets of flowers that were beyond anyone's imagination.

From January we began to implement the strategic changes which had been agreed by the church and the first and most obvious was that instead of meeting in three separate congregations on Sunday mornings, we all began to meet together in one place. Clearly, our church centre site in Calvin Road could not accommodate the numbers which had been meeting in three separate locations, so we knew we would need to rent a much larger space. But where? As we asked God and examined the options, we settled on the assembly hall of Glenmoor School for Girls (now Glenmoor Academy) in Ensbury Park.

The assembly hall at the Academy was ideal for us. Noticeably light, with large windows all down one side. Although we had to set up chairs, sound systems and other necessities at the two Congregations we had planted out, setting up at Glenmoor was much more demanding. There were, of course, many more people and that meant many more chairs. Arranging set-up teams was not the easiest. There was also all the work of setting down afterwards. Then there was the preparation of the rooms which were used for prayer and children and youth. But there was plenty of parking space and access to the Academy site was straightforward.

I will not easily forget meeting at Glenmoor Academy as one Sunday morning, following the worship, I stood up to give some news about Rob and Alison, from our team in Hong Kong. I knew exactly what I wanted to say, but nothing would come out of my mouth. Very quickly I realised I must be having a stroke of some kind. Was there a doctor in the house?! There were three doctors in the congregation that morning and I was off to hospital. The tests indicated I had suffered a transient ischemic attack (TIA) and I was off work for a week. Maureen looked at me, as only a wife can, and said: "I know what this is!" I had been under considerable pressure as Chair of Moorlands College on account of a set of events at College, plus, of course, we were going through many changes at church, hence Maureen's comment. If you had asked me if I suffered from stress, I would have replied very quickly in the negative. The fact is that sometimes we are not the best judge of knowing when we are about to cross the line between healthy pressure and stress that may break the bank, as it were. But, if you are married, you have a wife or a husband who does know, so best to listen! In the goodness of God, I did not suffer another TIA for twenty years.

✎

Over the previous few years, there had been a remarkable increase in the number of 11-17-year-olds attending our work for that age group. There were now 60 youngsters, with a Friday evening club, Sunday morning gathering and a monthly evening homegroup. It was becoming evident that the people who were leading this work were at their limit in terms of the time they could give. It was due to the excellent team, led by Adrienne, Peter and Jocelyn, and Helen, who had grown the youth work over the previous few years, that we were at a place where a full-time staff member was required.

In September 1997 Roger Constantine, who had trained at Moorlands College and had been leading the children's and youth work at a church in Essex for two years, was appointed to the staff. Roger was married to Sarah, both of them originally from Bournemouth and they had a young family. Maureen and I had met Roger and Sarah previously and we knew Gordon, their senior colleague in Essex. I asked Gordon's permission to approach Roger and Sarah about this post with us. Sarah had been involved with Roger in the 0-18 ministry in their previous situation and she would be increasingly involved with Roger here at Winton. Youth weekends and camps began to be a regular and strategic addition to the work. They were great fun for everyone involved, including staff and volunteers.

A review of the 0-18's work was commenced, and child protection procedures were introduced. A balanced biblical curriculum for 0-11 years and for 11-16 years was put in place and there was considerable evidence of spiritual growth. The work among 0-11's was also growing and all of this meant that there were now accommodation issues for all the groups. Although we were meeting at Glenmoor Academy on Sunday mornings, everything else continued to take place at our church centre in Calvin Road, which was proving to be increasingly inadequate on many fronts, but especially for the children and youth work. Renting the local YMCA facilities near us in Winton helped somewhat.

For many years, Roger and Sarah and the team working with them, arranged for the youth to attend Soul Survivor, an annual gathering of hundreds of teenagers from all over the UK. This was a highlight of the year when the Word and the Spirit combined through worship and teaching to bring many to faith in Christ. For others, the week enabled a deeper understanding and equipping to be effective followers of Jesus in their generation.

The Holiday Bible Clubs for the children in the school holidays became a much-anticipated annual event. Roger and Sarah loved arranging them and leading them and put together a superb team and programme. Some of the highlights were repeated each time, to the great delight of the boys and girls and to the team. Except, of course, if you were the team members chosen to be 'gunged' from head to toe at the end of the week with a slimy green liquid. Spiritual education and challenge were woven into these camps and holiday bible clubs with great care and much prayer. They were times when God was at work by His Spirit and many young lives were changed as they encountered the Living God.

Sarah's administrative gifts were not only a benefit to the children and youth ministry. She was responsible for formulating the church's Health and Safety Policy, introducing and maintaining our CRB checks and providing oversight for the volunteers. In a growing church, it is important to have someone who will coordinate the many volunteers who are involved, not least expressing appreciation for their consistent giving of themselves in service to God and to the church family.

✒

I spent two weeks with our church planting team in Hong Kong in April 1997. It was important to have some face-to-face time together as Hong Kong was due to return to the People's Republic of China in just a few months. Also, Rob and Alison, Jotham and Nathan were planning to return to Bournemouth on account of some health issues, which raised the need to strengthen the leadership team. Cheung Chau Christian Fellowship (CCCF) had adopted a cell approach to church, with at that time a Filipino Cell and an English-speaking cell. The English-speaking cell was about to multiply due to growth from an Alpha Course just completed. As well as Heather, who had prepared the way since 1994, it was agreed that the leadership team of the church would include a young Hong Konger, a Filipino and a couple from the USA. The CCCF leadership team had built relationships with an American Mennonite missionary and a colleague of his from the Philippines. Early in 1998, they began to share oversight of Cheung Chau Christian Fellowship in preparation for Heather's return to the UK, with the church in Winton continuing its financial and prayer support. Heather had spent four years helping to plant and lead CCCF and returned to Bournemouth in August 1998.

The latter half of the nineties saw more people in the life of the church, called by God into short or longer-term overseas mission, many looking towards China. There were prayer and work teams composed of all ages and also individuals and couples, again of different ages and at different stages of life, who responded to the Lord Jesus and His call to them

I thank God for what the Apostle Paul calls, "the obedience that comes from faith" in Romans 1:5. It was the obedience which flows from a living and venturing-on-God faith which moved Paul out into the foreign and cross-cultural Gentile world, having heard the unmistakable call of His risen and ascended Lord. It was the same obedience that continued to move others in the life of Winton Evangelical Church, both at this time and in the coming years, to give themselves to "the gospel of God... regarding his Son" (Romans 1:1,3), some to call people from other nations to "the obedience that comes from faith" and others to teach and preach that cross-cultural "gospel of God" here in the UK. The substance of the "gospel of God" is "Jesus Christ our Lord" (Romans 1:4). All of us who name the name of Jesus are called and sent out to live and speak "for his name's sake" (Romans 1:5). Christian mission is all about the name and glory of God's Son, Jesus Christ. Every church which names the name of Jesus Christ as Lord must have a central passion for Jesus, a passion that moves the whole church community to:

> ▶ ... call all... to the obedience that comes from faith for
>   his name's sake.
>
>   ● Romans 1:5 (NIV)

In the summer of 1998, Adrian and Sue and their family moved to Beverley in East Yorkshire, where Adrian became pastor of a local church. It was a joy for me to share in their welcome service at Beverley, but sad for all of us to say goodbye. Adrian had worked alongside Maureen and me in the Winton congregation until the end of 1996 and then as one of the Area Pastors.

In July 1998, as was the case from time to time since the first Week of Prayer and Fasting and Seeking God in 1987, the church gathered for a Week of Prayer. The week was shaped by the values God had given us: 'Loving God! Loving each other! Loving the lost!'

He spoke to us during those days through Scripture and prophecy. While listening to God, with the value of 'Loving the lost' before us, an illustration was given of a young woman dressed in a white blouse and denim dress, with working boots and a pitchfork. We understood this as a vision of the Church, the Bride of Christ (white speaking of the purity of the bride), dressed to work with the Bridegroom to gather in the harvest. Being in partnership with the Bridegroom, we are filled with His strength and power for the task. With reference to the building we had (our Calvin Road Church Centre premises) and any other building God may give us in the future (which at this point was ten years away), we were reminded that it is 'The Father's House'. The House is not ours, but His and He wants us to bring the poor, the blind and lame into 'The Father's House' (Isaiah 58:6-14 and Isaiah 61). This word from God to us as a church remained with us and shaped our vision and planning as the years passed until God's time came to give us new premises.

Towards the end of 1998, the church affirmed that the ministry of Maureen and me was a joint calling. This was obviously something that Maureen and I had known for many years and which had been evident to the church family. You may wonder why this was not recognised earlier. The fact was that women in ministry had been either a non-issue or a debatable issue in the UK church for many years. As our family had grown older, Maureen had grown into ministry alongside me and also in her own right, using the gifts God had given her. It had been a gradual and for us a welcome development, for which we thanked God. I was especially grateful to God. Maureen had been a member of the staff team for many years and had exercised leadership in line with her gifting, the church accepting and valuing her. It almost seemed superfluous that the church should take this step, but it was not. For Maureen, it was very affirming indeed. There had been many times when she had said to me, privately, how she felt she was involved in ministry in the church without ever having been appointed and affirmed by the church in the way new members of staff were always recognised. This had at times been something that had rendered her vulnerable to the suggestions and lies of the enemy. The church's recognition of our joint calling and ministry, (which took place at the same time as a recognition of Roger and Sarah's joint calling and ministry), brought about the matter of Maureen and Sarah being salaried. The gathered church community raised this question at the time and from 1999 Maureen and Sarah were salaried part-time.

When we had arrived to lead the church in 1978 the deacons had asked us if we would be interested in purchasing the manse (church house). We were delighted that they had thought about this and actually raised it with us, but there were difficulties. My salary was not remotely sufficient to support a mortgage with which to purchase the equity and at that time no one had even imagined the possibility of a shared equity scheme between the church and ourselves. In the end, nothing happened, as when the deacons sounded out the church about perhaps selling the manse to us, there were some who could not and would not contemplate the idea of the church not owning a house for the minister. So the deacons did not pursue the matter.

At that time, and for many decades previously, congregations of churches such as the Baptists, Pentecostal denominations and independent churches like our own, were used to having a manse, which they would rent to incoming ministers. The thought of paying sufficient salary to the minister, with which he could purchase a house on a mortgage, in the same way as quite a number in the congregation were doing, did not appear to occur to the congregations, or even to those who were acting in a church council role. If it did occur, to them, then there was little faith and expectation that God could provide this through the increased giving of His people. In fact, biblical principles of giving, like many other areas of Christian teaching and discipleship, were rarely ever taught.

This resulted in it being almost impossible for the majority of ministers to ever own their own home, or even being able to put money aside over the years when their usually not over-generous salary was being reduced each month by rent.

Another very unhelpful aspect of this practice of a manse system was that should there be a serious disagreement between whoever had leadership responsibility alongside the minister, then the minister could find himself and his family without a home. On a number of occasions over the years, I have seen the impact of this kind of scenario, causing worry and anxiety for the church leader and his wife, which only compounded the concern they already had. Indeed, the possible loss of 'their home' has been a reason why some ministers have remained in a church situation from which they should have moved on long since and that has only ever been to the detriment of both the church and the church leader.

This was certainly on my mind when my sense of God's direction for the church was different from that of some of the other leaders here in my first eight years. I knew that God had not asked me to leave. But the circumstances were such, at times, that Maureen and I were looking eagerly for a green 'Go' light from God. However, if we had decided to jump, even though we knew this was not what God was saying to us, where were we to jump to?

Given what I have said about the negative aspects of the manse system, you will not be surprised to know that I did not want to perpetuate the manse system here at Winton. Therefore, when we began to build a staff team in 1987, I strongly recommended that the church pay a good salary, equivalent to someone in a similar role in the secular world. This would enable staff to either rent or get a mortgage. In other words, choice would be provided.

I was delighted to see that choice become available to other staff, but our personal situation was that we remained in the manse system. There were times when I was resentful. This was an issue for me, but never for Maureen. I would go to God and tell him how ashamed and sorry I was and repent and ask His forgiveness. I would go away free and thankful and then, perhaps a year later, it would come and hit me over the head again. I remember Muriel, our long-time overseas worker from the church who we visited in France on holiday some summers, once sharing with us how there had been an issue in her life with which she had often struggled over the years and she would think it was resolved, then back it would come again. I was encouraged to think that Muriel, whom we always highly regarded for her life in God, also had her struggles.

God brought to my mind the words of an old friend of my father's. He said to me one day when I was probably about fifteen years old, "Always remember, David: if you honour God, He will honour you. God is no man's debtor." Maureen and I can look back and say with conviction and amazement: "Ain't that the truth!" We praise Him and worship Him for His faithfulness and overwhelming generosity to us in so very many ways, not the least in His amazing provision of our own home. And this is how God did it.

When we arrived in 1978, the deacons suggestion about us purchasing the manse could not be progressed at that time. Fifteen years later, in 1993, the church agreed that Maureen and I could purchase 24% of the equity of the church house. That proportion of the equity was as much of a mortgage as my salary was able to support at the time. That was how the situation remained until six years later, when a young accountant, who had only been a Christian for a couple of years, became a member of the church's finance group. Visiting me one day in my study at home, he indicated in a question he put to me that he presumed Maureen and I owned the house. I explained that, since 1993, we had 24% of the equity on mortgage. He asked some questions but made no comment. A few months later, the finance group, having examined the history, recommended to the church that I should be gifted 26% of the equity in recognition that the issue had not been progressed in 1978 and of course the value of the house had risen very considerably since that time. (There was a tax implication in such a gift of course). At that time in 1999, we were also able to purchase the outstanding 50% of the equity.

God wonderfully brought everything together through the care and concern of members of the finance group and the love and care of the church family. I received a considerable salary increase and as Maureen had just begun to be salaried part-time, these together enabled us to cover the increased mortgage costs. Maureen and I have never lost our sense of wonder and thanksgiving that we have our own home – it is almost an everyday praise theme.

CHAPTER 16

Growth and Grace

2000 – 2002

Despite all the lurid warnings that were circulating in the years immediately prior to the new millennium, the world didn't end in January 2000. The concern that computers would crash and the hype about Y2K turned out to be highly exaggerated. Here in the UK, Tony Blair was three years into what was to be a ten-year premiership.

In January 2000, the church commenced a new initiative: a teaching and training course which we called 'Foundations'. We had been aware for some time that there were many subjects and issues where there was little or no opportunity to provide appropriate teaching and equipping. We had in mind areas such as doctrine, ethics, church history and also leadership and preaching training, preparation for marriage, marriage enrichment and parenting. 'Foundations' was set up to help meet these needs. The courses ran on alternative months on Sunday evenings. The two courses for January 2000 were "Living and Telling the Good News" and "Spiritual Warfare Part 1".

The Lamplight Course, the discipleship course prepared and taught by Peter and the team he trained some years previously, was now included in the 'Foundations' programme as an ongoing element. Each course in 'Foundations', or each section of a longer course, such as Lamplight or Spiritual Warfare, was designed to last for four weeks. We knew that more people in the church community would be able to commit to a shorter four-week course for all kinds of practical reasons. Making 'Foundations' accessible was obviously key, in order that as many as possible were able to receive teaching and training. These courses covered a wide range of subjects and were a key Biblical education and practical Christian living tool in the church's ministry. 'Foundations' also opened up new opportunities to involve people in the life of the church to teach and train in areas where they had gifting and experience.

Since the 80s Maureen and I had become increasingly involved in preparing people for marriage. Up until that time, very few churches offered any help or counsel to those planning to marry. We recognised this as an area where we must explain to those intending to be married that pre-marital preparation was essential. I made it known that if a couple were beginning to think seriously about marriage, I would want to hear from them sooner rather than later so that we could commence working with them.

But it was not only marriage preparation. Sadly, the need to offer help and counsel to those already married had become increasingly apparent to us over our years in ministry. More than a few Christian marriages were far from being able to be described as relationship rich. Generally, women are much more willing to confess that their marriage needs help than men. Sometimes, for that reason, by the time we became involved, the relationship was beyond repair. One of the values of knowing your people well is that you can sometimes, but sadly not always, know who is struggling and you can then offer counsel and prayer ministry. Due to the lack of available marital and prayer counselling help in the area. we found ourselves being contacted by other local church leaders asking if we would see married couples who were in need. We were often involved in this way, but in due course, we had to limit ourselves, in the main, to our own church community. It was a huge regret that there were so few options for Christians looking for marital help. I was so thankful to God when a local Christian counselling service was set up, which was able to provide Christian professional help across a range of issues, including marriage. It was a privilege for me to be involved as a trustee.

For some time, we had been recognising our need to grow the staff team by appointing someone who had church leadership experience, was gifted in preaching and teaching, with a vision for the development of cell life and a heart and capacity to mobilise the church in evangelism and discipleship. A tall order! As the elders and senior staff began to have a clear view of the person specification profile and job description required, I thought I knew someone who would fit the bill.

In late 1994, Maureen and I had visited a church in Cambridgeshire, where Andrew Whitman was senior pastor. Maureen and I had a close friend, Geoff Larcombe who was on staff there and had been executive secretary of Regions Beyond Missionary Union in the years when we had been intimately involved in that Mission. On account of that relationship and knowing that Maureen and I had recently visited the Catch the Fire Conference in Toronto, we were invited to speak to the leadership team about our assessment and experience of that time. In the years that followed Andrew and I had kept in touch. He had trained at London Bible College, served on the staff of Campus Crusade for Christ and then led the church we visited. Since then, Andrew had moved to Norwich, where he was on the staff of a church where he had responsibility for training and teaching. In October 2000 Andrew and his wife Rosie and their two sons arrived in Bournemouth and Andrew commenced with us as Pastor for Training and Evangelism.

Andrew joined an elder's team of Roger Constantine, Andy Driscoll, Derek White and myself. Derek had become an elder in December 1999. Derek and his wife were joint directors of the Christian English Language Centre. At this time Andy Driscoll was just at the point of leaving the team, as he was commencing further study at Moorlands College. It was seven years since Andy and Carolyn first came to us, during their final year at Moorlands College. They had served on the leadership team at Hill View Community Church and subsequently, Andy became an Area Pastor and an elder. Following his further studies, Andy would once again join the team of elders in 2003.

Up until 2000, I had been responsible for the majority of the Sunday preaching. It was a privilege to open up the Word of God week by week and my approach was to seek to let the text speak. I was committed to expository preaching and loved taking a book of the Bible and working my way through it. Sometimes it would be a character study, Old Testament characters I particularly loved. Occasionally I would speak to a particular topic or theme, but primarily it was seeking to consistently work our way through the text and trusting the Holy Spirit to speak to God's people. I remember thinking, even then, that I would miss that so much when I retired. Yes, there will be the opportunity to preach elsewhere. But to preach God's Word to 'your own people' week in week out and to hear and understand the way in which the Holy Spirit was at work in their lives, is a unique privilege and gift from God. Nothing replaces that.

However, from 2000 I began to share the preaching. Some of the elders had preached from time to time, but now Andrew and Roger were involved on a regular basis, especially Andrew, for whom teaching was a primary gift. My responsibilities as senior pastor and lead elder had been ramping up for some years, not only with a growing staff team but in the wider church in the area, through the Send Your Fire network and my involvement at Moorlands College. I was grateful to God for the team around me and for their input into my life.

Maureen and I had led a Mastersun Holiday some years before to the Greek island of Cos, where you could gaze across the shimmering sea and feel you could almost touch Turkey. However, we discovered that if you were leading one of these, no way could it be described as a holiday. When other similar invitations came, wisdom suggested we should not accept. However, when we were invited to lead a Mastersun holiday in Austria in 2000, which included a visit to the Oberammergau Passion Play, performed only every ten years, we said 'Thank you very much!' The Passion Play was a powerful presentation of the trial, crucifixion, sufferings and resurrection of Christ and it was a privilege for us to experience that day. Remembering that we were still going to be leading a Mastersun Holiday, we ensured that we had arranged another time that year when we would be away together on our own in France.

We had been using Glenmoor Academy for Sunday mornings since January 1997 but we had continued to keep our eyes open for a possible new church centre site. Apart from Sunday mornings, we were using our premises in Calvin Road for everything else including the children and youth work, supplemented by renting other facilities. We had viewed a local Methodist Church building and also some United Reformed Church premises when we heard they were becoming available, but neither were appropriate from a number of perspectives. Land near the university, owned by the Talbot Trust, (which had been very generous to us ten years earlier when we refurbished our church centre), had been investigated but was not available. We had engaged a local estate agent to bring to our attention anything that fitted our requirements, but although we had viewed one or two possibilities, they had come to nothing.

Some of us had believed for many years that our new premises would be situated somewhere on Wimborne Road, the main thoroughfare through the areas of Winton and Moordown. Someone in the church family had told me some years earlier that they had been walking along Wimborne Road and had stopped outside the Bingo Hall. They believed God said to them at that time that the building was 'The Father's House.'

Now I need to take you back three years. One afternoon in 1997 I had decided to investigate this building. It was the former Moderne Cinema, opened in 1931, which had been functioning as a bingo hall for many years. If you look up and see the building to your right as you drive along Wimborne Road from Winton towards Moordown, the bingo hall appears on the skyline as a huge structure. But viewed from the pavement opposite, it appears much more restrained and comfortable in its environment.

I visited this particular afternoon and told the receptionist I didn't want to play bingo (which was proceeding in the main auditorium on the ground floor level) but requested permission to explore the premises. To my surprise, there were no questions and so I began by walking through to the main auditorium, where they were shouting the numbers. I investigated all the other rooms on the ground floor and then up the sweeping staircase to the first floor, from which there was access to the gallery. The gallery was huge and the old leather cinema seats were covered in layers of dust.

Continuing up the stairs past row upon row of seating, I came to a corridor running almost the width of the building with amazing views over the area. But there was more to come. At one place, steps led from the corridor up to the roof itself and, pushing open an access point, I stepped out onto the roof. I was taken aback by the height of the building, its vast expanse and the wide-ranging views across the town in every direction.

I finished my visit and exploration of the building and left with a strong conviction that this was to be our future church centre premises. We subsequently had the church's solicitors write to Gala Clubs, who owned the building, expressing our interest. But Gala was not interested. As God knew, we were not ready for this from many points of view. But God would get us ready and in due time He was to give us this building for His Kingdom and His glory.

In November 2001, the church gathered to decide upon our need for more space for our Sunday morning gatherings and indeed for our children and youth work in the week. We had been using Glenmoor Academy on Sunday mornings since 1997 and the church had continued to grow. We were now in need of more capacity. In our search, we had visited Winton Academy, whose premises were almost next door to Glenmoor Academy. The most suitable area of the College for Sunday mornings was their relatively recently constructed sports hall: great from the point of view of space, but no windows! After being used to four years of meeting in Glenmoor Academy's assembly hall, with one side of the meeting space almost all windows, that was a pause for thought. But we went ahead and brought a recommendation to the church family that we should move Sunday mornings to Winton Academy from Easter 2002.

The proposal was to use the building for Sunday mornings, as there was ample room for all ages and we could also rent other facilities there for Friday evenings youth work. The hire of the sports hall would cost £7,500 pa, as against £6,350 pa for our present use of Glenmoor Academy (without Friday evening use). There would be other costs involved: £18,000 in total for the purchase of chairs, sound equipment, soundproofing and all the other necessities we would require.

The elders and staff had been setting aside one day every month to pray and fast and seek God about a number of pressing issues, one of which was our obvious accommodation needs. As a church community, we had a 24/7 prayer week earlier in the year, when the same issue had been one of the matters for prayer. During that week of prayer God had spoken to us from Scripture:

> ▶ **"The children born during your bereavement**
> **will yet say in your hearing,**
> **'This place is too small for us;**
> **give us more space to live in.'**
> **Then you will say in your heart,**
> **'Who bore me these?**
> **I was bereaved and barren;**
> **I was exiled and rejected.**
> **Who brought these up?**
> **I was left all alone,**
> **but these—where have they come from?'"**
>
> ● Isaiah 49:20-21 (NIV)

> ▶ **" '... a city without walls... I myself will be a wall of fire**
> **around it,' declares the Lord, 'and I will be its glory**
> **within.' "**
>
> ● Zechariah 2:4-5 (NIV)

> ... "Oh, that you would bless me and enlarge my territory!
> Let your hand be with me...
>
> ● 1 Chronicles 4:10 (NIV)

We reminded ourselves of the promise of harvest in the 1987 Week of Prayer and Fasting and Seeking God. There were also recent words spoken to us from a local church leader: "God will give you more than you need; it will cost you more than you can afford".

Summing up all that God had said to us and was continuing to say to us, we believed that we were to expect to grow spiritually and numerically, going far beyond our present boundaries. It was at this time that we adopted this summary of what God intended us to be as a church: 'We exist to Love God, Love each other and Love the lost'.

Therefore, on that November evening in 2001, we agreed together, as a church community meeting in the presence of God, to go for it. We believed God was directing us to move, but that we were to continue to look to Him for more: more of Him most certainly and more in terms of place and space to meet. This move was not the end of the journey in terms of premises. Rather, it was like a stage in the journey to 'The Fathers House'.

On Palm Sunday, 24 March 2002 we began to meet at our new location on Sunday mornings and to use their premises for our youth work. I well remember being in the sports hall the evening before we had our first service there. The set-up team were laying out the new chairs – there were so many of them – the sound team were doing their experimenting and the musicians were getting acclimatised. I was filled with a huge sense of wonder and thanksgiving. I stood at the back of the sports hall, looking out over what seemed to be a vast array of chairs in this expansive area we were about to begin to use, and that Isaiah 49 question came to mind: "Where have all these come from?" It seemed to me unbelievable that God had brought us to a place where we needed this space and all these chairs. But He had. The word one of the leaders of Ichthus Christian Fellowship had given to me at the end of our church holiday in Exmouth in 1988 sprang to mind, 'God is going to give you 500 people'. That was fourteen years earlier and at the time I was like the disciple who said, "Lord, I believe; help my unbelief." The word God had given him for us then was on its way to fulfilment.

Ten years on from our first sabbatical, by the kindness of the elders and the church family, Maureen and I were about to plan for another. Up until this time, the church, like most others, did not have a policy concerning sabbaticals. But now the elders began to formulate a policy for senior staff for the years ahead.

Our three months of sabbatical would be divided into two: the first section taken in June/July 2001 and the second in 2003. During the last ten years, God had been drawing church leaders together in many places in the UK including our own area experience with the Send Your Fire network. From this networking had come prayer for towns and cities, mercy ministries of various kinds and evangelistic strategies. In our area, this could be seen in Prayer for Bournemouth, the Pregnancy Crisis Centre and Life in the Park. As a result of my involvement in helping to lead Send Your Fire, I wanted to discover and network with those who were similarly involved elsewhere. As a result, for the first month of my sabbatical, I visited church leaders who were heading up similar networks to SYF in various UK cities, discovering how God was working among them and the vision He had given them for their area.

Another element of the sabbatical in the summer of 2001 was a visit Maureen and I made to Kansas City, USA to spend a week at the International House of Prayer (IHOP). In 1994, when we were in Toronto for the first Catch the Fire Conference, we had heard Mike Bickle give a memorable preach from Song of Songs. He was then a pastor in Kansas City. In 1999 he set up IHOP, dedicated to 24/7 prayer ministry, including continuous, unceasing worship and intercession. It was a new experience to spend days in such an atmosphere. There was a sense of being bathed in the presence of God and receiving fresh insights into the character and ways of God. There were opportunities to attend teaching seminars and also to receive personal prayer. Maureen and I were blessed to receive from God and be strengthened and encouraged in Him.

We had followed the development of IHOP and their vision for houses of prayer around the world and we had talked with others in Bournemouth about the possibility of a Bournemouth Prayer House. A few months later, in October, SYF arranged for one of the leaders of IHOP, Kirk Bennett, to come to Bournemouth. The evening meeting was held at our church. Its purpose was for church leaders and churches in the area to learn more about the vision and purpose of IHOP and to begin to share the local vision for a House of Prayer in this area. A Prayer Room was commenced in Bournemouth and existed in various forms in the years that followed. There were other prayer gatherings too, drawing together those from many different churches who had the welfare of their community on their hearts.

Following that visit to Kansas and IHOP, we flew to Tampa, Florida for three weeks of holiday, personal reading and reflection. We are blessed to have been given valued friendships over the years and through the kindness and generosity of some friends, we had enjoyed some special holidays in their accommodation on the Gulf Coast of Florida, south of Tampa. Through these friends, we had been introduced to a Bournemouth couple, who had moved to the USA decades previously and led an Assemblies of God church in Sarasota, Florida. In 2001 they wanted to visit Bournemouth and so we arranged a house exchange with them. We did not doubt that we had the best of the exchange.

The house in which we spent those three weeks was situated on the edge of an inlet from the Gulf and the first night we were there it was 4th July, the American Day of Independence. The sky around Sarasota and the bay, including our inlet, was alive with fireworks – the colour and warmth of the evening air were wonderful! God gave us an incredibly special time with Him and with each other in an area which we have come to love. All of this is evidence of His Father heart and generous gifts to us through friendships He has provided.

CHAPTER 17

Room to Grow
2003 – 2005

The year 2003 marked 25 years since we arrived at Winton from London. On Sunday 28th September, the elders and staff team had arranged a surprise celebration to mark the occasion. It was a special morning. The sight of the staff team in various tartan regalia including kilts, performing an appropriate Scottish dance, will long live in the memory bank. Perhaps I need to clarify that this took place as an excursion at the time of the announcements.

Spring Harvest had been a blessing to Maureen and myself and to the church when we were involved in the late 80s. At that time, we heard about Alex and Peggy Buchanan, who were acting as pastors to the Spring Harvest Leadership Team. From the mid-70s, Alex had been engaged in a travelling, preaching and prophetic ministry at home and overseas. He was a friend and advisor to many churches and church leaders and to a considerable number of para-church groups, including the Evangelical Alliance.

During Alex and Peggy's involvement as pastors to the Spring Harvest team, he became concerned that those well-known church leaders needed a place where they could share their lives in a confidential environment. This led to him commencing what he inimitably called 'Blokes'. He invited around ten of these church leaders to gather with him three times a year for twenty-four hours.

Here is how Alex described those retreats when he sent me a letter of invitation to join Blokes 3: 'We have no set agenda… but we spend time in the Scriptures, in prayer and quietness. We laugh a lot and cry sometimes; we can also shout and scream if we want to, which we probably cannot do in our own churches.' There were some conditions for being involved in Blokes: 'Absolute honesty, total confidentiality-no sharing elsewhere. Total commitment to the dates – the retreat must be a priority.'

In 2001, quite out of the blue, (I had never met Alex personally, although I had some friends and colleagues who were involved in Blokes), he wrote to me inviting me to join Blokes 3. As you will realise, due to the value of these retreats and Alex's wise unwillingness to involve more than ten in each one, it meant that he subsequently commenced two more groups of leaders, Blokes 2 and Blokes 3. I had the privilege of being a member of Blokes 3 from 2001 and thank God for the relationships formed and the wisdom, discipline and blessings received. Journeying with the same group of guys, meeting up three times a year, hearing as each one had time and space to recount the joys and sorrows, the victories and heartaches and then gathering round to pray for each other, was an inestimable blessing to me.

In 2003 Alex invited me to take over the leadership of Blokes 3. He was still leading Blokes 1 and 2, but he was experiencing challenging health conditions and became unable to lead what had become nine retreats every year. I was responsible for the oversight of Blokes 3 for the next six years and I am thankful to God for the privilege. When I first accepted Alex's invitation to join Blokes 3 I knew no one else in the group, as they were all from London, the South-East and the Thames Valley corridor – I was the only interloper from the south coast. But some of those relationships have continued down through the years and have been a means of continuing encouragement and blessing.

From the very first, Alex and Peggy very generously gave of their time, wisdom (and humour) to us as a couple. They were always interested in what was happening in our lives, our family and the life of the church. They prayed for us, encouraged us, affirmed us and spoke truth to us in a way that strengthened us, although sometimes they could be scary. We had never had mentors in our earlier years, much as we had longed for such a provision, but they were a wonderful gift from God to us at a time when we were mentoring others.

Since the late 90s, Maureen and I had been spending increasing time with men and women in church leadership. Our first and foremost responsibility was to our staff team at church and as that was ever-increasing, it was no small thing. But with our involvement in the wider life and witness of the churches across the area since the commencement of the South Wessex Evangelical Alliance in 1988 and Send Your Fire in 1994, there were church leaders, especially married couples, who were looking for listening ears, just as we ourselves had been for so many years. Due to our history of looking but not finding help in earlier years, we had always said to God that if He could use us in that way for others, we were available. God certainly took us at our word! It was a privilege and joy to become privy to the struggles and disappointments, the vision and faith-filled lives of so many leadership couples and to journey with them year by year.

In May 2003 Alex and Peggy came to the church for a weekend of ministry. They spent time with the elders and staff team and Peggy spoke at an evening for women. Saturday was a men's breakfast event and then Alex preached on Sunday morning. Sunday evening included teaching on, and the opportunity to practise, the prophetic. Both of these dear saints were 'no nonsense' in what they taught and shared. They did not shrink from giving it to you straight from the shoulder, but because their love for their Lord and for you was so evident, the result was that you moved forward in God.

Some weeks before that weekend, most of the elders were at a 'Life in the Spirit' (LITS) conference at High Leigh, Hertfordshire. LITS began about 35 years ago, as a group of Reformed pastors, impacted by the charismatic renewal, gathered together in order to examine, in the light of Scripture, the new things God was doing in their lives. Some of the elders at church, myself included, had been attending the annual conference, with great benefit, for some years.

As a team of elders, we had been discussing, not for the first time over the years, whether as a church we should affiliate with any of the church streams. In the early 80s, when I was sorely in need of counsel and support, I was invited by Arthur Wallis to attend the monthly prayer days of the leaders of Southampton Community Church (SCC). At that time SCC was experiencing incredible growth and they were planting out congregations all over the Southampton area and beyond. Arthur Wallis was an itinerant bible teacher and author, much used by God in those early days of what was known as the house church movement. Two of his books, the Radical Christian and God's Chosen Fast are classics. He was on the leadership team of Cornerstone at this time, the name given to SCC and those congregations which had come into being through SCC. Those prayer days and the fellowship with the leaders of SCC were a blessing and encouragement in many ways. However, I did not feel any liberty from God to become part of Cornerstone or indeed New Frontiers International (NFI) although I had friends who were church leaders in NFI.

We had forged a fellowship link with Ichthus Christian Fellowship in 1997 (a link that would come to an end in 2004) which had been beneficial in our development as a church. The arrangement with Ichthus was relational, not structural, and we valued that aspect of our link with them. From time to time the issue of affiliation to one of the church streams, such as NFI, Salt and Light, Pioneer would arise. When it did, as a team of elders we prayed and thought it through, but so far there had not been any conviction that God was directing us to change our direction of travel, which was to be fully engaged with churches in our area and help resource the work of the Kingdom in the conurbation. However, the question was again on our agenda and we arranged to meet with Alex during the Life in the Spirit conference and seek his counsel.

Alex was, as always, straightforward in his questions, comments and advice. He asked us, "Why you would want to do that? You have the Ephesians 5 ministries among you as a group of elders". Alex believed that God's purpose for us was to be an Antioch / Minster church, in which we were already engaged in our role of assisting and supporting leaders and churches across the three boroughs of Bournemouth, Christchurch and Poole, and wider afield.

As elders, we had certainly believed for some years that God had directed us to pour our efforts and gifting into working together with other leaders and churches in our conurbation for the glory of the King and the good of His Kingdom. Alex affirmed that he believed we were 'on track' in this and we should not be looking to join up with a church stream. We were thankful to God, believing Alex's advice to be in line with our sense of God's direction for us over some years and we did not ever re-visit the issue.

I mentioned in an earlier chapter that effective administration is a necessity if church leaders are to be free to do what they were called to do. We had been served so well by a succession of office secretaries since 1987. They had all been very patient and flexible in dealing with their ever-changing roles as the church was developing and growing. In 1999 Alison Whyte had come on board as office secretary. We had ten years of working closely together and she was in essence also my PA. Being a 'high J' on the Myers-Briggs Temperament Analysis Course, Alison was superb at picking up the stuff that would otherwise be missed.

Her invaluable role would continue, but we were now at the point where we needed to appoint a senior staff member to lead the management and administration of the church. In January 2003 Greg Rawlings, who with his wife had been worshipping and serving in the life of the church for many years, took up the new post of Church Administrator. We were so thankful to God to be able to appoint someone of Greg's ability and testimony to Christ. He would be a pivotal member of staff in the months and years ahead, as God led us into projects where Greg's skills and gifts would be sorely needed. This appointment only served to highlight again our serious need for office space and, if possible, to have all the staff working at the same location.

In 2002 the elders set up the Human Resources Group (HRG). Employment law was becoming increasingly complicated and we needed to be on top of all our legal responsibilities. There was a long list of key issues to be addressed, including recruitment and selection procedures, contracts of employment, grievance and disciplinary procedures and policies to be prepared for Health and Safety and Equal Opportunities, to name but two. We were blessed to have people with the relevant skills, who were willing to serve and help the church in the area of human resources.

The formation of the HRG was the point at which we commenced an appraisal system for all staff, including myself. Since commencing to build a staff team in 1987 I had always regarded it as an essential and privileged part of my role to sit down regularly with staff members in order to ensure all was well with them in their personal and work situations. Setting in place an appraisal system was the opportunity to organise appropriate line management, involving other senior staff in the process apart from myself. These new, but very necessary, arrangements provided the trustees and elders with the security of knowing we had put in place responsible measures for protecting us all and enabling the personal and ministry development of the staff.

One of the immediate consequences of the establishment of the HRG was a recognition that the church was not structured in a way that was legally appropriate. For example, the HRG discovered that 'there is no legal entity which is able to act as the employer in staff contracts. This means that the staff do not have legal contracts of employment'. There were other issues too. The outcome was a recommendation that 'the church be structured as a Charitable Company'.

We had been thinking of changing the name of the church for some years. Winton Evangelical Church no longer seemed appropriate, as we were drawing people from across Bournemouth and our vision, while still including Winton, had widened to the conurbation as a whole. Indeed, the statistics of the over 400 adults, teenagers and children who attended the church, indicated that only 28% lived in the Winton area. The word 'Evangelical' meant nothing to the man in the street. It was a hindrance rather than a help. So there was a second proposal presented to the church in July 2003: 'That the name of the church become Bournemouth Community Church (BCC). The gathered church unanimously agreed with both proposals and in 2004 the church changed its name from Winton Evangelical Church to Bournemouth Community Church. The church became a Registered Charity and a Company Limited by Guarantee.

The appointment of the first trustees of the Charity was a significant moment. I knew church situations in our area where there had been serious disagreement between elders and trustees over crucial issues. In these situations, the elders who were trustees had been outnumbered by other trustees who, in some cases, were not even members of the church at all and they had been able to overrule the spiritual leadership. For that reason alone, it was important to ensure that in the newly named Bournemouth Community Church, the elders would have a majority among the trustees and that the senior pastor would be chair of trustees.

Having said that, an effective board of trustees requires an appropriate mix of gifts that will safeguard the affairs of the Charity. At BCC we have been very thankful to those members of the church who have served the Charity with their gifts, time and energy.

✗

In early July 2003, as a direct result of the excellent relationships among church leaders in the town through the 'Send Your Fire' network, an evangelistic outreach was held for a week in the Bournemouth Football Club stadium under the invitational heading, 'Meet Jesus'. The outreach was organised, led and funded by local churches and BCC was a primary resource church. There were stadium gatherings for worship, testimony and the preaching of the Gospel, while teams were engaged through the day in street witness and community service and engagement. There were 48 people who made commitments to Christ and 70 who renewed and re-affirmed their dedication to the Lord.

The previous year, 2002, Bournemouth church leaders began to meet together under the strapline 'Together for the Harvest'. This arose out of relationships we had built together through Send Your Fire and a desire to lay down our individual agendas in the conviction that each church has a part to play in God's strategy. We met monthly to pray and share together. We were able to pray into local issues and share together in local evangelistic opportunities such as summer Sunday evenings at the Bandstand in the Lower Gardens. Another plus from these excellent church leaders' relationships was 'Connect', which brought together leaders and people from different local churches on three or four Sunday evenings a year, where prayer was made for the town. Local community leaders, including politicians and senior police officers, came to share news and receive prayer. In 2004, a 40-day diary, 'Prayers for Bournemouth', was published. The first edition of 2000 copies was insufficient. Every Easter Sunday Bournemouth churches held a service at the Flame in the Square, which was erected in 2000 as a gift from the churches in Bournemouth to the town. Around this time the Bournemouth Prayer Room came into being, its aim being simply to encourage prayer for our town. The Flame, Connect and the Prayer Room were all expressions of our desire, that 24-hours a day, 365 days a year, worship, witness and prayer was being offered to God by more and more people across Bournemouth.

In September 2003 BCC commenced an Internship Programme led by two of the senior staff, who were also elders. The aim was to raise up younger leaders from within our own church family. We wanted young men and women to be Kingdom people and Kingdom builders for the rest of their lives. Two men and one woman completed the first year of the programme in June 2004. Each intern was self-financing and received 17 hours of supervised ministry, 2 hours of training and 1 hour of personal mentoring each week. This Internship Programme continued for many years. It was rewarding to have the interns working alongside the staff team and to see their growth in God and increasing confidence in the Gospel of his Son and in the exercise of the gifts they had received from Him.

The work among children up to 11 years of age had continued to grow steadily. There was a need for someone to build the work further and take up opportunities for school's work, and before and after school clubs. In April 2003, the church appointed Kirsty as Children's Worker. Two new weekday children's groups started: 5Alive for school years 1-2 and 7Up for Y3-Y5. These grew to such an extent that we had to rent Winton Primary School to accommodate the boys and girls attending. A new magazine-style children's church was also launched and along with the Holiday Clubs, our connections with children grew to over 200.

The pressure on our existing church centre premises at Calvin Road, Winton just kept growing exponentially. The Parents and Toddlers Group was bursting at the seams with 130 parents and children names on the books. All the weekly clubs for children and young people were experiencing increasing numbers on a regular basis. We were hiring extra minibuses to move children and youth to other sites, which of course were rented. The elders had been seriously considering moving to two Sunday morning services to accommodate the growing congregation but were reluctant to do so. Not having our own premises would make two services difficult to operate within the boundaries of our rental agreement with the School. It would also create huge personnel and logistical issues and the result would be two separate congregations – not an attractive proposition to us. Having prayed and thought through the pros and cons and discussed it with everyone who would be impacted, we came to the decision that was not the route for us to pursue. The sports hall, where we met, had capacity for over 400, but with some adjustment, it proved possible to seat up to 500. But of course, although the extra seating on a Sunday morning would help for a time, the pressures already mentioned on those operating the children and youth ministries continued, as did the unsatisfactory office accommodation for staff, with some of the team having to work from home.

All of these factors and pressures brought us to a significant moment when, in 2005, we launched 'Room to Grow' (RTG), a vision for one overall complex for BCC. A Room to Grow project team was put in place led by the Church Administrator. As an aid to helping us all to better understand the journey we were commencing, the elders and staff team viewed a video of the new premises of Peterborough Community Church, which revealed something of the scale of the project that was facing us. A 'Room to Grow' fund was established. The RTG project team also began exploring the sale possibilities of our church centre site, including planning permission for residential development in order to maximise the value of the site. The church engaged a professional firm to assist it in the search and possible adaptation or development of new premises. The firm had a wide range of skills which we required and had considerable experience in the kind of development which we anticipated.

From 2005 Room To Grow was one of the themes in the prayer life of the church which was taken up by adults and children alike. In the weeks of prayer in 2006 and 2007 and beyond RTG figured significantly. We all knew the pressures of 'camping out' as a church, which we had been doing now since 1997. We had been continuing to view and consider possible new premises year on year. Sainsbury's, the food supermarket, had moved out of premises on Wimborne Road, not far from our church centre site in Calvin Road. There was a 15-year lease and the annual rent was £234K. Eminently unsuitable. Punshon Methodist Church, opposite the Bournemouth International Centre (BIC), was also visited when we heard it was closing. We had no conviction that the location, although being central to the town and opposite the BIC, was where God wanted us to be situated.

Two of the lessons God had taught us over this journey in church leadership remained pivotal in these years of accommodation pressure with no apparent long-term answer.

The first was: 'Trust God and His promises at all times' with such promises like 1 Thessalonians 5:24 ringing in our ears: "The one who calls you is faithful, and he will do it."

The second was: 'Pursue the course God has given you to walk' and don't be deflected from that way or try to work out your own solution (shades of Proverbs 3:5 in The Message: "... don't try to figure out everything on your own!").

Since we began to build a staff team in 1987, building relationship together had been especially important. Gathering together in different contexts outside of a 'meeting' environment, whether that 'meeting' be engaging in worship and prayer or wading through an agenda, is essential to getting to know one another at a different level and discovering the gifts and interests that we each enjoy. Every year we would have a staff summer outing, usually involving walks and a pub lunch in the New Forest or somewhere similar. At Christmas, we would have a special meal together at a restaurant one or other of us could recommend. Tuesday morning staff meetings always had a coffee break when we could catch up on news of individual time away and holidays. The value of knowing each other well and understanding what makes each of us 'tick', cannot be underestimated. And it brings joy and appreciation!

Over the years during which this journey in church leadership has been pursued, in common with many church leadership teams, there have been many issues with which we have had to wrestle. For example, I have previously referred to the lack of teaching (which inevitably leads to a failure in practice) on subjects such as eldership, prayer and fasting and the theology of giving, to mention just a few. Another issue that became an increasing matter for searching the Scriptures, prayer and discussion, was that of women in leadership. To my memory, the first time it was discussed by leaders at BCC was in 1990. Since then, at various times it has been a matter the elders and senior staff considered carefully. Even before 1990, there was never any hesitation in releasing into ministry women who had evident gifting from God. The history of the church since that time provides clear evidence of the way in which God has called and provided gifted women to serve the church here and overseas to His glory and the blessing of us all. Some lead life groups, others on staff exercise oversight of various ministries. The key issue for us when considering any appointment in the life of the church has always been: is there evidence of calling, gifting and godly character? Gender itself, and gifting itself are never the criteria. Calling and gifting, witnessed by the leadership of the church, plus a life of integrity and Christlike character, are the essentials that cannot and must not ever be relegated to a lesser place.

However, although to our joy and blessing women continue to exercise leadership in various areas of ministry in the life of the church, in all our various discussions as elders we never came to a conviction that there was biblical evidence for women to be appointed to the role of an elder. There were times when I personally would have much valued the benefits of having women on the team of elders. As I know from the early years when Tony, Richard and I were elders and we used to meet one evening a month with our wives for a meal and discussion and prayer, our wives brought distinctive, wise and penetrating insights – along with humour! Having had a mixed-gender staff team all these years has been superb in every way and I am so thankful to God for that. However, neither I nor the other elders were able to move to the appointment of women as elders without having an assured biblical warrant.

CHAPTER 18

Looking Ahead

2006 - 2007

A t this point, I was just over three years from arriving at the age of 65. That age is not now the natural terminus that it used to be. Back then 65 was still reckoned to be the appropriate point in most situations at which retirement beckoned. I had not yet decided if I would retire at 65. With a serious attempt at objectivity (and asking my wife just to make sure!) I did not think or feel that I was short of what was required to lead the church effectively. However, there were other factors to be considered. Maureen was a few years older, and she was still actively engaged in the life of the church. In so many ways it had been a joint ministry and if I carried on, I knew Maureen would want to do so too. Also, I had seen God build an elders and staff team who were gifted and able. If God wanted to appoint one of the elders to follow me, I could hold up proceedings if I remained longer than was best for everyone. While growing up in Scotland and also since coming south, I had seen many churches, when the minister retired or moved to another church situation, enter into what seemed to be interminable interregnums. Maureen and I had often discussed this and were very sure that we did not want such a situation to develop at BCC when it was God's time for us to 'retire'.

In early 2006 I arranged for the team of elders to have a day away together at Moorlands College so that we could begin to give attention to the issue. This was the first time we had a serious discussion, but it was good to give it an airing, as it were. We all knew that the decisions we would need to take on the journey that lay ahead of us would be crucial for the health and welfare of the church. Over the next couple of years we prayed much, corporately and individually, as we had discussions at various points along the way. It was important that we were able to talk freely together, listening as each one shared their thoughts and convictions. The immediate question was whether one of the existing eldership was God's choice to take up the mantle of senior pastor. I thank God for the team of elders that God gave me over my final years of leading BCC. Each elder had oversight of a particular portfolio of the church's ministry. They were a quality bunch of guys – gifted, able and none of them a push-over or a yes-man. They were thoughtful, honest and expressed their views with conviction and grace. Most of all, they were Word and Spirit men, who loved Jesus and His church. BCC was well-blessed with God's provision of leadership for His church at this significant time in its history.

By the end of 2006, Maureen and I were sure that God was indicating to us that I should conclude my years as senior leader of BCC in 2009 and I communicated that to the elders.

Meanwhile, there were quite a few changes taking place in the staff team. At the end of 2007, Andrew laid down the oversight and development of life groups, (BCC's cells), but continued to have oversight of evangelism and discipling. Roger took over the cell role from Andrew, while still being the elder with oversight of children and youth ministry. In 2008 Sarah concluded as youth worker after eleven years. She continued on staff as Children and Youth Director, while assisting Roger with the oversight of Life Groups and Life Communities. Maureen had been reducing her hours over the previous couple of years and was now working a three-day week, providing oversight to the women's ministry and continuing her one-on-one counselling and discipling work, plus partnering with me in marriage preparation and marriage enrichment.

In January 2006 we appointed Lucy as BCC's Community Worker. Lucy graduated from Moorlands College in 2004 and then entered on our one-year internship course. During her year as an intern, Lucy researched how we could better serve the local community, developing links with the police, local agencies and the Council. Over the past ten years, BCC had established an excellent reputation in the community, through the weekly parents and toddlers group and children and youth clubs. We wanted to extend this provision by establishing parenting groups and family support. Lucy's appointment was part-time and she continued working part-time in her physiotherapist post. A year or so later Bournemouth Council came on board with some funding, which enabled Lucy to work for the Council two days a week and the other days for BCC.

Tim Miller, a third-year student at Moorlands College, approached me in the summer of 2005 asking if he could have a placement at BCC for his final year which was just about to start. Initially, I was doubtful, as we already had our complement of placement students for that academic year. However, when I asked him what he had in mind he told me he wanted to be able to understand how a larger church operated, in other words, could he sit in on elders and staff meetings? My hesitancy in taking on another student placement for the year was mainly down to the fact that someone appropriate on staff had to be responsible for the supervision and that was a significant and often time-consuming task. However, bearing in mind what Tim wanted to do, I was probably the appropriate staff member. So I agreed. In the year 2005-2006 I had the opportunity to get to know Tim well and as he was attending staff meetings, so did the other staff. In due time Sarah roped him in to do sessional work alongside her in the youth work programme. I learned that Tim's intention after graduation was to spend some years in Africa. His home church had an active relationship with a work in Zambia. When he shared with me some of the detail of what was in view for him there, I suggested to him that he was perhaps not ready for what he had in mind.

In the summer of 2006, we had an unexpected vacancy on the youth work staff and we offered Tim a one-year part-time contract which he accepted. Another one-year part-time contract followed and during those two years, he studied for his M.A. with the London School of Theology. In September 2008 Tim was appointed Children's Worker. A year later he began to work alongside Sarah, our Children's and Youth Work Director, leading the teams who were working with children and youth. By 2010 Tim was asked to be responsible for the oversight of Life Groups and Life Communities and in 2011 he was appointed as an elder.

Andrew had been heading up evangelism and discipling for the previous six years. Alpha courses, which had been an integral part of BCC's outreach for ten years, came under Andrew's leadership and oversight. One of the key benefits of Alpha is that it requires Christians to speak to friends and family about Jesus and invite them to the Course. As a result, we saw people sharing their faith with more confidence and many came to faith. Andrew had also been increasingly involved in an equipping role, as he was gifted in training and mentoring. This resulted in others being trained to lead and assist in the Alpha courses and in other evangelistic and discipling tools which he introduced. One of these was the Freedom in Christ (FIC) course, which we began at BCC in early 2007 and which continues to be a much-used discipling instrument in the life of the church.

There had been a distinct lack of an appropriate discipling tool for new Christians in many UK churches for years. But it is more than fair to say that we came to regard the Freedom in Christ course as highly recommended for Christians who had been on the road for many years, not just for new believers. Maureen and I often said to each other, "If only this course had been available in the early 80s when we started at Winton." It covered so much essential ground, for lack of which many followers of Jesus have been held back from experiencing true freedom in Christ. In the late eighties, I did a Sunday evening series on 'Discovering our true identity in Christ'. Under God, it proved to open a door for many Christians in understanding and being secure in who they were in Christ. The books of Dr Neil T Anderson, first published in the UK in 1992, were the precursor to the Freedom in Christ course.

When the church developed a sabbatical policy, the intention was that full-time salaried elders should be able to have a three-month sabbatical after seven years of service and ministry. The purpose of a sabbatical is to provide time and space for personal study and reflection and to give an opportunity to examine and experience other situations which will assist in personal and skills development and future ministry. Such times are invaluable if the preparation is careful and covered in prayer. In 2004 Roger and Sarah had two weeks in the USA visiting some youth projects, but for various reasons, it had not been possible for them to set aside an extended period at that time. But in 2006 they had a two-month sabbatical, when they spent time in South Africa working with an orphanage and visiting Metro Ministries, who have work among three thousand children. They also spent some time in the UK examining different church leadership structures.

In 2008, Andrew, who had been on staff for eight years, had a two-month sabbatical to research and prepare for his dissertation in connection with a Master of Ministry degree, which he completed a few years later.

In the summer of 2006, a team of nine from the church went to Athens, Greece, where Jo Bassham, one of our overseas workers was serving with an agency called Nea Zoi (New Life). One of the team, Chris Lombard, studied at Moorlands College from 2007 and in his final year, he and his wife Amanda had a six-week College placement with Nea Zoi in Athens. After Chris graduated they worked with that agency in Greece and then later moved to Romania where they served with an organisation that operates a shelter for victims of sex trafficking, most of them children. Since 2017 Chris and Amanda and their family have lived in Athens, working with victims of sex trafficking and refugees.

In 2008 there were two short-term BCC teams serving overseas. It was two years since Roger and Sarah had spent some of their sabbatical in South Africa and they now returned to South Africa, leading a short-term multi-age team of thirteen from BCC. Sixteen people were on a team to Nepal, where BCC overseas workers Bill and Janet Ashwell had been since 2005. This team, with an age range from18-65, was led by Andrew and Sheila Muir. Andrew was the BCC elder with oversight for our cross-cultural ministry and the Missions Care Team. He was Executive Director of International Care Network, a Christian charity that he and Sheila had set up in Bournemouth with a strategic ministry to asylum seekers and refugees. A few years later their ministry among these refugees led Andrew and Sheila to live and work in Afghanistan.

Bill and Janet had recently purchased land at Godavari on the south side of Kathmandu and the team helped by digging foundations and making mud bricks. The land would house a small organic demonstration farm and a training hall for alternative building techniques and Aquaponics. While in Nepal the team were able to travel and experience life well away from Kathmandu, including riding on elephants and seeing rhinos and crocodiles! Bill and Janet said of that team visit: "They were wonderful times and we very much appreciated everyone who made the sacrifice to come and serve with us. Fellowship times were sweet and never to be forgotten."

Church leaders have a continuing responsibility to ensure that their overseas workers know they are loved, valued and honourably financed. Also, that they and their ministry are the subject of consistent prayer by the church family, publicly as well as privately. This does not have to be carried out by the senior leader. But, it is the senior leader's responsibility to ensure that this is covered effectively, if at all possible as part of an elder's oversight portfolio, or by a respected member of the church who carries Christ's heart for his worldwide church.

Over the years, gender-specific ministries had not been a priority. What had been strategic for very many years were the prayer gatherings of men and women, meeting separately. This was something that God just did. There was no planning about it. In the eighties, Maureen and a few of the women in the church began to meet together in our home to pray for one another. A few of these women had husbands who were not yet in Christ and so early on this led to them together praying for these men to be born anew. In time, that grew into a larger group of women, praying for one another, their husbands and families. This group of women became known as Grapevine and they continued to meet weekly and pray for their families and the wider church. Women of Prayer, which is the successor to Grapevine, meets every week at the LIFEcentre, BCC's home, of which much more in due course.

As a result of the prayers of the women, the men began to gather to pray at the church centre in Calvin Road at 7am before work. Some of those husbands, who came to Christ through the prayers of the women, became strategic in the development of those morning prayer times. The men were primarily calling on God to save other men and that the Holy Spirit would grow them in Christ and take them deeper in Him. Men have continued to meet to pray for one another and for the life and witness of the church.

Gender-specific ministries did begin to develop around 2006. A group of women began to arrange occasional gatherings, usually twice a year under the great name of Chat Chocolate and Change (CCC). Sometimes these were held at the church centre in Calvin

Road and sometimes in a hotel. The reason CCC came into being was to bring together women in the church and to provide an informal meeting point, where they would feel able to talk and share about issues relevant to women. At this time, some of the women were unsure of their value, identity and giftings. These gatherings, initiated by the women on the staff team, were primarily for BCC, but there were certain times when women from other churches were invited. Some very gifted speakers who came to Chat Chocolate and Change included Priscilla Reid and Fiona Castle. As a result of these gatherings, many women at BCC began to step forward with new confidence in who they were in God.

It is a well-known fact that it is not so easy to find the same enthusiasm in men to gather together as is readily discovered in women. (Unless of course, it is food or football, preferably both!) However, M2 came into being around the same year as CCC commenced. Smaller groups of men had enjoyed meals out together over the years. M2 built on this and arranged special teaching courses, at the church centre and sometimes in hotels. Saturday prayer breakfasts were a constant, sometimes with visiting speakers. In 2008 about 40 men had a weekend away together in Dorset, a very enjoyable and valuable time for everyone.

Room to Grow (RTG) continued to be a focus for prayer. The ongoing search for appropriate premises continued to be led by Greg whose job title had been changed from Church Administrator to Operations Manager to better reflect the development of his role. So far, although other possible premises had been investigated, there was no progress on a new site for BCC. However, in 2006 a double-fronted shop, 533-535 Wimborne Road, just 2 minutes from our church centre in Calvin Road, became available for purchase. Greg had been looking for premises to rent for office space and this possibility was presented. The property appeared to be ideal. Wimborne Road was the main thoroughfare traversing Winton, so this would give us a frontage on the main road and would provide space for offices and a community advice and information centre. It required change of use permission, which we had been told the Council would look on favourably. The church met to consider this purchase which would cost around £200K plus about £15K refurbishment costs.

One question the church family was asking was whether it was possible to use the money in the Room to Grow Fund, already given towards the purchase of a large multi-purpose church centre, for the purchase of this property. We agreed together that if we purchased 533-535 Wimborne Road it would be sold as and when God provided the new multi-purpose site for the church. There was £165K in the Room to Grow Fund, with substantial promised funds still to come. In August, the gathered church believed this was from God and agreed to move ahead. A gift day was arranged and provided enough for us to complete the purchase. Buying, refurbishing and beginning to use 533-535 Wimborne Road was an important step on the journey to the new church centre a few years down the track. We called the premises LIFEhouse and it was opened with joy and thanksgiving to God on Saturday 9th June 2007.

CHAPTER 19

Completing the Course

2008 - 2009

O ne morning, just a few months later, in early January 2008, Greg, our Operations Manager, telephoned me, "David, the Bingo Hall is on the market!" It was just over ten years since my recce around those premises. I had asked Roger and Andrew, both of them elders and senior staff, to have a look themselves and they agreed the premises would be superb for us as a church. But we had not mentioned the possibility to the church. As Greg was heading up the search project, he knew about our thoughts on the subject. The Bingo Hall was originally built as a cinema and opened in 1931, just three years before our forerunners had built and opened our church centre premises in Calvin Road. Those saints could never have imagined that the huge building they had seen being built not too far away on the main thoroughfare in Winton, would be the subject of a possible purchase by their successors 83 years later.

On 13th February, the elders met on the site of the Bingo Hall and then again on 20th February, accompanied by the firm of architects we had engaged to help us a few years earlier. They had considerable experience in converting buildings for church and community use and could supply external advice and counsel. Also accompanying us were some BCC members, who were involved in the building and construction industry. Their united assessment was, "It is an excellent building with amazing potential and generally in sound condition. It appears to be ideal for our purpose". The Gala Estates Manager was present, the Bingo Hall being owned by Gala Clubs. He was a Christian and told us there were no other enquiries at that time, but that the premises would be marketed in two weeks' time. We arranged an elders' meeting for appropriate consultation and decision and called the church community to gather on Monday evening 3rd March.

We reminded ourselves that God has a pathway through for us: He knows the way, just as in the history of Israel at the Red Sea. Prayer in small groups followed. The proposal from the elders was that the church should make an offer, subject to a full structural survey and change of use agreement, for the premises at 711-715 Wimborne Road, formerly a cinema and used as a Bingo Hall by Gala Clubs. I reminded the church of the prophetic word brought to us in February 2001 by a local church leader: "He will give you much more than you need. But it will cost you much more than you can afford. But much more than you can imagine will be achieved as you trust Him for this and act accordingly." We then viewed a DVD of the Gala Hall and Greg gave us a presentation of what it could look like once renovations had been made.

The Gala Hall: 28,000 sq ft with 2x2 bed flats above 2 small shops on either side of the entrance. It was on the market for £1.85M +VAT. The cost of renovation and refurbishment was reckoned to be £1M. Our present church centre in Calvin Road was 3,300 sq ft and its value estimated at around £400K.

I underlined the principle which over the years we had come to recognise as our first priority when considering any issue which carried a substantial financial cost. It was this: "First and foremost, the question is not 'How much will it cost?' but rather, 'What is God saying?'" Questions and discussion followed. It was agreed that if the purchase went ahead, a proposal to sell our premises in Calvin Road would come to the church. Also, the LIFEhouse,

533-535 Wimborne Road, bought in 2006, would be sold, as we had agreed at the time of purchase, so that the funds, originally given for a multi-purpose site for the church, would be ploughed back into their original purpose. The agreement of the trustees of the Bournemouth Community Church Charity was necessary for any purchase of the Gala Hall and the sales of the church centre in Calvin Road and the LIFEhouse in Wimborne Road. The elders and the trustees were in full agreement together, the importance of which I emphasised earlier when I described the 2004 formation of the Charity.

Prior to coming to our decision together as a church, we remembered the straightforward manner in which the Lord Jesus spoke to His disciples when teaching them about the cost of following Him. If we were to move ahead with making an offer and our offer was accepted, then the sacrifice involved for us all would be considerable, certainly more than anything else we had ever faced as a church. However, as we had benefited in inheriting our existing church centre in Calvin Road, through the obedience and sacrifice of those who had gone before us, so we wanted to provide for those who will follow after us at BCC. We wanted to leave a legacy that will bless the community and enable more and more lost people to find a place of refuge and healing in Christ. I reminded the church that many years before, one of the church family was walking past the Gala Hall and heard God say to her concerning it, "The Father's House".

Following a period of prayer and reflection, the gathered church overwhelmingly agreed that the elders should make an offer on the premises, giving freedom to act within the figures of £1.25M and £1.8M. Following that meeting, the church made an initial offer of £1.4M and then, when that was not accepted £1.675M, which was accepted on 25 April. However, that acceptance by Gala Clubs had not yet been ratified by its Board.

At an April meeting of the church family, the elders brought a proposal to sell the church centre in Calvin Road, so that the church would be ready to move on the sale without having to call everyone together, perhaps at short notice. Permission was given to sell, if necessary. In May, the church centre was placed on the market, with instructions that it was not to be sold until the purchase of the Gala Hall was confirmed. A number of enquiries were made concerning the purchase of our church centre, including the prospect of it being demolished for a block of flats. We had no peace about that. In November, the premises were sold for £390K to the Egyptian Coptic Church, as a centre for them in this area of southern England.

On 25th January 2009, we held a special Thanksgiving Service as we prepared to vacate our church centre building in Calvin Road. A presentation of the history of the building, with photographs from the foundation laying, was prepared and we worshipped and thanked God for those who sacrificed to see the church come into being and these premises erected to the glory of God.

Let's break off from that journey for a moment, as other very important new ventures were taking place in 2008. For some time, the elders had been considering introducing Life Communities alongside our small groups called Life Groups. Three presentation evenings had been arranged for the church family so that the elders could introduce the concept. The aim was to commence some small groups which would seek to build friendships through special interests such as Badminton, Football, Extreme Sports and other interests that were 'not' sport related. There was a powerful DVD which we used to illustrate the way in which these Life

Communities could be envisaged as lifeboats being launched out to reach those who were struggling and needed rescuing. These plans for Life Communities had been laid in 2007 for launching now in early 2008, not knowing of course that the issue of the Gala Hall would arrive at this time. But, realising that God knew about the timing, we proceeded. After all, loving and reaching the lost is key to who we are in Christ and why BCC was birthed. Whether or not we were moving to new premises did not change that. So the three evening presentations went ahead, using one of the lecture halls at Bournemouth University, about a couple of miles away. In September, the first three Life Communities were launched: Venture, Down to Earth and Friends First. The same month saw 40 attending the autumn Alpha Course.

In May we heard that an application had been made to English Heritage that the Gala Hall be declared a listed building. That decision would have had quite an impact on the building's saleability and our plans for it. However, in the goodness of God, English Heritage decided not to list the building. Subsequently, in July, the elders decided to enter a new, reduced offer for the building of £1.3M.

We had written out to former members of BCC to inform them of our plans to purchase the Gala Hall and many generous gifts were received. The Gift Week for our purchase of the Gala Hall took place from 7-14 September 2008 which was also a Week of Prayer and Fasting. £415K was given, including Gift Aid to be reclaimed. During that week, the church also received a gift of property, with a value of around £200K. This was a remarkable moment. A couple who had been worshipping at BCC and who were trustees of a redundant church building, came to me during the gift week to tell me that God had directed them and the other trustees to make a gift of their building to us, to enable BCC to go ahead with what they believed to be God's will for us. Thank you, Lord! It is a reminder that, walking in God's will and way opens up opportunities to experience God's miraculous provision, which would otherwise never be known.

With the offer of £1.3M and the gifts of £415K, £885K was still required to proceed with the purchase. The additional £885K required was mostly wrapped up in BCC's assets: our church centre in Calvin Road, LIFEhouse, purchased a couple of years previously and the property donated during the gift week, a total combined value of around £800K. A letter was sent to the church family outlining all these facts and many other details, including the estimated costs of renovation and refurbishment of the Gala Hall at £1M. This sum would be required to do necessary work on the roof, renewing the frontage, creating offices and moving the LIFEhouse facility into one of the two shops on either side of the entrance to the building. It would also cover the next phase, which would fully refurbish the premises providing a 1000-seater auditorium, a children's youth and community area, a coffee and serving area, and other extensive facilities.

In October, in light of the size of mortgage we would have to take to bridge the funding gap between the £415K received to date and our offer of £1.3M, the elders decided to reduce our offer for the Gala Hall from £1.3M to £850K, with a willingness to go to £1M if required to seal the purchase. One of the many remarkable providential aspects of this whole journey to purchase the Gala Hall was that it took place at a time of economic recession in the UK. During 2008, while our negotiation to purchase was going on with Gala Clubs, as far as we know they never received an offer from any other prospective purchaser. In ordinary economic times, there could have been more than a few other bidders for the site. In the goodness of God, a member of the church family provided a loan to cover the funding gap, so we did not require a mortgage to finalise the purchase. That loan was repaid from the sale of the assets mentioned earlier. In November, Gala Clubs agreed to sell the building to BCC for £1M. Contracts were exchanged on the 10th December 2008 and completion was on the 4th March 2009.

Our Father in heaven is the best property advisor and the best economist! He gave His church a building of 28,000 sq ft as against our original church centre of 3,300 sq ft. Our new multi-purpose centre is more than eight times larger in square feet terms and yet it only cost two and a half times more (£1M as against £400K). In our Lord's post-resurrection meeting with His disciples by the Sea of Galilee, He showed Himself to be the very best fisherman. Although the disciples who had made their living from the Sea had been fishing all night and had caught nothing, they obeyed the Master's word and placed the net exactly where He directed:

> ► ... they were unable to haul the net in because of the large number of fish.
> Then the disciple whom Jesus loved said to Peter, "It is the Lord!"
>
> ● John 21:6-7 (NIV)

Indeed it is!

While these significant decisions regarding buildings were being taken, the elders had been continuing to talk and pray together about the appointment of my successor as lead elder and senior pastor. In December 2007, the elders had sent a detailed letter to every person committed to the life of BCC, outlining that Maureen and I would be retiring from our respective roles at BCC in March

2009 and that I would also be retiring from the leadership of the team of elders and as an elder. I spoke briefly about this on a Sunday morning in December 2007 and that was followed by an evening in January 2008, when the church community gathered to hear further information and ask appropriate questions. On that occasion, the church was invited to share with the elders the names of anyone they believed may be an appropriate candidate for the elders to consider.

We drew up a list of people who had been mentioned to us by the church family and also included people we knew ourselves and considered could be possible candidates for the role. A Person Specification and Job Description had been prepared and an information pack was made ready. During these months, the elders contacted some of those who were known to us, for exploratory conversations. We also advertised the post in the Christian Press. Throughout 2008 every Monday had been set aside as a Prayer Day. Prayer Days and Weeks of Prayer had been integral to the life of the church since 1987. Over these years, the church family had never been short of matters for praise and prayer, nor were they now.

Advertising for the senior pastor role, as you might imagine, brought in many and varied applications from the UK and overseas. In August, the elders perused the details of those who had applied and made a shortlist for interviews in September. Following these interviews, in our prayer and discussions as elders, we thanked God for the godly and gifted candidates with whom we had spent time. However, we had no conviction that we had met the person God had appointed as the next lead elder and senior pastor at BCC. The elders then agreed individually to set aside the following week for prayer and reflection concerning my suggestion to them that Roger, a member of the team of elders and who had been on staff since 1997, be considered as my successor as lead elder. When we met following that week devoted to seeking God, the elders unanimously agreed and affirmed that Roger should be invited to take up the role. After having had time to discuss with Sarah and seek God, Roger accepted our invitation. All the way through this process it had been particularly important for the staff team to be kept appropriately informed and involved. They were delighted to know that the elders had invited Roger and that he had agreed.

✎

From January 2009 I moved to a four-day week and Roger and I used the coming weeks to begin to prepare for the transfer of my responsibilities over to him. For some years, Maureen and I had asked God to enable such an 'in house' transfer to take place, thus avoiding what could be a lengthy interregnum. Although I was sad to be looking at my final weeks leading BCC, I was full of thanksgiving to God for the way in which He had worked all things in accordance with His will. The church family were at peace, indeed quietly excited that my successor was in place and that God had wonderfully provided for BCC to enter the new season ahead in our new multi-purpose church centre. We had been 'camping' in schools since 1997 and the search for new premises had been on our minds for all those years. Now there was the prospect of having God-given premises from which to seek to continue and grow further BCC's witness to the Lord Jesus and His Gospel.

I was so grateful to God and I could see His love and wisdom in the timing of these significant events. With my banking background, I was possibly the best person to be leading the church through the whole capital project of the purchase of the Gala Hall. But I was very sure that Roger and his wife Sarah were best suited to the creativity required to oversee the renovation and refurbishment of our new church centre. Throughout 2008 the elders had obviously discussed together what we wanted to do with the building, in the light of our mission and staffing priorities. If God had brought in someone from outside the elder's team to lead the church at the very time we had completed the purchase, it would have been a big ask for them to suddenly orientate to this huge project without being involved in the history leading up to it. As it was, we were all reading off the same page.

I handed over the Chair of BCC Trustees to Roger in early March 2009. I am so grateful to God for the quality of those who served as trustees from the time we set up the Registered Charity in 2004. So many people serve in the local church and often their contribution is unseen and unheralded. But without those who serve year in, year out, no local church could effectively function. Finance officers in any church have an important role to play. It is crucial that they are people full of faith and integrity. They also need to be able to 'speak truth to power' to quote a phrase. BCC and I especially have been so thankful to God for the people who have served as finance officers over the years. But the role of BCC's Finance Officer from 2003 to 2009 was particularly onerous. Freddie led the Finance Group through those years and was a strategic help to the church, especially in the purchase of what became the LIFEhouse at 533-535 Wimborne Road in 2006/7 and in the purchase of the Gala Hall at 711-715 Wimborne Road in 2008/9. The fact is that no church can operate legally and effectively, or grow its life and witness, without the strategic help of members of the church family who are willing to place their time and gifts at the disposal of the Lord Jesus and His Church. There are so many people who have served God and the church community at BCC that I cannot begin to mention them all. One of the reasons why so few names are mentioned is that once you begin, where do you stop? Thank you, one and all, in Jesus' name!

On Sunday 8 March 2009 the church gathered as usual in the morning at Winton Academy to commission Roger as lead elder and senior team pastor. It was a memorable occasion. Joy and thanksgiving pervaded everything that took place that morning. Participating with us in the service were two people who were mutual friends of Roger and myself and indeed of BCC. Gordon Tuck, who had been the lead elder at Woodford Baptist Church when Roger was on staff there before coming to us in 1997 and now led Testwood Baptist Church near Southampton and Dr Steve Brady, Principal of Moorlands College, who had ordained Roger to the Christian Ministry. Gordon, Steve and all of us as elders had the privilege of laying hands on Roger and praying the anointing of God upon him for this new season. I passed the 'mantle' of lead elder and senior team pastor on to Roger and preached on the theme of Biblical Leadership. What great cause for thanks to God.

On Sunday 15 March 2009, we gathered as a church community in our new building, the Gala Hall, to thank God together for His gift of it to us for His glory and the Gospel of His Son. For most of the church, it was their first experience of walking into the building and seeing its extensiveness and potentiality. There was a very gaudy cinema-style carpet running through the whole of the ground floor and of course, no seating, as the fixed tables and chairs used for bingo had already been removed by teams from the church during the previous week. So there were no chairs! We sat on the carpeted floor when we weren't standing and praising God. It would be some months before we would be able to cease using Winton Academy for Sunday mornings and move into the Gala Hall, which was renamed The LIFEcentre. Meanwhile, the firm of architects had met with Roger and the refurbishment project team and had set out their order of priorities.

When we entered the year 2009 I was more than aware that the next few months would be the last times I would be privileged to preach to God's family as their pastor. It was something, of course, I had known was coming for many months, but that did not make it any easier. Yes, God willing, there would be many opportunities to preach the Word of God in many places in the months and years that lay ahead. But nothing ever replaces preparing and preaching consistently to the people God has given you to teach, shepherd, love, care and pray for over years. As you engage in personal and pastoral interaction with the 'flock of God', (and it is vitally important that you do) the Holy Spirit makes clear to you the areas of grace and truth He is directing you to emphasise in your teaching and preaching. There is great joy in observing the increasing freedom that Jesus promised coming into people's lives when they know, truly know and live out, God's truth. Being able to witness those godly changes, those life-transforming changes in the lives of people you have seen come to Christ or in others who are His but were well and truly 'stuck' for lack of hearing and understanding and applying truth in the power of the Holy Spirit, that is one of the many special joys of ministering to the same congregation over a substantial period of years.

I was in no doubt as to the theme for the final March Sundays. It would be to recount again the foundational issues for which we stood as a church. On 1st March I preached on the Bible as the Word of God, its authority for faith and practice and its centrality in the history of BCC and in my personal history. On the 8th, Roger's commissioning, it was 'Biblical Leadership' from Deuteronomy 31:1-8 and Joshua 1:1-9. On the 15th, the Thanksgiving Service for the Gala Hall, I preached from 1 Chronicles 16:8-36, the song of praise to God on the arrival of the ark of the covenant of the Lord in the tent that David had prepared for it. On 22nd I took as my theme the Holy Spirit from Mark 1:1-8 and John 16:5-15 'BCC is a Word and Spirit church'. Something took place that final morning for which I was totally unprepared. As I began to prepare to preach, someone way back in the far-left hand corner of the hall, began to clap. Then someone else near the front stood and began to clap and suddenly everyone was on their feet clapping, which seemed to go on for ages. I was choked with emotion, amazed and deeply moved. How thankful I was to God. How rich the church family which He had set around me.

The church had arranged a thanksgiving service to God for the over 30 years that Maureen and I had been at BCC. It took place at Winton Academy on Saturday 28 March 2009. Lloyd Griffiths and the worship band led us. What a blessing Lloyd, our long-term worship leader, had been to the church and to me personally over so many years. Roger Smith, a church leader representing the local Send Your Fire Network and Tony Seymour, our first full-time staff member appointed way back in 1987, both spoke. Geoff Larcombe, representing my years of involvement with Regions Beyond Missionary Union and Latin Link and Graham Roberts, representing local church leaders, both brought greetings. Steve Brady spoke on behalf of Moorlands College and my participation as a member of the Board there over many years. It was so good to have Fiona, Kevin and Stuart, our daughter and sons, contributing their own thoughts. My parents were also there. Sarah Constantine and Adrienne Wilson spoke with some humour about Maureen's ministry over the years and her penchant for bargains when food shopping.

Roger Smith preached and Maureen and I were overwhelmed by the gifts given to us by both the church and the staff team. The elders prayed over us and committed us to God's purposes in the coming years. A DVD of the day was produced which was a special and memorable gift to us. Then there were refreshments and time to speak to people who had come from near and far: family members, personal friends, and so many who had been involved in the life of the church over the years and had contributed to its life and witness during their time. It was emotional and exhausting and wonderful!

CHAPTER 20

Who Am I?

2009 – 2011

I had heard accounts of people from all kinds of different working backgrounds, including Christian ministry, who were not prepared in any way for the huge change of gear involved in moving from an absorbing working life to a season where there is no set pattern of life to shape the days; where purpose appears to have taken wings. It is not difficult to imagine some of the issues that could arise in life at this juncture. If who you are is predicated on the job you do and its success or otherwise, when retirement arrives (and indeed long before) you are going to face some large issues in areas such as security, significance and self-worth. For someone who is 'in Christ', the 'who am I' question should not be onerous. If you have been making the journey with Jesus during your working years, walking with Him as a child of His Father and yours and enjoying the life of the indwelling Holy Spirit, then sure there will be many changes to face, but the question of 'who am I' will not be one of them. God's unchanging love and faithfulness continue whatever our change of circumstances may bring.

But perhaps in the pressures of ministry and the stresses of life, you have lost sight of your place in the heart of Jesus; perhaps it is longer than you care to remember since you gazed on the hands of your Father, on which is written in indelible and eternal letters, your name. If this is you, you are not alone. Many Christians, including those who lead churches, have found themselves in such a situation. You are also, more importantly and significantly, not alone because the wonderful truth is that Jesus is Emmanuel, God with you! He called you to Himself by His Spirit. He has entered into a covenant, sealed by His blood shed for you, that He will never cease from loving you and nothing can ever separate you from Him. And again, as at the first, the Lord Jesus invites you to 'Come'.

> ▶ "Are you tired? Worn out? Burned out on religion?
> Come to me. Get away with me and you'll recover
> your life. I'll show you how to take a real rest. Walk with
> me and work with me—watch how I do it. Learn the
> unforced rhythms of grace. I won't lay anything heavy or
> ill-fitting on you. Keep company with me and you'll learn
> to live freely and lightly."
>
> ● Matthew 11:28-30 (MSG)

I suppose you could call Sunday 30th March 2009, the first day of the rest of my life. Actually, what I did, the morning after that very wonderful and emotional farewell to leading Bournemouth Community Church, was walk ten minutes down the road to a local church in our area of Bournemouth. On the way, I saw someone I knew very well indeed on his way to worship at BCC. His bicycle came to a halt and he said to me, "Well, David this is mighty strange!" He was right. It sure was very strange indeed.

Maureen and I had talked together, from time to time, about our desire to remain at BCC after I handed over the senior leadership. The received wisdom among church leaders and churches of all kinds at that time (and this had been true for many years) was that if you retired you did not remain in the same church. Why did this view prevail? One reason could be either that you were glad to get away or the church was glad to see the back of you. Another could be insecurity: insecurity in the retiring leader and/or in the incoming leader which would more than likely result in all kinds of unhelpful problems. For Maureen and me, our preference was to remain in the life of BCC, but without any leadership role of any kind. I had mentioned this to the team of elders in the year leading up to our 'retirement' and they had made it clear that they would want us to continue to worship at BCC. The elders and staff teams had come into being during my leadership, so they knew me very well and I knew them very well. They were well aware that I would not be continuing in any leadership role and they also knew I did not suffer from insecurity.

However, for Maureen and me, there was still a question mark over whether we could remain at BCC. If the new senior leader was someone from outside of the elder's team, someone who didn't know me and whom I didn't know, then it might be wiser for us not to continue in the life of the church. As it was only a few months before I was due to step down that we knew who the new senior leader would be, up until then we were unsure if we would be able to continue in the church community. However, when Roger accepted the elders and church's invitation to follow me as lead elder and senior pastor, there was no doubt that we could remain. Roger and I had worked together for over eleven years and for the last few years he had effectively operated as my number two. Insecurity was not an issue for him either. He knew my weaknesses and I knew his. There was mutual honour, respect and appreciation between us. Maureen and I were very thankful to God that we could remain in the life of a church family we loved and who cared for us.

In chapter two I mentioned a number of key issues which Maureen and I have discovered to be essential in our learning to follow Jesus on this journey of church leadership. One of these is to guard your time with God, your wife or husband, and children. Sadly, when some married people retire, they discover that their husband or wife is almost a stranger. Church leaders are not immune to this scenario. They may have been busy with what used to be called 'the work of God' but have failed to invest in their marital relationship (and also sometimes the lives of their children). Investing in these primary relationships is very clearly a godly work to which we are called to give priority. The Word of God in Ephesians 5, and I write and speak obviously from the perspective of a husband, is very plain about our responsibility and privilege in this regard:

> ▶ **Husbands, love your wives, just as Christ loved the church and gave himself up for her...**
>
> ● **Ephesians 5:25 (NIV)**

Investing tender love and caring compassion in your marriage, whether you are a man or a woman, pleases God and honours Him. This is very much included in what it means to live life in the Spirit. Romans 8:5 reminds us:

> ▶ ... those who live in accordance with the Spirit have
> their minds set on what the Spirit desires.
>
> ● **Romans 8:5 (NIV)**

The prospect of having more time together when the daily demands of leading a local church have eased should bring joy and anticipation to both of you. Whether it does or not will reflect if you have been making 'what the Spirit desires' a priority in the strategic matter of your marriage relationship.

Maureen and I had done some careful thinking about our plans from the end of March through to the end of 2009. Knowing that we were going to come to the end of a way of life that had been so fulfilling and so busy, we knew it was wisdom to have some well thought out plans in place. We had the joy of knowing we would be returning to the church family at BCC in due course, but how long should that 'due course' be and what would we do with the intervening time? We had suggested that we would return to BCC in January 2010 and the elders had been content with that. It would give nine months for us to be 'out of the way' and for Roger and the church to adjust to the change of leadership. During that time, if the previous years had been anything to go by, there would be new people arriving at BCC who would not know who we were when we came back. That could only be healthy for everyone concerned.

As we had thought about life after concluding that major season of ministry, we had a desire to be able to spend some time each year back in our home area of Aberdeen and Aberdeenshire. A few years previously, we had spent a week in a friend's mobile home on a caravan park in what is often called 'Royal Deeside'. Deeside is the valley of the River Dee, which flows east from the Cairngorms National Park to Aberdeen and the North Sea. On its journey, the river passes through the Balmoral Estate, much loved by the Queen and where she has her Scottish home, Balmoral Castle. On that holiday Maureen and I had thought that if we could purchase a mobile home in that caravan park it would be ideal for the years ahead. The site was only thirty miles from Aberdeen by a beautiful loch near the village of Aboyne: what could be better? We were able to buy just what we wanted in 2006 and had already used it for some holidays.

So our plan for April to December 2009 was to have April in Aberdeenshire. May/June would see us on the Gulf Coast of Florida in accommodation which, through the kindness of friends, we had been able to use at times over the years. July and August we would be at home here in Bournemouth, worshipping in churches in the area and then we would return to Aboyne for September and October. A further two months at home would follow before again being part of the church community at BCC. It was important to have thought through those nine months and we enjoyed a special time together, relaxing, enjoying different scenery and climatic conditions, especially in Florida(!) and asking God about our future. We were saying to Father: 'Here we are, what now?' The verses from Jeremiah which Derek Prime had given me in my last year at London Bible College, were just as relevant and true now, in this new season, as they had ever been:

> ▶ **For I know the plans I have for you," declares the Lord, "plans to prosper you and not to harm you, plans to give you hope and a future."**
>
> ● **Jeremiah 29:11 (NIV)**

There was great joy in knowing that we were no less loved or valued by the Lord Jesus now than we were when we were leading His church at BCC. God knew the plans He had for us. and we were content that He would unfold them in His time.

One very special aspect of our time in the States was our visit to the Billy Graham Library in Charlotte, North Carolina. We had flown to Washington DC and very much enjoyed visiting the well-known sights. We then drove south and visited Charlotte on our way to Sarasota on the Gulf of Mexico coast. Maureen, when a teenager in Aberdeen, came to faith in the Lord Jesus watching the Billy Graham film, Souls in Conflict a record of the 1954 London Haringey Crusade. When we were preparing our route from Washington to Florida, the Billy Graham Library was top of the list to visit. We spent almost a whole day there. It was absorbing and evocative as we were reminded again and again of how God had chosen to use this very ordinary, but dedicated and anointed man, to reach so many people around the world with the Gospel of Christ. In a clearing in the trees, at the perimeter of the Library, was the burial place of Billy's wife Ruth, who had died just two years previously. On the stone were these words: 'Construction complete. Thank you for your patience.' We left with a personal sense of great thanksgiving for the way God had used Billy's ministry in Maureen's life and with a renewed desire to consistently love and serve Jesus through all our remaining years.

Before we move on, we were, by and large, disappointed and sometimes saddened by quite a few of our visits to local churches during the months of 2009 when we were at home in Bournemouth. 'Why?' you ask. Lack of welcome would be the one thing that stood out. I do not mean that we were expecting to be recognised and welcomed. In fact, we deliberately tended to visit churches where we would not be known. But time and again there appeared to be no designated welcome team or individual and we would go into the building and sit down without anyone greeting us or speaking to us. Very seldom did anyone in the congregation make any attempt to enquire if it was our first time in the church or broach any question or simply smile and say, "Good morning!" We would take the initiative and say, "Good morning!" but it did not elicit anything further than a return "Good morning!". We thought that if we were prodigals seeking to return to God and His people, or if we had been without faith at all, but venturing, we would not have been enthusiastic about coming again. Yet, in the story Jesus told to illustrate the heart of God, the father runs to meet the prodigal. Jesus Himself says, 'Come to me!' The Holy Spirit invites, "Look to Jesus". There appeared to be little correlation, sadly, between the heart and compassion of the Trinity and the way in which these churches were, or were not, in fact, welcoming visitors. Surely, an appropriate welcome is basic and of huge value, and there is never a reason for it to be missing from any community of God's people.

In January 2010, it was time for us to return to BCC. We had missed being part of the church family, so you would think we would be 'over the moon' as the first Sunday approached. But we were not! I was particularly nervous. What was I nervous about? I cannot now remember specifics. But I was! Probably, it was recognising that everything would be different. How would I feel about it and how would we find our place, our new and very different place, in the life of the church? How would that work?

Well, it was absolutely fine of course! We were hugged and welcomed and deliberately sat in the back row. We looked around and there were quite a lot of people we didn't recognise. That was good! We were glad that, as before, new people were arriving and making BCC their home. We reached out to some people near us we didn't know. We welcomed them and asked how long they had been coming to BCC. When they asked us if we were new, we simply said something like, "Not really, but we have been away for a while." We had people asking us if we were new to the church, or how long we had been in the church on many occasions during our first year back at BCC and we were so glad. The church was reaching out to people they didn't know and welcoming them. It didn't matter in the slightest that they did not know our history at BCC.

But you may be thinking, " Come on, how was it really not to have any leadership role and to 'just' be one of the congregation? Well, let's answer these two questions in that order.

First of all, I can say, hand on heart, that I did not miss the lack of having any part in the leadership of the church.

I knew it had been God's time for me to bow out of those God-given privileges and responsibilities and I was full of thanksgiving for the years He had given me in that role. As I have said previously, I was also at peace that Roger was God's appointed successor to me. Would I always agree with all the decisions that he and the leadership team would take in the years ahead? No! But it was now their responsibility to lead the church in the way they believed God was directing them. After all, in my years leading the church, there were more than a few times when there were those who did not agree with some of my leadership decisions. That goes with the territory. My role now, as far as BCC was concerned, was to pray for Roger and the elders and staff team, share with them, when asked, any wisdom I might have and serve Christ and His church in any way that would help to build and strengthen this community of the redeemed. As I have continued to enjoy close trusting relationships with Roger and the leadership over the succeeding years, there have been ongoing opportunities for us to discuss the life and direction of the church together. But I do so in the glad knowledge that they now bear responsibility before God for the life, worship and witness of the church. And, as you will read, I have had the privilege of preaching and sharing in appropriate key events.

However, there was one thing I knew beforehand that I would miss very much, and I did, and that was preaching the Word of God Sunday by Sunday. To preach through a section of the Bible or follow a theme through week by week to the people God has given you is the greatest of privileges. Maureen and I both missed being part of the staff team. It was a great mixed-age and mixed-gender team and we found not being with them a real wrench. We also both missed pastoral and counselling involvement, one-on-one and two-on-two, which had been an integral element of our ministry. However, the Lord soon opened up many opportunities for us in those areas which will become apparent later.

But I think I hear someone asking: 'How did the church family deal with you still being around? Did they try to 'burn your ear' if they were unhappy with leadership decisions?' No, in the main that didn't happen very much, for which we were thankful. Only on a few occasions did Maureen and I have people asking us what we thought about issues they were not so sure about. In those situations, we suggested to them that they spoke to the elders or an appropriate staff member. They got the message and understood our need to stand aside.

Now for the second question: How was it 'just' to be a member of the congregation?

To answer that I have to go back to what I was saying at the beginning of this chapter concerning facing retirement with all its life changes. I mentioned then that if your identity is tied up with your working role; if that is the primary or only area in which your security, significance and self-worth is rooted, then that unhealthy identity environment in which you have been swimming, perhaps as a 'big fish', will result in you being like a fish out of water when you are no longer in that pool. Mercifully, my identity was not tied up with my role in church leadership. My primary identity was and is as a loved child of the Father. Subsidiary identities are as a loved husband, father and grandfather. So when the question comes: "How was it 'just to be a member of the congregation'?" I can respond: "it was OK." There was no trauma, no shaking of my personal foundations. An old song comes to mind, which may sound somewhat twee and yet:

"All may change, but JESUS NEVER, Glory to His Name".

The fact is that nothing is forever, except the love of Father, Son and Spirit. Working life and roles are not forever. My life with Maureen is not forever: we are at the time of life when we know that one of us will have to face the loss of the other and then live on without them. So the question of where our security is founded, our true identity, is crucial if we are to know, truly know, peace whatever our circumstances.

I am writing this eleven years after I became 'just' a member of the congregation at BCC. I can continue to say:

"It's been OK." There are many people in the church community now who do not have any relationship with me, or I with them; they would not have a clue that I ever led BCC. That is as it should be in a large and growing church.

Maureen and I have the joy of seeing people coming to faith and growing in God and others, who we have known for decades, continuing to enjoy God and His people and witness to His saving and keeping power.

A question for you. Is your identity primarily and securely in God, Father Son and Holy Spirit? Are you generously and consistently investing in your relationship with the Triune God, the only relationship you have which is a forever relationship? Apart from the glorious fact that living life this way is to know and experience the One who is the fairest among ten thousand, you will also find yourself echoing the words of the hymn writer:

"Through all the changing scenes of life,
    In trouble and in joy,
The praises of my God shall still
    My heart and tongue employ.

- (Nahum Tate 1652-1715 and Nicholas Brady 1659-1726)

✗

During the few days between Christmas 2009 and the new year, when things were quiet, I decided to have a look at a property website I had often heard mentioned but had no reason to consult previously. As I detailed in an earlier chapter, God had wonderfully enabled us to purchase the church manse as our own home, on which there was still a mortgage. There was therefore no rush to move, although we had decided that it would be wise to move to a smaller house at some point in the next year or two. So, more out of interest to see the website than seriously thinking of looking for somewhere, I turned on the computer and looked for bungalows in our area. To my surprise, there was a new-build chalet-bungalow at the end of our road. We both thought- that's strange. We had no recollection of ever seeing such a house. But the road where we had lived for these many years is a long one. So the next day we took a walk to that end of our road and discovered this house somewhat hidden away and just across the road from an attractive area of woodland where our family had often walked our lovely Labrador 'Shona' in years gone by. We decided to arrange to view it and immediately loved it. We had never looked for a house to buy before, so it was rather a strange experience. We decided it would be wise to look at a couple of other similar houses for sale in the area but ended up coming back to the one at the end of our road. We were able to purchase it later in January and discovered that the builder was a Christian about to retire and this was the final house he had built for sale. He had completed the house at the end of March 2009, exactly the time we concluded at BCC. Our home had been a lovely house in which to bring up our family, so we were glad to sell it to a young family from the church.

So now there was a panic to downsize before we moved in April. The panic was mine as I had accumulated so much paperwork over the years, not to mention books. I went through one shredder in the process and culled my bookshelves somewhat, most of the books going to the Moorlands College library or to the students. After so many years in our home, 32 to be precise, the leaving of it was, remarkably, not too emotive. We were just so thankful to God for the new home He had provided for us, which was more than we could ever have expected or even hoped for. The next few months were taken up with settling in and for me, enjoying re-arranging the garden.

Towards the end of 2009, Steve Brady and Colin Bennett, Principal and Vice-Principal of Moorlands College, had sounded Maureen and me out about becoming Chaplains at the College. I had resigned from the Board of Trustees in 2008 after serving for twenty years, so I knew the College and the staff well. There had been an obvious need for Chaplains for some years, but finance to employ someone was in short supply. We had told Steve and Colin that we were not making any decisions about our future until early 2010. As we thought and prayed it through, we believed this was something we could do, and that God was asking us to do. We commenced as Chaplains in September 2010 and continued through until 2014. Every Wednesday we made our way the seven miles to Moorlands just in time for lunch with the students and then spent the next hour with a different tutor group each week. The rest of the afternoon was taken up with individual students who had booked in to see us. Those extra years involved in the life of the College were a great privilege for us both, especially in the opportunity it gave us to journey with many students during those significant years in their lives. While studying at College, many of them were discovering that there were areas of their lives in which damage had been sustained. They came to recognise their need to forgive, receive healing and find their resources in God for the months and years ahead. There were those who were unsure of their identity in Christ and needed to find security in the character of God and His forever choice of them to be His children.

Bible colleges are drawing their students from a world where so many have suffered insecure and sometimes abusive childhoods and teenage years. They have been living in a society where God's pattern for life and living has been completely jettisoned in favour of living for self and for the moment and where nothing is off-limits. Living like that is dangerous and damaging for every kind of health, spiritual, mental, emotional, relational and psychological. Coming to faith does not automatically erase the impact of painful and often life-changing experiences. But being 'in Christ' and having the indwelling Holy Spirit, means that heaven's resources are available for everyone who will recognise and confess their need and then humbly come and ask. Over the years we have discovered that many Christians, be they new in the faith or on the journey for years, are unaware of the damage they have sustained, and which is hindering their experience of the fullness of life that Jesus promised to those who are His. Others are only too aware of their personal need and suffering but are unaware of how to access help. Church leaders and bible colleges have a responsibility to preach and teach in such a way that those who are in need realise they are not alone. Along with that they also have a responsibility to the Lord Jesus and to those in their care to provide the appropriate pastoral help. In other words, to ensure that those who have the God-given heart and gifts to help are available (and known to be available). There are times when we all need a 'skin face' to come alongside us and pray with us and for us as we come to Jesus, the great physician of our soul.

If people training for ministry in God's Kingdom are not helped into healing and health while training, they may well come to grief later and others too may suffer in the fall-out. We have witnessed this in a number of situations known to us and because of the world in which students live and in which they will be serving, the needs in this regard are only going to become greater.

Our primary area of ministry has been the local church and sad though we are to mention it, many leaders do not know their people enough to be able to recognise the issues which debilitate and hinder growth in holiness and joy. There is a very evident need in many congregations of God's people to hear preaching from the Word of God which teaches the fullness of the Christian's inheritance in Christ and the ministry of the Holy Spirit to lead them into that fullness. Then, of course, alongside anointed preaching, the provision of appropriate pastoral and prayer ministry is crucial.

On Sunday 28 November 2010 there was a very special thanksgiving service at BCC for the completion of the first phase of the refurbishment of the Gala Hall, now called the LIFEcentre. It was eighteen months since we had met for the first time in the Gala Hall and thanked God for His gift of the premises to us and now, here we were, able to use the LIFEcentre week by week. I was given the privilege of recounting the journey God had taken us on as a church which had brought us to this point. There were, of course, people who had come into the church over these months who did not know the story of God's wonderful provision.

Just a week or so later, Andrew, one of BCC's elders, and his wife Sheila moved to Kabul, Afghanistan where they were to serve until 2017. Andrew and Sheila had been at BCC since 1999 and around that time founded International Care Network (ICN) as a response to the arrival of five hundred asylum seekers and refugees in Bournemouth. Leviticus 19:34 was the seed which went on to grow the large tree of ICN:

> ▶ **The foreigner residing among you must be treated as your native-born. Love them as yourself, for you were foreigners in Egypt. I am the Lord your God.**
>
> ● **Leviticus 19:34 (NIV)**

Twenty years later, ICN has helped 4000 people of many different ethnic and language groups and has a staff of fifteen drawn from various local churches. Their work with asylum seekers and refugees brought Andrew and Sheila into contact with many Afghans and then, with God's heart and at His calling, they served in Afghanistan for seven years.

CHAPTER 21

Home and Away
2011 - 2012

2011 was going to be a memorable year for us, with some very special times and also two unexpected and sad events, one directly affecting our family. On Sunday 30th January, I participated in the morning service at BCC praying with the elders for Tim, as he was appointed an elder.

In March 2011 I was in Nepal for three weeks visiting two of BCC's overseas workers, Bill and Janet. Maureen didn't come with me as due to her renal condition we had decided some years previously that it would be unwise for her to travel to certain areas of the world. I had never been able to visit Bill and Janet since the church had commissioned and sent them out in 2005, so it was a great joy to spend time with them in situ in Kathmandu. It was so good to see the land they had purchased where they were developing an aquaponics business and on which two teams from BCC had worked in 2008. The training Bill and Janet were providing here for Nepali Christians would enable rural communities to improve their diet and to earn enough to support themselves. I was able to visit a Government orphanage, in which Janet was involved and where there was a great need for care and compassion. She had been a light in a dark place there for many young girls, some of whom it was a joy to meet.

It was a special privilege to be in Nepal. Growing up, we had many missionaries who stayed in our home in Aberdeen while they were speaking about their work overseas at various local churches and events. Some of these missionaries had been pioneers for the Gospel in Nepal and I remember looking at many slides of this amazing country, never imagining that one day I would be able to visit. In earlier years, there had been some who knew the call of God to Nepal, but at that time the country was still closed to the Gospel. So those missionaries had lived and worked on the northern border of India, praying for the nation to open and reaching Nepali's who crossed back and fore into India. Nepal joined the United Nations in 1955 and gradually the door opened for Christian missionaries to enter. There was a need for mission agencies to work together to gain admittance and so the United Mission to Nepal (UMN) was born.

One person I very much wanted to meet was Pastor Robert Karthak. I had often heard his name mentioned over the years from Regions Beyond Missionary Union personnel working in Nepal with the UMN. He was a pioneer church leader in those early years of the Gospel in Nepal and founded Gyaneshwor Church in the centre of Kathmandu. He was in his late eighties when we met and now, at the time of writing, he is in his nineties and still preaching. Bill and Janet belong to one of the churches planted out from Gyaneshwor and I worshipped with them there one Sunday. I met with Robert at his city-centre church. After reminiscing about some of the pioneer missionaries he had worked with, some of whom I had known well, he talked about the situation as it was now in 2011. Since that time, the church in Nepal has continued to grow, but it is under increasing pressure from Government restrictions and clampdowns, with expatriate Christian workers also finding it increasingly difficult to obtain permission to remain. But the church in Nepal is well-founded and a living witness to Christ in a nation where spiritual darkness is very evident.

While in Kathmandu it was also good to meet up with Phil, whose grandmother Joyce was a great encouragement to Maureen and me in our early years at BCC and who has been a long-term friend and intercessor for us both over the years. Phil was working with UMN and two years later I had the joy of preaching at his marriage to Pratiksha, who also served with UMN, at the English celebration of their wedding in Berkshire.

Kathmandu is an amazing city. Going pillion on Janet's scooter through the centre of the city was an experience to remember. I visited Patan Durbar Square in the heart of the city, full of ancient monuments, temples and shrines, a reminder, if needed, of the thick darkness which can only be penetrated and broken open by Jesus, the Light of the World. I had the very special opportunity to trek for four days with Bill and Janet in the Annapurna Himalayan Range above Pokhara. I cannot begin to describe the stunning mountain vistas or the sunrises and sunsets over the snows of the Annapurnas. Maureen and I had the privilege of visiting missionaries and Peruvian churches in the Andes in the 80s and 90s. Being back in another of the high places of the earth, the Nepali mountain people reminding me in many ways of the Quechuas in Peru, was another gift from our amazing Creator and Father.

I arrived back from Nepal at the end of March and two weeks later we celebrated Maureen's 70th birthday. I had set this up, amid tight security, before the Nepal visit. Maureen is not an email girl so I was able to send out invitations without her knowing and wonderfully, no one let the cat out of the bag. I had arranged, on the Saturday of her birthday, that we would use the large new cafe area at the BCC LIFEcentre, with refreshments available and people able to come and go during the afternoon. I told Maureen we were going out to celebrate her birthday and we set off in the car, without her having a clue where we were going. After a deliberately circuitous route, which caused her to guess our destination wrongly a few times, we ended up at the LIFEcentre and to her huge surprise and initial embarrassment, she was greeted by a crowd of family and friends.

In early July a dear friend died very unexpectedly and suddenly. John was away from home at the time, on his annual visit to his alma mater, Cambridge University. This was a very great shock for his wife Sandie. John, an exceptionally fine consultant surgeon, had come into our lives thirty years before. We had met in the early eighties, through our shared desire to see local church leaders working together. Our friendship grew and over the years John and I regularly enjoyed evening pub meals in the New Forest, sharing each other's lives and praying for one another and the church leaders across the area. I was privileged to lead and preach at his thanksgiving service on 19th July at Ringwood Parish Church, where John had often preached as a lay reader.

Three days before John's thanksgiving service, on Saturday 16 July, both my father and mother died. My parents had moved to Bournemouth many years before and lived just a mile from us. It was so good to be near to them and to be able to help them both in practical ways, especially when Dad had to enter hospital some weeks earlier, as he cared for my mother, whose dementia had slowly worsened in the two years since I retired from leading BCC.

The hospital indicated that my father would need care, as and when he left hospital and so we arranged for my mother to enter a local care home, which we thought would be just for a week or so until Dad joined her there. About a week later, Dad died in hospital. The same day, a few hours later, Mum died in the care home, without hearing that Dad had died and with no medical cause. I remember taking an early morning walk the next day, a Sunday, trying to come to terms with the suddenness of this totally unexpected situation.

I was blessed by God to have them as my parents. The influence of my father's integrity and my mother's love and their prayers for me from before I was born, provided a firm foundation for me in terms of personal security and stable family life.

At the time, you do not understand the huge value of such an inheritance, but you sure do as you move out into life and grow older. Most of all, through them I was exposed to the Gospel, biblical teaching and a home where men and women who loved and served Christ often came to stay.

We had a graveside service on a very beautiful summer's day. Then followed a Thanksgiving Service at their home church, not far from where they lived. My brother Philip and I shared our reflections on our parents' lives. To say goodbye to both parents on the same day was a tough one for us both. Maureen's grandparents, who had brought her up as their daughter, had died in Aberdeen many years before, as had Maureen's birth mother, to whom she had always been close. We were now the senior generation in both our families.

Twice in that year, 2011, I was in Scotland leading funeral and Thanksgiving services for friends who had died. One in January in Aberdeen and another in December in Edinburgh at our home church during the sixties, Charlotte Chapel. In fact, looking back now, in the eleven years since retirement I see that I have been involved in almost forty funeral and Thanksgiving services for those who have preceded us to heaven. I thank God for the friendships He has given Maureen and me over the years. Some of those who have gone before, were very dear, much-loved friends and we miss them. But how they have enriched our lives!

I mentioned my involvement with Alex Buchanan and his initiative in bringing church leaders together. After my years in Blokes 3 with Alex and then the experience of leading Blokes 3 myself until 2008, I had a strong desire to facilitate something similar for church leaders in this region. As I have referred to previously, for many years before we retired Maureen and I had the privilege of meeting regularly with younger local church leaders and their wives in a mentoring context. We believed this was something we should pursue and so in January 2012 I commenced Blokes South, after Alex's model that had blessed and helped me.

I began with five men. Maureen and I had been meeting up with them and their wives for some years. Within a few months, those five men had suggested fellow church leaders who wanted to participate and we were at what I believed to be the maximum workable number of ten. Bournemouth YMCA had recently bought a large house in Studland, a few miles from Bournemouth on the road to Swanage in the area known as The Purbecks. It proved ideal for us in that it was not far to travel for most of the men, but it was a world away from our usual urban area. We met three times a year from 10am Monday until lunchtime Tuesday. We worshipped and heard from the Word of God at the outset and ended on Tuesday sharing communion together. Monday evening, we would go out for a pub meal together. The rest of the time, one by one, we shared our lives together and prayed for one another.

Maureen began to meet with the wives of these church leaders, again three times a year, but usually only for a day rather than overnight. Girls South was their name – perhaps 'girls' is a euphemism, but there you are. In 2015 I commenced Blokes South 2. The men in Blokes South 1 had colleagues leading other churches who were keen to join us, but we were at our maximum of ten. Other church leaders had also contacted me, enquiring if I was going to commence another group. So Blokes South 2 began and there were now twenty leaders in the two groups, from churches in Wiltshire, Hampshire and Dorset. Maureen also commenced Girls South 2 for the wives. It had been such a joy to see how quickly the men, (women have always been better at this!), many of whom did not know each other, sharing their lives with one another. Church leaders have an ongoing need of a safe and confidential place where they can unload about their own personal lives, their marriage, family and church situations. But not only unload. They need a place where they are accepted and valued and will receive counsel, prayer and ongoing steady loving commitment from those who are their peers.

Through my involvement with these men, there have been many opportunities to preach in their churches and spend time with them and their leadership teams. Maureen has often commented to me, when we have heard both husband and wife speak about an issue, 'you sometimes wonder if it is the same issue!' That will not surprise you if you are married. Hence the value of being able to work together in this situation, as we did as Chaplains at Moorlands College and indeed as we did for years at BCC. This has been and continues to be a rare privilege for us both. We are so thankful to God for the quality and passion of these couples, whom He has called to lead His church in these days. Sadly, we have known too many church leaders whose marriages and/or ministries have been broken. How we long that Alex Buchanan's model of consistently gathering groups of leaders to journey together and pray and support one another was operating all across the UK.

In May 2012 I again had the opportunity to make a visit to someone from BCC working for Jesus overseas. Jonathan, whom I had known since he was but a lad, had commenced two years of training with Youth With A Mission (YWAM) in Singapore in 2010. Now he was with YWAM in Myanmar (Burma) on their School of Frontier Mission, involved in teaching English, evangelism and discipleship. I had arranged to spend some days with him, based in the capital Yangon (Rangoon).

However, there were other reasons which also contributed to bringing this visit to SE Asia together. For some years I had known a pastor from Bangalore, India. We first met at the Life in the Spirit Conferences, referred to in an earlier chapter and he had preached at BCC. Samson had invited me to visit his church, to preach one weekend and to speak at a pastors' conference the following week. As I was thinking about Myanmar and Bangalore, I also realised it provided an opportunity to visit my nephew, Duncan, who at that time was working with a charity, Water Aid, just north of Delhi. I planned to combine these three visits and suggested to Stuart, our younger son, that he might come with me to spend time with Duncan and Jonathan.

Stuart and I flew to Bangkok, Thailand via Delhi and enjoyed two days together exploring that fascinating city, its river artery and the remarkable 1782 Grand Palace, not to forget Thai kick-boxing, which we discovered as we were looking for somewhere to eat on our first evening. On the third day, we were at the airport early for a 6.30am flight to Myanmar, where Jonathan met us. During the five days we were with him, we were able to see something of the faded colonial splendour that was Yangon. Stuart and I stayed in an amazing lakeside hotel built by the Russians many years before. It too had a rather fading glory. However, since then Myanmar has become a popular tourist destination and we would not be able to afford to stay at that hotel now.

Just along the lakeside from the hotel was Aung San Suu Kyi's home (pronounced: Ang Sang Su Chee). We drove past the house on a number of occasions and the crowds outside left you in no doubt as to her popularity with the people of Myanmar. At that time, 2012, Aung San Suu Kyi had been in some form of detention or another since 1989. She was referred to by the people as 'Mother' due to her years of attempts to bring democracy to this nation, ruled by the military. Her detention ceased soon after we were in Myanmar and she received the Nobel Peace Prize in recognition of her fight for democracy. However, this democracy icon has slipped from grace since then, due to her defence of the accusations against Myanmar for their treatment of the Rohingya Muslim people. The military is accused of crimes against the Rohingya, who fled over the border to Bangladesh and now live in their tens of thousands in one of the largest refugee camps in the world.

However long before the Rohinga persecution hit the news, the military government has had a decades-long history of oppressing the mainly Christian ethnic people groups of the Karen, Kachin and Chin and it continues to this day.

I had the opportunity of joining the Myanmar YWAM team, spending time with their team leader and sharing the Word of God with them. They are involved in many varied ministries in Yangon, including a clinic and HIV centre and English language classes. Jonathan and I had valuable time together and talked and prayed about his future, as he was due to leave Myanmar in the not-too-distant future. In fact, five months later, in October, I had the joy of marrying Jonathan to Su Jin at BCC! Jonathan met Su Jin while with YWAM in Singapore and they have gone on to serve God together on staff with YWAM in Singapore, then in leading a YWAM base in South Korea, Su Jin's home nation. In 2018 they moved to live in Okinawa, Japan, where they are language learning and building community through various outreaches, home gatherings and evangelism.

While in Yangon, it was a joy to meet a local pastor, who I had been in touch with for some years, initially through a mutual friend. He leads a church in Yangon, is a teacher/trainer who also does remarkable work outside the capital. He travels to neglected rural areas, where he sets up discipling and training schools for young people who have come to Christ so that they can reach their own people with the Gospel. I have continued to be in close touch with him and his strategic ministry in this very needy Buddhist nation.

After five days with Jonathan, Stuart and I flew via Bangkok to Delhi, India where Stuart's cousin Duncan met us. We were then driven by a friend of Duncan's to Jaipur, an interesting introduction to Indian driving and Indian roads. Jaipur, with a population of three million, is the capital and largest city in the State of Rajasthan. Apart from an unscheduled weekend in Delhi, when returning home from our sabbatical in Asia in1991, I had no experience of India, nor had Stuart. Duncan had suggested a few nights in Jaipur, then train back to Delhi. We three stayed in a hostel, which was a tall, narrow building with the cheapest open-air eating place you can imagine on the roof-top. The food was amazing and the eating area was decorated with more lights than you could throw a stick at. Gazing out over the rooftops, on sultry evenings, with all the sounds drifting up from the streets below, was just the ticket.

The next day, we took a tuk-tuk, an auto-rickshaw or motorised rickshaw, to the Amber Palace, a 16th-century hill-top fort just outside Jaipur. There was the opportunity to take an elephant ride up to the fort and we did, three of us on three elephants. The rudimentary seating mechanism, which was supposed to hold you fast, broke loose soon after my elephant began to move. As the elephant made its ponderous way up the hill road to the Fort, I was seriously concerned about being thrown over the wall into the lake far below. Stuart and Duncan appeared somewhat amused at my predicament and my futile attempts to attract the attention of the young man who was walking with the elephant. It was certainly one for the memory bank. By the by, the Amber Palace and Fort are well worth visiting, but I would suggest perhaps giving the elephants a miss.

We had two full days in Jaipur, in the searing heat, but then it was a 5am start to catch the train to Delhi, which was a fascinating experience both in terms of the in-carriage population and the passing scenes through the window. We were in Delhi by 11am and in the afternoon we visited the Red Fort and generally explored the centre area. The widespread begging and the sight of so many seriously disabled people were distressing. The next day I was due to fly south to Bangalore, so it was time to say goodbye. Stuart had another day with Duncan in Delhi, then he had to fly home as his two weeks of holiday from work were up. I arrived in Bangalore in the early afternoon, to be met on the airport concourse by Samson and two young men from his church holding high a welcome banner, much to my embarrassment.

They took me for a Chinese meal, at which point Samson told me I would be speaking at a youth gathering that evening. There were about eighty young people present. I spoke from 2 Timothy 1:6-10, 'Fan into flame the gift of God'. There was a great sense of the presence of God, with many receiving prayer. The two Sunday morning services at 7am and 9.30am were packed out, downstairs and upstairs. I preached from Song of Songs 2:14. Queues of people waited for prayer. Immediately following praying for so many, Samson took me to preach at a much smaller church nearby, where the church and pastor were going through some tough times. Samson was seeking to help and support that church and other similar weaker causes. After a meal, it was time for the evening service at 6pm, with three hundred present, perhaps half the numbers of the morning services. Again, the hunger for God was so very evident. Late evening, I called Maureen. It was good to know that Stuart was back home safely.

Samson's father, who I was able to meet, founded the church. 99% are converts from Hinduism. There is a very special anointing on him, including the gift of healing. In fact, many of those who now worship at the church first came to him because of their physical needs and having received prayer and healing in the Name of Jesus, subsequently came to faith in Christ.

The Pastors' Conference began on Monday. There were about 120 church leaders present. I preached that day from Colossians 1:24 - 2:3, on the theme of 'Suffering and joy in the life and ministry of a church leader.' It was a privilege to spend time in many one-to-one and group conversations. In the evening, Samson took four of the young leaders and me out for a Thai meal. It was stimulating to see and hear their passion for Jesus and desire to see God moving powerfully in their city. I heard accounts of the suffering of many believers. Persecution, including beatings and killings, are not uncommon, especially in rural areas. Since my visit and the arrival of the Narendra Modi Government in 2014, with its radical Hindu power base, the persecution and suffering of Christians and Muslims have ramped up considerably.

Tuesday was one of the church's regular prayer and fasting days. As we arrived at the church premises, there were over a hundred, on their knees, crying out to God, praising and worshipping, all at the same time. Later I spoke from Matthew 6 and Isaiah 58 on prayer and fasting. Then one after another prayed, standing or kneeling and as each prayer was being offered, all would speak their 'Amen'. My attention was drawn to one woman and as I did that verse came to mind, "She who has been forgiven much, loves much". I asked Samson's father about her afterwards. He told me that she had been set free from many demons, bound up with her Hinduism and he said, "Her love for Jesus and gratitude to Him knows no bounds."

There followed what seemed a never-ending line of people who were coming for healing, some for pains and sicknesses and some for family members, especially husbands. It is the first time I have ever sat on a chair to pray for people, but that is what Samson and his father suggested I did. They knew this was going to take some time. After a meal at Pizza Hut, then an hour's sleep, I spoke at a men's meeting in the evening. There were about seventy, mostly between the ages of twenty and forty. I loved their unaccompanied singing, one man leading off and then the others joining in, clapping all the while. It reminded me, just a little, of singing in the Free Church of Scotland in the Highlands. The precentor will start with the first line, there being no instruments of any kind, then the congregation will follow. There the comparison definitely ends. Definitely no clapping in the Free Church of Scotland. Prayer followed, the men being as noisy as the women, then more praise, with all arms lifted high.

The next day, I had lunch with Samson's parents and heard more about the work of God in the founding of the church. Then Samson gave me a tour of Bangalore and I prepared for the flight home the next day. Samson is no longer a bachelor! He is now married to Shiby, they have two children and he continues to lead this vibrant gospel church and its outreach into many surrounding districts. The situation for churches and pastors in India continues to become more hazardous and leaders like Samson need our prayers.

In my earlier visit to Nepal in 2011 and now in this visit to Myanmar and India, I have referred to the growing political pressures on the church in these nations and also the increasing level of persecution Christians are suffering.

I hope I am wrong in what I am about to say, but I think it is more than possible that the church in the UK is by and large ignorant of the conditions under which so many of their brothers and sisters are living in other nations. In the history of Christianity, there has never been a time when the worldwide church of Jesus Christ has been subject to opposition and persecution as it is today. Are UK Christians aware of this? If they are aware, is it simply a general knowledge of that fact or is there any detail to their awareness?

How would most Christians in the UK hear about the conditions of the Church in other nations? A comparative few would hear through overseas mission periodicals and a few via broadsheet newspapers or the radio/television news, whether accessed by traditional means or by their phone. But clearly, the major route by which people who love Jesus will hear detail that would provide prayer fuel would be through their local church. That is where I fear there is a breakdown, which has led to what I believe to be a severe ignorance of the conditions in which brothers and sisters are living across the world. Does your local church provide information about the suffering church and does the leadership encourage and seek to stimulate individual and corporate prayer in this regard? For some years I have used an excellent resource for information and prayer produced by the Barnabas Fund, which provides hope and aid for the persecuted church. Their bi-monthly prayer diary provides daily information on the suffering church. The current issue I am using refers to the conditions of believers in thirty-five nations from every area of our world. In this free publication is information that can serve individual or small group prayer, and provide, for church leaderships, accurate and up-to-date information with which to help the people of God they lead to fulfil their responsibility to God and to His suffering people.

> ▶ **Continue to remember those in prison as if you were together with them in prison, and those who are mistreated as if you yourselves were suffering.**
>
> ● **Hebrews 13:3 (NIV)**

> ▶ **I urge you, brothers and sisters, by our Lord Jesus Christ and by the love of the Spirit, to join me in my struggle by praying to God for me. Pray that I may be kept safe...**
>
> ● **Romans 15:30-31 (NIV)**

Barnabas Fund: 9 Priory Row, Coventry CV1 5EX
Email: info@barnabasfund.org

Soon after I returned home from India, Maureen and I set off by car for a holiday in Italy. Over the years we have often visited France in the summer and enjoyed three weeks in a mobile home on a campsite, but this was our first visit to Italy. We took our time driving through France including a weekend at one of our favourite places in France, Annecy.

The town is set on the shores of the beautiful lake of the same name which lies at the foot of towering mountains to the east. There are innumerable cafes by the river that runs through the town and feeds into the lake.

We had rented a self-catering flat just a couple of miles from Lake Garda. The Italian Lakes are stunning! We enjoyed exploring Lake Garda which has pleasure boats crisscrossing the Lake, from which there are superb vistas in every direction. So many picturesque lakeside towns, with seemingly endless tree-lined promenades and glorious flowering oleander everywhere. The drive back to France and home led through the Mont Blanc Tunnel to Chamonix, where some years before while staying in Annecy, we took the lift to the top of the mountain.

We were thankful for time away together. In the three years since we retired, life had become busy. We were glad to be involved in what we believed God wanted us to do, but valued weeks away at our mobile home in Aberdeenshire and the kind of holiday we had just enjoyed. Early on, after we had retired, we had decided together that I would limit preaching away from BCC to twice a month, as we wanted to keep our roots in the church well-watered. I was also preaching at BCC from time to time and we were both involved in pastoral situations. It was also good to be able to continue our relationship with Moorlands College by preaching at College Chapel and lecturing on various occasions. But if you added in weddings and funerals, leading church weekends and the many times we spent with people in need of some kind or another, life was certainly as busy as we wanted.

Having been in church leadership in the area for well over thirty years, there were many different situations where it was thought we might be able to help. In 2010 we had been approached by the elders of a church who needed ongoing help and counsel. We met with the leadership on a regular basis and I was involved in preaching there regularly. Our involvement with that church community continued for about seven years. About a year or so later, another church, who were encountering some difficulties, asked us to step in and help in a similar way. In both of these church situations, our involvement continued until new pastoral leadership had been appointed.

I had been involved as a trustee for Christian charities of all kinds over the years, but I was now gradually reducing those commitments. There were only a few at this stage and one was International Care Network (ICN), in connection with its founders, Andrew and Sheila Muir. Their move to Afghanistan found another BCC member, Andrew Barber, taking the helm of leadership at ICN from 2011 to 2014 when he and his wife Mi Jung and their family moved to live and work overseas. The other charity I was still involved with was the Oaks Counselling Service. For many years, leaders and people from other churches would contact Maureen and me, enquiring if we would be available to see people with presenting issues or suggest others who may be able to help. There was a very evident need for such a service in the area. In 2000 The Oaks was birthed and has provided a channel through which many people, with varying needs, have been helped by qualified Christian counsellors.

CHAPTER 22

Full Circle

2013 – 2020

Two special family events were to feature in 2013. In February our daughter Fiona was married to Steve in Hampshire. Fiona qualified as a counsellor in 2012 and is a pastoral staff member in a Hampshire college. At the time of writing, she is under huge pressure at work from the rising tide of mental health issues among teenagers during the COVID pandemic. Social media has a lot to answer for in this regard. Her description of the lack of wise and loving parental relationships in the lives of many of these youngsters provide a deeply concerning insight into the family breakdown in our nation.

In September Maureen and I celebrated our golden wedding anniversary! We had booked a New Forest country hotel for the day. The weather was superb and it was very special for us to have all our family and some close friends celebrate with us. It was one of those times which appear to come with increasing rapidity as the years pass, when you cannot believe how old you are until you look at your children and grandchildren. We have so very much for which to thank God.

During the next two years, we lost three of those friends who had been present on that special day, David, Jean and Val. Their going to heaven was glory for them, but a severe loss for their loved ones and for us. David had been our best man and I had been his.

He and I had first met at a holiday at Capernwray Christian Holiday Centre when we were both teenagers. Maureen felt the loss of Jean and Val particularly. Friends you make when you are younger are not easily replaced as you get older. Jean came to Christ within our first year at BCC. She had an immediate appetite for the Bible and for books that would aid her growth in God. She was a woman of prayer, wisdom and grace. At bible college, I was told that the pastor and his wife should never have close friends in the congregation. I understand why that advice was given to us as students, but it is not always necessarily wisdom from heaven. It depends on the people and situations concerned and most importantly, listening to the Holy Spirit. Jean and Maureen became friends. Maureen could tell Jean anything about her own struggles and frustrations and knew Jean would never repeat anything, ever. And Jean, like a true friend, would tell Maureen what she needed to hear. In March 2014, BCC gathered, with her family and we celebrated her life and testimony to Jesus.

Much earlier in this journey, I mentioned the Clan: four couples whose friendship began while the men were at London Bible College, (now London School of Theology). One of those couples, Keith and Val, had recently moved to Braintree, Essex and later Keith was invited to lead a church in the town. In January 2014 I preached at their welcome service. In June 2015 Val died after a brief illness. She was one of Maureen's best friends outside of Bournemouth and they had known each other for 45 years. As with Jean, Maureen and Val could talk to each other with no holds barred. Val was straightforward, feisty, in the good way I love about Maureen. Val walked with Jesus. Just eighteen months since I had preached at their welcome service, Maureen and I were both speaking at the thanksgiving service for her life.

Our time as Chaplains at Moorlands College concluded at Easter 2014 and something I never thought I would witness took place: Maureen spoke to the student body, with the lecturers present, at the weekly Chapel Service which marked our farewell. That was a first – and she would say, definitely a last!

At the beginning of 2014, I began to be aware that one of my hips was becoming increasingly painful. We were due to be in Portugal in the early summer for the marriage of a couple from BCC. As I had agreed to conduct the ceremony, I decided to have my hip condition investigated, as if I was not going to be able to marry them, the sooner they were aware of that the better. I was told that it was a rapidly deteriorating condition, which I had gathered by the pain. I would need a new hip. Sadly, we were not able to share in their wedding and I had my new hip fitted the first few days in June. I was only in hospital for three days, but it was the first hospital stay since my tonsils were extracted as a lad. I am so thankful to God that my health has been so robust over the years, especially when Maureen's health has been much less assured.

I mentioned previously that Tim, who had come to BCC for his third-year placement while at Moorlands College and had subsequently joined the staff team, had been appointed an elder in 2010. His intention, after his third-year placement with us, had been to serve God in Zambia. God's timing for Tim and Zambia was not then, but in 2014, having been on staff for some years, and securing his MA through the London School of Theology, Tim moved to the north of Zambia to teach at Fiwale Hill Bible College, not far from the large mining city of Ndola. Tim invited me to come to visit him and speak at the bible college's annual alumni conference in July 2015. I did not need a second invitation. I flew to Lusaka, the capital of Zambia, via Dubai and Tim met me at the airport. Ndola, the nearest city to the bible college, was about a five-hour drive north from Lusaka and on the way we visited the cafe and extensive bookshop attached to Operation Mobilisation's centre in the country.

Fiwale Hill Bible College is in a rural area, about four miles down a dusty road, just off the main highway. Tim was teaching mainly biblical studies, plus some hermeneutics and systematic theology. The conference lasted over five days and it was a privilege to teach from Matthew 5 on the subject of the Kingdom of God, drawing out the implications of Kingdom living from the Beatitudes. The student body attended all the sessions and it was particularly helpful to me to hear from those who had been through the College and were leading churches, both urban and rural. It became clear that much of the television ministry that many Christians in Zambia were listening to was pushing a 'prosperity gospel' and that this was having a deleterious impact on many believers and distressing many of these pastors. This is perhaps one of the major challenges to the church in Zambia. Indeed, when I was in Lusaka later, I was able to see some of the huge, overly expensive and ornate buildings, which those who were preaching this 'gospel' had erected in recent years.

The growth of Islam in Zambia was also very evident and my return journey to Dubai found me on an aircraft, the majority of whose passengers were devoted followers of the Prophet. The men were unrestrained in their washing rituals in the men's washrooms prior to the flight. But perhaps even more concerning than the preaching of a prosperity gospel and the growth of Islam was the legalism in conservative churches and the resistance to and fear of the work of the Holy Spirit. Not too dissimilar a situation, then, to the presenting attitudes in many conservative evangelical churches in the UK when I came out of bible college in the seventies.

On the Sunday following the conference week I preached at Ndola Christian Fellowship, where Tim worshipped and often preached himself. The congregation was comprised of a fair number of expatriates working in the mining industry, missionaries such as Tim and of course, Zambians from Ndola and the surrounding area.

After I had told Tim I would be able to come to speak at the College, he had asked me if I could stay on for another week.

If so, he said he would take a week's holiday and we could travel together. As with his original invitation, I was delighted with the idea. We drove south to Lusaka and stayed overnight at a Christian guest house. The next day, continuing south, we drove the seven hours to Livingstone and the Zimbabwe border. I enjoy road travel, especially through geography that is entirely new to me. It had been good to be able to see something of the area around Fiwale and Ndola at times during the conference week, especially a couple of visits to a small safari park, Nsobe, where we escaped for a couple of hours of peace (and steak!) by the beautiful lake. But the further we drove south from Lusaka, the more the landscape changed. Less flat and agricultural, more hills and much less population in evidence. More of what I tend to think of as an African landscape, where you expect the head of an exotic animal to appear at any moment above the long grass. Many trees too, with their leaves turning brown, the rains having ceased in April. The vegetation was drying up at pace.

Livingstone, named after David Livingstone, the Scottish missionary and explorer, is situated on Zambia's southern boundary, with Zimbabwe to the south-east and Botswana to the south-west. The mighty Zambezi River marks the border. The next day we enjoyed exploring Livingstone, especially having coffee and chocolate cake in the grounds of a hotel immediately overlooking the Zambezi. But as good as chocolate cake and coffee are, the sight of the Victoria Falls, which Livingstone named after Queen Victoria, was breathtaking. The month of July, when we were there, was reckoned to be the best time of year to see the Falls, as the flow of water is less in the dry season. If there is too much water, the excess mist and spray tend to minimise your ability to see the stunning vista. The native people described the Falls to Livingstone as 'the water that thunders'. We walked a little above the Falls, where you were safe, just. We sat on a rock near where the Zambezi crashes over into the void and marvelled.

Could you top that experience? Tim had said he wanted to gift me a day on safari and although such an experience had never been on my bucket list, it was memorable. (Ever since then, when there is a programme on TV about elephants, I have to see it!) The next morning, we drove about an hour to a point on the Zambia/ Botswana border. We crossed the Zambezi on quite a small craft, guardedly watching the hippos cavorting in the river, then on to Chobe National Park in Botswana, where the guide met us. Tim and I were his only guests that day, so we could ply him with questions at any point. We saw so many animals, including giraffe, zebra, cape buffalo, antelopes, warthogs and crocodiles and many varieties of exotic birds, but as I have mentioned, the elephants stole the show for me. In the afternoon we were out on the Chobe River with the guide, watching family groups of elephants crossing right in front of us.

In the evening, back in Livingstone, we drove down to the Zambezi again. I had heard people eulogise about evenings in Africa. I had been privileged to often visit South America and Asia, but this was my first taste of Africa and I now knew what they meant. There had been an evening the previous week in Fiwale when we had a meal with a family and afterwards Tim and I had walked the short distance to his home. I looked up at the Southern sky and it was a stunning sight I will always remember. The other African evening that was stored in the memory bank was this one, down by the banks of the Zambezi. Quite a number of people were sitting around eating and drinking in the sultry air, lazily watching the sun chasing the horizon. It was the place where passengers boarded or embarked from river craft providing tourists with sunset cruises. We sat and enjoyed pizza and beer, watching the river and the hippos, while the sky changed from pink to deep crimson, to black sprinkled with sparkling diamonds.

The next day we drove north to Lusaka and the airport: Dubai and Heathrow for me and Fiwale Hill Bible School for Tim. The following year, 2016, Tim moved to Kaniki Bible University, also near Ndola, to teach similar subjects plus eschatology. Both at Fiwale and Kaniki, Tim's biblical input and opportunity to speak into those issues I have mentioned, and many others which were and still are facing the Zambian Church, was a gift from God to those training for church leadership in the nation. In early 2018 Tim returned to Bournemouth and took up the post of Teaching Pastor at BCC.

On 28 April 2016, our first great-grandchild arrived. Lydia Grace, born to our granddaughter, Lucy. We couldn't believe that we had a great-grandchild! Surely, we cannot be that old?! Lydia was and continues to be a delight. We had the joy of participating in her dedication at the local Vineyard Church.

For some months Maureen had become increasingly breathless. In one sense this was not too surprising as it was one of the symptoms of her exceptionally low renal function. Maureen was now at stage five renal failure, which is the final stage before dialysis. However, the renal consultant's opinion was that this level of breathlessness was down to more than her renal condition. He recommended that we arrange to see a heart specialist and that resulted in Maureen having an angiogram. During that procedure, Maureen suffered a stroke and ended up on the cardiac ward of Bournemouth Hospital. The stroke primarily affected her balance and mobility. She was told later that the result of the angiogram had been that she needed four stents to ease the blood flow in some of her arteries. The consultant warned that having the stents fitted could cause another stroke. Maureen decided to proceed, and that procedure went ahead without harm. Thank you, Lord. It took some months, but, generally, Maureen recovered very well from the stroke and of course, her breathing was easier.

While Maureen was in hospital, Peter was a patient at the same time. Peter, you may remember, was a member of staff and an elder for some years at BCC. He and his wife Linda pioneered the planting out of our second congregation in 1992. While visiting Maureen I was also able to visit Peter and one day, to Maureen's amazement, he was at the end of her bed visiting her! Peter had had a serious health condition for many years: in fact, that is how he and I first met. A relative of Peter had asked if I would visit him in hospital. At that time, in 1983, he was not a Christian, but a few months later he began to come to church and soon came to faith in Christ. Within two months of Maureen and Peter being in hospital, Peter died. He was only 57 and was the first of a number of brothers and sisters at BCC, who God took to Himself very much earlier than we would have expected. Our heart went out to his wife Linda and the family. I had the privilege of preaching at the Thanksgiving Service for Peter's life. I mentioned earlier that almost every month since we retired from leading BCC, we were saying goodbye to co-labourers from these years together, or to dear friends who had been in the church or whom we knew from other situations. As Maureen began to comment around this time and even more since then, "I think we now know more people in heaven than we do on earth."

Each year we made the 600-mile journey by road to visit our mobile home in Aboyne, Aberdeenshire. Usually, we were there somewhere around Easter and then in late August, each time for about 4/5 weeks. By this time, it was ten years since we had bought our Scottish retreat and we so enjoyed being able to spend time back in the area where we were both born and raised. The site is a small, privately owned, caravan park situated by a small loch around which is a very pleasant walk from which you can catch sight of Mount Keen, the most easterly of the "Munros", the name given to the 282 mountains in Scotland which are over 3000 ft. There are many trees, some of which are tall Caledonian pines, the occasional red squirrel and a great variety of birds. As there are no entertainment facilities or shops on site most of those who own the mobile homes are in the older age group, like us. So, it is quiet which suits us down to the ground. There are many other walks available alongside the nearby River Dee. There is also the old railway line, which is now a fantastic walking and cycling path, that used to run from Aberdeen to Ballater and carried the Royal Family on the last leg of their journey to their summer retreat at Balmoral Castle. Of course, you are also only a couple of miles from The Cairngorms National Park, a vast area of natural beauty and high mountains.

In September 2017, while we were in Aboyne, Roger, who followed me as senior pastor at BCC when I retired in 2009, was in contact to tell us that the condition of Sarah, his wife, had worsened. Knowing that Sarah was very ill, we had said to Roger before we went north a few weeks earlier, that we would come back at any time. I wrote about Sarah at the time that she and Roger came on staff at BCC in 1997. Sarah was first diagnosed with cancer in 2000 but had never let her condition hold her back from living life well for Jesus. You only truly knew Sarah, if you knew her in the context of her love for Jesus and the children and youth to whom she gave herself unreservedly.

We returned to Bournemouth. Sarah passed into the presence of her Lord on 12 October. I preached at BCC on Sunday morning 15 October from John 14:1-6 and led the committal service on 23 October. The Thanksgiving Service for her life and ministry was later the same day at BCC. It was, in every sense of the word, a Celebration. The ground floor worship area of the LIFEcentre had been creatively and beautifully decorated and was full to overflowing. So many had come to thank God for the gift of Sarah and to stand with and support Roger, and their daughter Emma and son Joshua.

N

In May 2018 Maureen and I were able to have a holiday again in Sarasota, on the Gulf of Mexico coast of Florida. Through the generosity and kindness of our long-standing friends here in Bournemouth we had visited their condo on a number of occasions over the years and those holidays had always been such a blessing to us both. The property is on an 11-mile long, off-shore, outlying island, which you reach by crossing three bridges from the mainland. It was nine years since we had been there; in fact, our last visit had been the summer we had retired from BCC. You can see the ocean from the apartment, walking there in just a couple of minutes. Those miles of beaches are only accessible to residents so, walking the shore is a quiet delight. An amazing variety of shells and birds of every kind: sandpipers, egrets, herons, oyster-catchers and the rather superb, surface-of-the-sea-skimming pelicans. Many are the times while leading BCC when I walked this beach and talked with the Lord. There was one particular occasion when the Lord helped me to open my hands and release to Him a very strategic issue that I so much wanted to sort out myself. In due time, in His way, God sorted it, wonderfully of course! That stretch of shore is for me a precious place. I often thought of Hudson Taylor, walking the beach at Brighton and hearing God speak to him about workers for inland China.

Maureen is not really a beach person. But there are so many beautiful places away from the beach, but nearby, where you can sit in the shade, with the water lapping at your feet and gaze out over the inland waterways between the island and the mainland, soaking in the beauty or reading a good book. One of our favourite places to visit is the Marie Selby Botanical Gardens. They sit alongside Sarasota Bay, with its tidal lagoons and views of the great sweep of the inland waterway. The display of wild orchids in the Gardens is truly amazing. There is also The Ringling, combining the home of the Ringling Circus Museum and the largest university art centre in the USA, all situated in sixty-six acres of grounds and gardens with spectacular views of the Bay.

We have always worshipped at The Tabernacle Church when we have been in Sarasota. It has an interesting Bournemouth connection. I mentioned earlier that in 2003, as part of a sabbatical, we did a house exchange with the pastor and his wife, who were born and brought up in Bournemouth. Neville and Lorette had moved to the USA in their twenties and Neville had led the Tabernacle with vision and energetic faithfulness for thirty-one years, retiring just a little before I did. So on this visit, in May 2018, we worshipped again at The Tabernacle and it included Pentecost Sunday. The service was led by an anointed worship leader and the pastor, who had succeeded Neville, spoke into the theme of the day with clarity, grace and power. The last time we had visited in 2009 Dr R.T. Kendall (Westminster Chapel, London 1977-2002) had been preaching. It had been good to see and hear him again, after having benefitted from his ministry in the UK and the many books he has authored.

In 2015, our older son Kevin had moved from Bournemouth to the Midlands. He worships in an excellent Assemblies of God church, just north of Coventry. Through his work, he met Angela and they were married at their church in September 2018. It was a glorious day and the reception was held in a country hotel a few miles away. Kevin's family, Daniel, Laura and Lucy (our grandchildren) from his marriage to Debbie were there and Lydia, Lucy's daughter, our great-granddaughter, now two years old.

As you have been following our journey, you will have recognised that two of our three children were married when we were leading BCC. But as you have read on, you will have realised that both our elder son and our daughter have remarried. It's a truth that 'no one is an island'. The conclusion of these two marriages has brought pain to the four people directly involved and of course to their children and parents. How often have we heard friends of our generation comment sadly on the totally unexpected turn of events that have touched their children's lives – and therefore theirs too. Never for a moment did we imagine that our son and daughter and their children would walk this road. It was so sad to see the impact on them and to experience our own subsequent loss. We are so very thankful to God for His limitless love which knows no boundaries and provides grace and forgiveness.

March 2019 brought us to the milestone of ten years since that memorable handing over of the mantle of leadership of BCC to Roger. During those years Roger had lost Sarah, the love of his life and partner in ministry. Only he knows how tough his personal road has been, but his testimony to God's sustaining and empowering grace has been clear to all of us. The refurbishment of the LIFEcentre has long since been completed, but in the last few years, an internal staircase has now been erected in the main auditorium to provide ease of access between the ground and the gallery areas. The worship and ministry of the church community continue to give testimony to the grace of our Lord Jesus Christ and His Gospel.

I have been writing during the COVID-19 pandemic. Maureen and I are so grateful to God for these past eleven years when, in response to our question to Him in 2009, "What now, Lord?" He has given us the joy of continuing to walk with Him and share His love and compassion with others. As Steve Farrar said in his book 'Finishing Strong', 'it's not how you start that matters. It's how you finish'. Psalm 92:14 talks about "bearing fruit in old age... staying fresh and green." It has been our desire to be just that in this season of life and to continue to speak out the testimony of v15, 'The Lord is upright; he is my Rock...'

The key principles we referred to in chapter two remain as wisdom for the journey. They are just as relevant now as they have been while we have been learning them from the Lord over these five decades. It is 50 years since I graduated from London School of Theology, when it was London Bible College and since I was ordained at Charlotte Chapel, Edinburgh. It is fifty years since I commenced at Westbourne Grove Baptist Church in Notting Hill, London. The changes in society and in ways of 'doing church' have been many and varied and have altered life in many remarkable and unexpected ways. When you are living through these changes as they take place, although some do take you by surprise at the time, generally they soon become part of the accepted landscape. But when you use the rear-view mirror, you often do a double-take. It is somewhat like looking at a photograph of someone taken many years before, who you knew then and have seen regularly and so have not noticed how much they have changed. But now, as you look at that thirty-year-old photograph: Wow! They really have changed! Did they really look like that then? The world, our nation and the church in the UK are quite different today compared to 1970. But those key lessons God has been teaching us remain the same in their truth and their efficacy. They continue to speak with the same resonance and power today as ever because the God we love and serve is the Unchanging One. His Son, the Lord Jesus Christ, is the same yesterday today and forever. His Spirit continues His sovereign work throughout the earth.

Let me then come back to these foundational lessons which are clearly set out in God's Word and which He has, in His grace, underlined to us again and again as bread for the journey in the many different seasons of life.

1. *Walk humbly with God*

Micah 6:8 sets this out in memorable fashion. Let the Word of God and the Spirit of God daily teach you what this means. This verse also directs us to act justly and love mercy in all our relationships with others.

> ▶ He has shown you, O mortal, what is good.
>   And what does the Lord require of you?
> To act justly and to love mercy
>   and to walk humbly with your God.
>
> ● Micah 6:8 (NIV)

> ▶ He guides the humble in what is right
>   and teaches them his way.
>
> ● Psalm 25:9 (NIV)

2. *Forgive and keep on forgiving*

In Matthew 18:21-35, Peter asks Jesus where the limits are when it comes to forgiving. The Master's reply rocked him back on his heels. Forgiveness must be without limit and from the heart.

> ▶ Then Peter came to Jesus and asked,
>> "Lord, how many times shall I forgive my brother or sister
>> who sins against me? Up to seven times?"
>
> Jesus answered, "I tell you, not seven times,
>> but seventy-seven times.
>
> ● Matthew 18:21-22 (NIV)

3. *Keep your spirit clean*

'Let's keep our spirits clean' became the phrase Maureen and I would speak to each other when things became tough. We knew we were 'done for' in our walk with God and our ministry if we allowed our hearts, minds, and spirits to become sullied by ungodly responses to people or situations.

> ▶ Create in me a pure heart, O God,
>> and renew a steadfast spirit within me.
>
> ● Psalm 51:10 (NIV)

4. *Trust God and His promises at all times*

> ▶ The one who calls you is faithful, and he will do it.
>
> ● 1 Thessalonians 5:24 (NIV)

> ▶ But the Lord is faithful, and he will strengthen you
>   and protect you from the evil one.
>
> ● 2 Thessalonians 3:3 (NIV)

> ▶ Trust in the Lord with all your heart
>   and lean not on your own understanding;
> in all your ways submit to him,
>   and he will make your paths straight.
>
> ● Proverbs 3:5-6 (NIV)

The verses from Proverbs were given to me by my parents when I began in ministry and they sure are wisdom literature.

5. *Pursue God and the course He has given you to walk*

Jeremiah 1:4-19 tells us not to be deflected from the way God has shown you how to live or from the way He has shown you to lead His people. But pursue Him and follow the course He has set out for you with grace and courage.

> ▶ "... You must go to everyone I send you to
>   and say whatever I command you.
>
> ● Jeremiah 1:7 (NIV)

6. *Guard your time with God, your wife or husband, and your children*

Ephesians 5:15 - 6:4 teaches us to let love, compassion and care mark out our foundational relationships at all times. Your first calling is to love the Lord your God with all that you are and then to love your wife or husband, and children, in that order of priority with the self-same love.

> ▶   "Be very careful, then, how you live –
>   not as unwise but as wise,
>   making the most of every opportunity...
>
>   ● **Ephesians 5:15 (NIV)**

7. *Keep on seeking after God*

Let it be the consistent choice of your will. There are always times, seasons when the last thing you want to do is seek God. At such times let your will be aligned with your Father's in heaven, who eternally loves you and whose Son, the Lord Jesus Christ, offered up Himself for you.

> ▶   One thing I ask from the Lord,
>   this only do I seek:
>   that I may dwell in the house of the Lord
>   all the days of my life,
>   to gaze on the beauty of the Lord
>   and to seek him in his temple.
>
>   ● **Psalm 27:4 (NIV)**

> ▶ ... When my heart whispered, "Seek God,"
> my whole being replied, "I'm seeking him!"...
>
> ● Psalm 27:8 (MSG)

"God thirsts to be thirsted after." – Augustine

I remember reading a fascinating description of beautiful wedding saris being handwoven in the Indian city of Varanasi:

> 'The gold, the silver, the reds, the blues – all the marvellous colours threaded together are spectacular. These saris are usually made by just two people – a father who sits on a platform and a son who sits two steps down from him. The father has all the spools of silk threads around him. As he begins to pull the threads together, he nods, and the son responds by moving the shuttle from one side to the other. Then the process begins again, with the father nodding and the son responding. Everything is done with a simple nod from the father. It's a long tedious process to watch. But if you come back in two or three weeks, you'll see a magnificent pattern emerging.'

This is an evocative image. You and I may be moving the shuttle, but the design is in the mind of our Father. The son has no idea what pattern is emerging, he just responds to the father's nod. As I retrace the years there are many threads, each one contributing to the pattern the Father intended in my life.

So also, with your life. I am reminded of a church social in Aberdeen when I was probably about eleven years of age. On these occasions, it was common for someone to do a recitation. The one I remember, which obviously made quite an impression on me at the time, was about our lives being like a tapestry. The difficulty is that we are looking at the back of the tapestry and all we can see is a tangle of threads and knots, which is not at all attractive and makes no sense to us at all. But, with all these different threads, the Father is weaving a beautiful pattern and when we see Him, we will for the first time gaze on the front of the tapestry of our lives. And we will be amazed at the multi-coloured, multi-dimensional pattern He has woven. That wedding sari will be spectacular for His glory.

This God we love and serve is the God who knows us and loves us.

And the Lord Jesus Christ knows you and loves you. In John 21, as Jesus comes alongside his three-times denying disciple Peter, the question Jesus poses cuts to the core, 'Do you love me?' Three times Peter answers in the affirmative. Then Jesus tells Peter that he still has a future with Him. The future is summed up in the words: 'Follow me'. When Peter then asked about Jesus' plans for another disciple, Jesus answered, 'What is that to you? You must follow me'. (John 21:22).

Peter left with a song in his heart from that lakeside breakfast encounter with Jesus: 'I am forgiven! Jesus still loves me! He still has a purpose for me!' The Lord Jesus knows you and He loves you and He has a purpose for you. That purpose is to follow Him. Do not look at others. Do not compare yourself with them.

Jesus' word to Peter was: 'You must follow Me'. Learning to follow Jesus is the work of a lifetime, taken day by day. It involves steadily gazing upon Jesus.

Today, whatever day or point in your life you are at as you read these words, the road ahead of you is one on which you've never been before. Your Father in heaven, who truly loves you more than you can ever know, says to you: 'Keep your eyes on My Beloved Son'. And in the words of Mary, the mother of Jesus, to the disciples: 'Do whatever He tells you.'

▶ **Discipline in a Long-Distance Race**

Do you see what this means—all these pioneers who blazed
the way, all these veterans cheering us on? It means we'd
better get on with it. Strip down, start running—and never
quit! No extra spiritual fat, no parasitic sins. Keep your
eyes on Jesus, who both began and finished this race
we're in. Study how he did it. Because he never lost
sight of where he was headed—that exhilarating finish in
and with God—he could put up with anything along the
way: Cross, shame, whatever. And now he's there, in the
place of honor, right alongside God. When you find
yourselves flagging in your faith, go over that story again,
item by item, that long litany of hostility he plowed
through. That will shoot adrenaline into your souls!

● **Hebrews 12:1-3 (MSG)**

ABOUT THE AUTHOR

David Craig lived in Aberdeen and Edinburgh, working in one of the Scottish banks where he qualified as an Associate of the Insttiute of Bankers in Scotland. He trained at London Bible College (now London School of Theology) and had a student pastorate in a Buckinghamshire village church.

From there he commenced ministry at Westbourne Grove Baptist Church (now Westbourne Grove Church) in Notting Hill, London which he led for eight years. There followed a ministry of over thirty years at Bournemouth Community Church during which time the church went through various phases of growth including planting out congregations locally and overseas and the purchase of a large multi-purpose building for worship, witness and community engagement.

David was a trustee of Moorlands College for twenty years, including four years as Chair of Trustees. His heart to see church leaders supporting and praying for each other and for churches to engage in evangelism and community action together has been a continuing passion, as has Christ's commission to His church to 'go and make disciples of all nations'.

David lives in Bournemouth and is married to Maureen, with a family of three, two of whom are married and they now have six grandchildren and one great-grandchild.